PAUSE
FOR
POWER

Stephen G. Hatfield
1999

A YEAR IN THE WORD

PAUSE
FOR
POWER

WITH

WARREN W.
WIERSBE

Chariot Victor Publishing
A Division of Cook Communications

Chariot Victor Publishing,
a division of Cook Communications, Colorado Springs, Colorado 80918
Cook Communications, Paris, Ontario
Kingsway Communications, Eastbourne, England

Unless otherwise noted, Scripture quotations are from the *Holy Bible:
New International Version* ®. Copyright © 1973, 1978, 1984 by
International Bible Society. Used by permission of Zondervan Publishing
House. All rights reserved. Quotations marked KJV are from the
Authorized (King James) Version. Quotations marked TLB are from *The
Living Bible*, © 1971, Tyndale House Publishers, Wheaton, IL 60189. Used
by permission. Other quotations are from *The Bible, A New Translation*
© 1950, 1952, 1953, 1954 by James A.R. Moffatt and *The New Testament:
An Expanded Translation* by Kenneth S. Wuest, © 1961 by the William B.
Eerdmans Publishing Company. Used by permission.

This book was originally published as twelve paperback editions in 1994
and 1995, compiled by Stan Campbell, who also wrote the personal reflec-
tion questions. Each devotional reading is adapted from Warren Wiersbe's
"Be Series."

Editor: Greg Clouse
Cover Design: Kevin Simpson

© 1998 by Warren W. Wiersbe. All rights reserved.
Printed in the United States of America.

1 2 3 4 5 6 7 8 9 10 Printing / Year 02 01 00 99 98

CONTENTS

RENEWAL

30 Daily Readings from the Book of Romans

YOU'VE PROBABLY NOTICED DURING POLITICAL CAMPAIGNS THAT MANY OF the candidates promise to do "new things" to solve the old problems. Whether it's a "new frontier" or a "new deal" or a "new vision," the promise is the same: it's time for renewal. It's time for a change!

When Paul wrote to the Christians in Rome, one of his themes was *making a new beginning.* He explains how the Gospel of Jesus Christ is the answer to the "old problems" everybody confronts—problems like sin, guilt, defeat, and broken relationships. The heart of every problem is the problem of the heart, and only through Jesus Christ can we have new hearts so that we can make new beginnings in life.

Renewal begins with a new relationship with God, which Paul calls *justification,* a basic biblical doctrine that every child of God must understand. Spiritual renewal that begins with justification continues with *sanctification,* a new power to overcome sin and a new motive for living. Paul tells us how the new life in Christ enables us to be good friends, good citizens, and good servants of God in the midst of a wicked world.

As Paul reasons about God's marvelous plan of salvation and explains how it works, you'll discover how practical this "renewed life" really is, and how "justified" people can experience renewal—"newness of life"—in their daily walk with the Lord.

It's time for a change! It's time for renewal! And the Epistle to the Romans points the way.

Scripture: Read Romans 1:1-7

"You also are among those who are called to belong to Jesus Christ" (Rom. 1:6).

THE RIGHT STUFF

When you study Romans, you walk into a courtroom. First, Paul called Jews and Gentiles to the stand and found both guilty before God. Then he explained God's marvelous way of salvation—justification by faith. At this point, he answered his accusers and defended God's salvation. "This plan of salvation will encourage people to sin!" they cry. "It is against the very Law of God!" But Paul refuted them, and in so doing explained how the Christian can experience victory, liberty, and security.

There were Jewish believers in the Roman assemblies and they would naturally ask, "What about Israel? How does God's righteousness relate to them in this new age of the church?" In chapters 9–11 Paul gave a complete history of Israel, past, present, and future.

Then he concluded with the practical outworking of God's righteousness in the life of the believer. When you sum it all up, the Book of Romans is saying to us—*"Be right!"* Be right with God, with yourself, and with others! The righteousness of God received by faith makes it possible for us to live right lives. Rome needed this message, and we need it today: *Be right!*

Applying God's Truth:

1. What is one situation you're facing where you need to experience more victory? Liberty? Security?

2. How has God's righteousness been evident in your past? Your present? How do you expect Him to work in your future?

3. What are your goals as you begin to read through the Book of Romans?

Scripture: Read Romans 1:8-15

"I am obligated both to Greeks and non-Greeks, both to the wise and the foolish. That is why I am so eager to preach the gospel also to you who are at Rome" (Rom. 1:14-15).

WHEN IN ROME ...

Paul's special commission was to take the Gospel to the Gentiles, and this is why he was planning to go to Rome, the very capital of the empire. He was a preacher of the Gospel, and the Gospel was for all nations.

Rome was a proud city, and the Gospel came from Jerusalem, the capital city of one of the little nations that Rome had conquered. The Christians in that day were not among the elite of society; they were common people and even slaves. Rome had known many great philosophers and philosophies; why pay any attention to a fable about a Jew who arose from the dead? Christians looked upon each other as brothers and sisters, all one in Christ, which went against the grain of Roman pride and dignity. To think of a little Jewish tentmaker, going to Rome to preach such a message, is almost humorous.

Paul arrived in Rome a prisoner as well as a preacher. In Jerusalem he was arrested in the temple, falsely accused by the Jewish authorities, and eventually sent to Rome as the Emperor's prisoner to be tried before Caesar. When Paul wrote this letter, he had no idea that he would go through imprisonment and even shipwreck before arriving in Rome! At the close of the letter (15:30-33), he asked the believers in Rome to pray for him as he contemplated this trip, and it is a good thing that they did pray!

Applying God's Truth:

1. Paul directly confronted the pride of Rome. What are some of the obstacles *you* face as you try to present the Gospel to others?

2. If you knew that presenting the truth of Jesus to others would involve shipwreck, imprisonment, and other similar hardships, would you be at all reluctant to share the Gospel? Why or why not?

3. Do you have the assurance of knowing that other people are praying for you? If not, what can you do to arrange some prayer support?

Scripture: Read Romans 1:16-17

"In the gospel a righteousness from God is revealed, a righteousness that is by faith from first to last, just as it is written, 'The righteous will live by faith' " *(Rom. 1:17).*

LUTHER, WESLEY... AND YOU?

On May 24, 1738, a discouraged missionary went "very unwillingly" to a religious meeting in London. There a miracle took place. "About a quarter before nine," he wrote in his journal, "I felt my heart strangely warmed. I felt I did trust in Christ, Christ alone, for salvation; and an assurance was given me that He had taken away my sins, even mine, and saved me from the law of sin and death."

That missionary was John Wesley. The message he heard that evening was the preface to Martin Luther's commentary on Romans. Paul's Epistle to the Romans is still transforming people's lives, just the way it transformed Martin Luther and John Wesley. The one Scripture above all others that brought Luther out of mere religion into the joy of salvation by grace, through faith, was verse 17: "The righteous will live by faith." The Protestant Reformation and the Wesleyan revival were both the fruit of this wonderful letter.

Imagine! You and I can read and study the same inspired letter that brought life and power to Luther and Wesley! And the same Holy Spirit who taught them can teach us! You and I can experience revival in our hearts, homes, and churches if the message of this letter grips us as it has gripped men of faith in centuries past.

Applying God's Truth:

1. What do you think would need to happen before you could experience revival in your church? In your home? In your personal life?

2. What is the #1 transformation you desire for your life?

3. Why do you think the message of "living by faith" made such a difference for Luther and Wesley?

Scripture: Read Romans 1:18-32

"Although they knew God, they neither glorified him as God nor gave thanks to him, but their thinking became futile and their foolish hearts were darkened" (Rom. 1:21).

ACCEPT NO SUBSTITUTES

Man knew God; this is clear. But man did not want to know God or honor Him as God. Instead of being thankful for all that God had given him, man refused to thank God or give Him the glory He deserves. Man was willing to use God's gifts, but he was not willing to worship and praise God for His gifts. The result was an empty mind and a darkened heart. Man the worshiper became man the philosopher, but his empty wisdom only revealed his foolishness.

Having held down God's truth and refusing to acknowledge God's glory, man was left without a god; and man is so constituted that he must worship something. If he will not worship the true God, he will worship a false god, *even if he has to manufacture it himself!* This fact about man accounts for his propensity to idolatry. Man exchanged the glory of the true God for substitute gods that he himself made. He exchanged glory for shame, incorruption for corruption, truth for lies.

Applying God's Truth:

1. Why do you think some people are so resistant about honoring God?

2. What are some false gods that people today turn to?

3. Do you personally know people who reject God and turn to substitutes? Can you do anything to influence and/or help these people?

Scripture: Read Romans 2:1–3:20

"To those who by persistence in doing good seek glory, honor, and immortality, he will give eternal life. But for those who are self-seeking and who reject the truth and follow evil, there will be wrath and anger" (Rom. 2:7-8).

CONSISTENT ACTIONS

God had given Israel great material and spiritual riches: a wonderful land, a righteous Law, a temple and priesthood, God's providential care, and many more blessings. God had patiently endured Israel's many sins and rebellions, and He even sent them His Son to be their Messiah. Even after Israel crucified Christ, God gave the nation nearly forty more years of grace and withheld His judgment. It is not the *judgment* of God that leads men to repentance, but the *goodness* of God; but Israel did not repent.

In verses 6-11, Paul was not teaching salvation by character or good deeds. He was explaining another basic principle of God's judgment: God judges according to deeds, just as He judges according to truth. Paul was dealing here with the consistent actions of a person's life, the total impact of his character and conduct.

True saving faith results in obedience and godly living, even though there may be occasional falls. When God measured the deeds of the Jews, He found them to be as wicked as those of the Gentiles.

Applying God's Truth:

1. What are some obvious blessings of God that people—even many Christians—tend to overlook too often?

2. How does the goodness of God lead people to repentance?

3. An unsaved person can certainly do good things. Do you think he or she can *consistently* have good character and conduct? Explain.

Scripture: Read Romans 3:21-31

"All have sinned and fall short of the glory of God, and are justified freely by his grace through the redemption that came by Christ Jesus" (Rom. 3:23-24).

COST VERSUS VALUE

Salvation is free, but it is not cheap. Jesus had to die on the cross in order to satisfy the Law and justify lost sinners. The best illustration of this truth is the Jewish Day of Atonement described in Leviticus 16. Two goats were presented at the altar, and one of them was chosen for a sacrifice. The priest then put his hands on the head of the other goat and confessed the sins of the people. Then the goat was taken out into the wilderness and set free to symbolize the carrying away of sins.

Dr. G. Campbell Morgan was trying to explain "free salvation" to a coal miner, but the man was unable to understand it. "I have to pay for it," he kept arguing. With a flash of divine insight, Dr. Morgan asked, "How did you get down into the mine this morning?" "Why, it was easy," the man replied. "I just got on the elevator and went down."

Then Morgan asked, "Wasn't that too easy? Didn't it cost you something?"

The man laughed. "No, it didn't cost me anything, but it must have cost the company plenty to install that elevator." Then the man saw the truth: "It doesn't cost *me* anything to be saved, but it cost God the life of His Son."

Applying God's Truth:

1. How do you think the phrase, "You get what you pay for," applies to salvation?

2. Does the fact that your salvation is free mean that you're under no obligation to God? Explain.

3. Can you think of an analogy for a specific unsaved friend that would parallel the elevator anecdote used with the coal miner?

Scripture: Read Romans 4:1-15

"What does the Scripture say? 'Abraham believed God, and it was credited to him as righteousness'" *(Rom. 4:3)*.

SOME THINGS NEVER CHANGE

Dr. Harry Ironside, for eighteen years pastor of Moody Church in Chicago, told of visiting a Sunday School class while on vacation. The teacher asked, "How were people saved in Old Testament times?"

After a pause, one man replied, "By keeping the Law." "That's right," said the teacher.

But Dr. Ironside interrupted: "My Bible says that by the deeds of the Law shall no flesh be justified."

The teacher was a bit embarrassed, so he said, "Well, does somebody else have an idea?"

Another student replied, "They were saved by bringing sacrifices to God."

"Yes, that's right!" the teacher said, and tried to go on with the lesson.

But Dr. Ironside interrupted, "My Bible says that the blood of bulls and goats cannot take away sin."

By this time the unprepared teacher was sure the visitor knew more about the Bible than he did, so he said, "Well, *you* tell us how people were saved in the Old Testament!"

And Dr. Ironside explained that they were saved by faith—the same way people are saved today!

Abraham is the father of all who believe on Jesus Christ and are justified by faith. If you are a Gentile, you can never be a natural descendant of Abraham; but you can be one of his *spiritual* descendants. Abraham "believed God, and it was credited to him as righteousness."

Applying God's Truth:

1. Prior to this reading, how would you have responded to the question: "How were people saved in Old Testament times?"

2. Since faith was behind the ceremonies of the Old Testament, what should faith inspire *us* to do today?

3. What do you think is entailed in being a "spiritual descendant" of Abraham (privileges, responsibilities, etc.)?

Scripture: Read Romans 4:16-25

"[Jesus our Lord] was delivered over to death for our sins and was raised to life for our justification" (Rom 4:25).

A LEGAL MATTER

Justification is the act of God whereby He declares the believing sinner righteous in Christ on the basis of the finished work of Christ on the cross. Each part of this definition is important, so we must consider it carefully.

To begin with, justification is an *act*, not a process. There are no degrees of justification; each believer has the same right standing before God. Also, justification is something *God* does, not man. No sinner can justify himself before God. Most important, justification does not mean that God *makes* us righteous, but that He *declares* us righteous. Justification is a legal matter. God puts the righteousness of Christ on our record in the place of our own sinfulness. And nobody can change this record.

Do not confuse justification and sanctification. Sanctification is the process whereby God makes the believer more and more like Christ. Sanctification may change from day to day. Justification never changes. When the sinner trusts Christ, God declares him righteous, and that declaration will never be repealed. God looks upon us and deals with us as though we had never sinned at all!

Applying God's Truth:

1. Since justification is an *act* that God does, what is *your* responsibility?

2. Can you give a personal example to explain the difference between justification and sanctification?

3. Do you feel you have a good understanding of justification and sanctification? If not, what resources and people can you consult?

Scripture: Read Romans 5:1-11

"We know that suffering produces perseverance; perseverance, character; and character, hope" (Rom. 5:3-4).

THE HOPE SEQUENCE

Justification is no escape from the trials of life. But for the believer, trials work *for* him and not *against* him. Suffering builds Christian character. The sequence is: suffering—perseverance—character—hope. Our English word *tribulation* comes from a Latin word *tribulum*. In Paul's day, a *tribulum* was a heavy piece of timber with spikes in it, used for threshing the grain. The *tribulum* was drawn over the grain and it separated the wheat from the chaff. As we go through tribulations, and depend on God's grace, the trials only purify us and help to get rid of the chaff.

For many months I visited a young man in a hospital who had almost burned to death. I do not know how many operations and skin grafts he had during those months, or how many specialists visited him. But the thing that sustained him during those difficult months was not the explanations of the doctors, but the promises they gave him that he would recover. That was his hope. And the thing that sustained his hope was the love of his family and many friends as they stood by him. The love of God was channeled through them to him. He did recover and today gives glory to God.

Applying God's Truth:

1. Do you think it's possible to have perseverance, character, and hope *without* sufferings? Explain.

2. Can you think of a recent personal trial that helped make you a better, stronger, person?

3. How can personal trials result in your giving glory to God?

Scripture: Read Romans 5:12-21

"But where sin increased, grace increased all the more, so that, just as sin reigned in death, so also grace might reign through righteousness to bring eternal life through Jesus Christ our Lord" (Rom. 5:20-21).

WE NEED A GOOD REIGN

Grace was not an addition to God's plan; grace was a part of God's plan from the very beginning. God dealt with Adam and Eve in grace; He dealt with the patriarchs in grace; and He dealt with the nation of Israel in grace. He gave the Law through Moses, not to replace His grace, but to reveal man's need for grace. Law was temporary, but grace is eternal.

But as the Law made man's sins increase, God's grace abounded even more. God's grace was more than adequate to deal with man's sins. Even though sin and death still reign in this world, God's grace is also reigning through the righteousness of Christ.

An Old Testament story helps us understand the conflict between these two "reigns" in the world today. God rejected Saul as the king of Israel, and anointed David. Those who trusted David eventually shared his kingdom of peace and joy. Those who trusted Saul ended in shame and defeat.

Like David, Jesus Christ is God's anointed King. Like Saul, Satan is still free to work in this world and seek to win men's allegiance. Sin and death are reigning in the "old creation" over which Adam was the head, but grace and righteousness are reigning in "the new creation" over which Christ is the Head. And as we yield to Him, we "reign in life."

Applying God's Truth:

1. What is your definition of God's "grace"? What is a personal example?

2. Without God's grace, how do you think the religion of Christianity would be different?

3. To what extent do *people* determine which of the two "reigns" is more in control?

17

Scripture: Read Romans 6:1-4

"We were therefore buried with him through baptism into death in order that, just as Christ was raised from the dead through the glory of the Father, we too may live a new life" (Rom. 6:4).

THE LIVING DEAD

Historians agree that the mode of baptism in the early church was immersion. The believer was "buried" in the water and brought up again as a picture of death, burial, and resurrection. Baptism by immersion (which is the illustration Paul is using in Rom. 6) pictures the believer's identification with Christ in His death, burial, and resurrection. It is an outward symbol of an inward experience. Paul is not saying that their immersion in water put them "into Jesus Christ," for that was accomplished by the Spirit when they believed. Their immersion was a picture of what the Spirit did: the Holy Spirit identified them with Christ in His death, burial, and resurrection.

This means that the believer has a new relationship to sin. He is "dead to sin." If a drunk dies, he can no longer be tempted by alcohol because his body is dead to all physical senses. He cannot see the alcohol, smell it, taste it, or desire it. In Jesus Christ we have died to sin so that we no longer want to "continue in sin." But we are not only dead to sin; we are also alive in Christ. We have been raised from the dead and now walk in the power of His resurrection. We walk in "newness of life" because we share His life. "I have been crucified with Christ and I no longer live, but Christ lives in me" (Gal. 2:20).

Applying God's Truth:

1. In what ways have you demonstrated that you have "died to sin"?

2. Which sins do you find most difficult to remain "dead" to?

3. What steps do you take to "stay dead" when tempted by old and alluring sins?

Scripture: Read Romans 6:5-23

"Anyone who has died has been freed from sin" (Rom. 6:7).

DON'T BE A BETWEENER

Too many Christians are "betweeners": they live between Egypt and Canaan, saved but never satisfied; or they live between Good Friday and Easter, believing in the Cross but not entering into the power and glory of the Resurrection.

A tremendous fact is introduced in this section of Romans: the old man (the old ego, self) was crucified with Christ so that the body need not be controlled by sin. The phrase "done away with" in verse 6 does not mean annihilated; it means "rendered inactive, made of no effect."

Sin wants to be our master. It finds a foothold in the old nature, and through the old nature seeks to control the members of the body. But in Jesus Christ, we died to sin, and the old nature was crucified so that the old life is rendered inoperative. Paul was not describing an experience; he was stating a fact. The practical experience was to come later. It is a fact of history that the believer died with Him, and "anyone who has died has been freed from sin" (v. 7). Not "free *to* sin" as Paul's accusers falsely stated, but "freed *from* sin."

Applying God's Truth:

1. How do you feel about being "united with [Jesus] in His death"? (6:5) Why?

2. Using a percentage, to what extent do you feel you've "entered into the power and glory of the Resurrection"?

3. What things can you do to experience more fully the life and freedom Jesus has made possible for you?

Scripture: Read Romans 7:1-6

"By dying to what once bound us, we have been released from the law so that we serve in the new way of the Spirit, and not in the old way of the written code" (Rom. 7:6).

TWO EXTREMES

Something in human nature makes us want to go to extremes, a weakness from which Christians are not wholly free. "Since we are saved by grace," some argue, "we are free to live as we please," which is the law of *license*.

"But we cannot ignore God's Law," others argue. "We are saved by grace, to be sure; but we must live under Law if we are to please God." This is the extreme expression of *legalism*.

What really is "legalism"? It is the belief that I can become holy and please God by obeying laws. It is measuring spirituality by a list of do's and don'ts. The weakness of legalism is that it sees *sins* (plural) but not *sin* (the root of the trouble).

In my pastoral experience, I have counseled many people who have suffered severe emotional and spiritual damage because they have tried to live holy lives on the basis of a high standard. I have seen the consequences of these attempts: either the person becomes a pretender, or he suffers a complete collapse and abandons his desires for godly living. I have seen too that many legalists are extremely hard on other people—critical, unloving, unforgiving. Paul wanted to spare his readers this difficult and dangerous experience.

Applying God's Truth:

1. Do you tend to lean more toward the extreme of license or the extreme of legalism? In what ways?

2. What do you feel are the major problems that result from legalism?

3. How would you suggest that people could remain absolutely obedient and faithful to God without falling into the snare of legalism?

Scripture: Read Romans 7:7-13

"But sin, seizing the opportunity afforded by the commandment, produced in me every kind of covetous desire. For apart from law, sin is dead" (Rom. 7:8).

THE REBEL WITHIN

Something in human nature wants to rebel whenever a law is given. I was standing in Lincoln Park in Chicago, looking at the newly painted benches; and I noticed a sign on each bench: "Do Not Touch." As I watched, I saw numbers of people deliberately reach out and touch the wet paint! Why? Because the sign told them not to! Instruct a child not to go near the water, and that is the very thing he will do! Why? Because "the sinful mind is hostile to God. It does not submit to God's law, nor can it do so" (Rom. 8:7).

Believers who try to live by rules and regulations discover that their legalistic system only arouses more sin and creates more problems. The churches in Galatia were very legalistic, and they experienced all kinds of trouble. "If you keep on biting and devouring each other, watch out or you will be destroyed by each other" (Gal. 5:15). Their legalism did not make them more spiritual; it made them more sinful! Why? Because the Law arouses sin in our nature.

Applying God's Truth:

1. What rules and regulations do you find most frustrating? Why?

2. What are some forbidden things that tend to arouse your curiosity or attract your interest?

3. If rules and regulations are a source of problems, should they be done away with? If not, what other options do we have?

21

Scripture: Read Romans 7:14-25

"I do not understand what I do. For what I want to do I do not do, but what I hate I do" (Rom. 7:15).

HUMAN ERROR

The Law cannot give life: it can only show the sinner that he is guilty and condemned. This explains why legalistic Christians and churches do not grow and bear spiritual fruit. They are living by Law, and the Law always kills. Few things are more dead than an orthodox church that is proud of its "high standards" and tries to live up to them in its own energy. Often the members of such a church start to judge and condemn one another, and the sad result is a church fight and then a church split that leaves members—or former members—angry and bitter.

As the new Christian grows, he comes into contact with various philosophies of the Christian life. He can read books, attend seminars, listen to tapes, and get a great deal of information. If he is not careful, he will start following a human leader and accept his teachings as Law. This practice is a very subtle form of legalism, and it kills spiritual growth. No human teacher can take the place of Christ; no book can take the place of the Bible. Men can give us information, but only the Spirit can give us illumination and help us understand spiritual truths. The Spirit enlightens us and enables us; no human leader can do that.

Applying God's Truth:

1. What are some mistakes you've made in the past when trying to eliminate a difficult problem? Did you possibly put too much trust in a human resource rather than a godly one?

2. Who are some celebrities who promise answers to various personal problems? Why do you think people "buy into" so much blatant self-promotion and sales tactics?

3. How can you benefit from the wisdom of other people without putting *too* much value on their advice?

Scripture: Read Romans 8:1-17

"Those who are led by the Spirit of God are sons of God" (Rom. 8:14).

LEVELS OF LIFE

To be unsaved and not have the Spirit is the lowest level of life. But a person need not stay on that level. By faith in Christ he can move to the second level. The evidence of conversion is the presence of the Holy Spirit within, witnessing that you are a child of God (v. 16). Your body becomes the very temple of the Holy Spirit (1 Cor. 6:19-20).

What a difference it makes in your body when the Holy Spirit lives within. You experience new life, and even your physical faculties take on a new dimension of experience. When evangelist D. L. Moody described his conversion experience, he said: "I was in a new world. The next morning the sun shone brighter and the birds sang sweeter . . . the old elms waved their branches for joy, and all nature was at peace." Life in Christ is abundant life.

But there is a third level of experience for which the other two are preparation. It is not enough for us to have the Spirit; the Spirit must have us! (Rom. 8:12-17) Only then can He share with us the abundant, victorious life that can be ours in Christ. Because He is "the Spirit of life," He can empower us to obey Christ, and He can enable us to be more like Christ.

Applying God's Truth:

1. What friends can you think of in each of the three levels of life: (1) People who do not have God's Spirit; (2) People who do have the Spirit; and (3) People under the control of the Spirit?

2. How has the Holy Spirit changed your perspective on life?

3. Can you think of ways to allow God's Holy Spirit to have more control over you?

Scripture: Read Romans 8:18-39

"We know that in all things God works for the good of those who love him, who have been called according to his purpose" (Rom. 8:28).

No Condemnation

The believer never need faint in times of suffering and trial because he knows that God is at work in the world, and that He has a perfect plan (vv. 28-29). God has two purposes in that plan: our good and His glory. Ultimately, He will make us like Jesus Christ! Best of all, God's plan is going to succeed!

How can we Christians ever be discouraged and frustrated when we already share the glory of God? Our suffering today only guarantees that much more glory when Jesus Christ returns!

There is no condemnation because we share the righteousness of God and the Law cannot condemn us. There is no obligation because we have the Spirit of God who enables us to overcome the flesh and live for God. There is no frustration because we share the glory of God, the blessed hope of Christ's return. There is no separation because we experience the love of God (v. 35). We do not need to fear the past, present, or future because we are secure in the love of Christ.

Applying God's Truth:

1. Looking back over your life, can you see how some of your trying situations have resulted in good?

2. What is one thing you are suffering with right now for which you can *see* no possible way for God to ever use for good? Do you have the faith to *trust* Him to do so?

3. Can you truthfully say that you feel no condemnation from God? No obligation? No frustration? No separation? Which of these areas do you feel needs the most attention?

Scripture: Read Romans 9:1-13

"I could wish that I myself were cursed and cut off from Christ for the sake of my brothers, those of my own race, the people of Israel" *(Rom. 9:3-4).*

AN EMPHASIS ON ISRAEL

It seems strange that Paul would interrupt his discussion of salvation and devote a long section of three chapters to the nation of Israel. Why didn't he move from the doctrinal teaching of chapter 8 to the practical duties given in 12–15?

To begin with, Paul was considered a traitor to the Jewish nation. He ministered to Gentiles and he taught freedom from the Law of Moses. He had preached in many synagogues and caused trouble, and no doubt many of the Jewish believers in Rome had heard of his questionable reputation. In these chapters, Paul showed his love for Israel and his desire for their welfare. This is the personal reason for this discussion.

But there was a doctrinal reason. Paul had argued in Romans 8 that the believer is secure in Jesus Christ and that God's election would stand. But someone might ask, "What about the Jews? They were chosen by God, and yet now you tell us they are set aside and God is building His church. Did God fail to keep His promises to Israel?" In other words, the very character of God was at stake.

So the emphasis in chapter 9 is on Israel's past election, in chapter 10 on Israel's present rejection, and in chapter 11 on Israel's future restoration. Israel is the only nation in the world with a complete history—past, present, and future.

Applying God's Truth:

1. Of what you know about Israel's history, what would you say were its most glorious periods? Its lowest points?

2. If you had been a devout Jew during the first century, how do you think you would have felt about Paul? Why?

3. What do you think God has in mind for Israel's future?

Scripture: Read Romans 9:14-21

"Is God unjust? Not at all! For he says to Moses, 'I will have mercy on whom I have mercy, and I will have compassion on whom I have compassion'" (Rom. 9:14-15).

JUSTICE, MERCY, AND SOVEREIGNTY

Moses was a Jew, Pharaoh was a Gentile; yet both were sinners. In fact, both were murderers! Both saw God's wonders. Yet Moses was saved and Pharaoh was lost. God raised up Pharaoh that He might reveal His glory and power; and He had mercy on Moses that He might use him to deliver the people of Israel. Pharaoh was a ruler, and Moses was a slave, yet it was Moses who experienced the mercy and compassion of God—because God willed it that way. God is sovereign in His work and acts according to His own will and purposes. So it was not a matter of righteousness but of the sovereign will of God.

God is holy and must punish sin, but God is loving and desires to save sinners. If everybody is saved, it would deny His holiness, but if everybody is lost, it would deny His love. The solution to the problem is God's sovereign election.

A seminary professor once said to me, "Try to explain election, and you may lose your mind; but explain it away, and you will lose your soul."

God chose Israel and condemned Egypt, because this was His sovereign purpose. Nobody can condemn God for the way He extends His mercy, because God is righteous.

Applying God's Truth:

1. As you read this section of Romans, do any questions come to mind? If so, with whom can you discuss your questions?

2. When God shows mercy to some people, does that mean He's being unfair to others? Why?

3. When you can't fully understand God's working, what do you do to maintain your faith?

Scripture: Read Romans 9:22-33

"The Gentiles, who did not pursue righteousness, have obtained it, a righteousness that is by faith; but Israel, who pursued a law of righteousness, has not attained it" (Rom. 9:30-31).

GRACE RIGHTEOUSNESS VERSUS LAW RIGHTEOUSNESS

Paul wrote of divine sovereignty and then human responsibility. Note that Paul did not say "elect" and "nonelect," but rather emphasized faith. Here is a paradox: the Jews sought for righteousness but did not find it, while the Gentiles, who were not searching for it, found it! The reason? Israel tried to be saved by works and not by faith. They rejected "grace righteousness" and tried to please God with "Law righteousness." The Jews thought that the Gentiles had to come up to Israel's level to be saved, when actually the Jews had to go down to the level of the Gentiles to be saved. Instead of permitting their religious privileges (vv. 1-5) to lead them to Christ, they used these privileges as a substitute for Christ.

No one will deny that there are many mysteries connected with divine sovereignty and human responsibility. Nowhere does God ask us to choose between these two truths, because they both come from God and are a part of God's plan. They do not compete; they cooperate. The fact that we cannot fully understand *how* they work together does not deny the fact that they do. When a man asked Charles Spurgeon how he reconciled divine sovereignty and human responsibility, Spurgeon replied: "I never try to reconcile friends."

Applying God's Truth:

1. In what ways have you recently observed the evidence of God's divine sovereignty?

2. In what areas have you exercised your human responsibility?

3. If you had a friend pursuing "Law righteousness," what advice would you offer to help him or her experience the freedom of "grace righteousness"?

Scripture: Read Romans 10:1-13

"Since they did not know the righteousness that comes from God and sought to establish their own, they did not submit to God's righteousness" (Rom. 10:3).

WILLFUL IGNORANCE

I srael was ignorant of God's righteousness, not because they had never been told, but because they refused to learn. There is an ignorance that comes from lack of opportunity, but in their case, it was an ignorance that stemmed from willful, stubborn resistance to the truth. They were proud of their own good works and religious self-righteousness.

The godly Presbyterian preacher, Robert Murray McCheyne, was passing out tracts one day and handed one to a well-dressed lady. She gave him a haughty look and said, "Sir, you must not know who I am!"

In his kind way, McCheyne replied, "Madam, there is coming a day of judgment, and on that day it will not make any difference who you are!"

Everything about the Jewish religion pointed to the coming Messiah— their sacrifices, priesthood, temple services, religious festivals, and covenants. Their Law told them they were sinners in need of a Savior. But instead of letting the Law bring them to Christ (Gal. 3:24), they worshiped their Law and rejected their Savior. The Law cannot give righteousness; it only leads the sinner to the Savior who can give righteousness.

Applying God's Truth:

1. Do you think most ignorance about God is due to lack of opportunity to hear about Him, or a resistance to the truth?

2. In what ways do your church sacraments and traditions point to Christ?

3. Can you think of people who seem to be so absorbed with tradition and ceremony that they miss the reality of a personal relationship with Jesus?

Scripture: Read Romans 10:14-21

"How beautiful are the feet of those who bring good news!" (Rom. 10:15)

BEAUTIFUL FEET

We must never minimize the missionary outreach of the church. While this passage relates primarily to Israel, it applies to all lost souls around the world. They cannot be saved unless they call upon the Lord Jesus Christ. But they cannot call unless they believe. Faith comes by hearing, so they must hear the message. How will they hear? A messenger must go to them with the message. But this means that God must call the messenger and the messenger must be sent. What a privilege it is to be one of His messengers and have beautiful feet!

As I was writing this chapter, my phone rang and one of the businessmen in our church reported another soul led to Christ. My caller had had serious spiritual problems a few years ago and I was able to help him. Since that time, he has led many to Christ, including some in his office. His phone call was to give me the good news that one of his associates had led a friend to Christ, another miracle in a spiritual chain reaction that has been going on for three years now.

Some of us share the news here at home, but others are sent to distant places. In spite of some closed doors, there are still more open doors for the Gospel than ever before; and we have better tools to work with.

Applying God's Truth:

1. Who is your ideal model for what an evangelist should be? What characteristics of the person do you admire?

2. Who are some people that *you* could reach with the Gospel who might not hear from anyone else?

3. On a scale of 1 (least) to 10 (most), to what extent do you feel your church is committed to evangelistic outreach?

Scripture: Read Romans 11:1-15

"What Israel sought so earnestly it did not obtain, but the elect did. The others were hardened" (Rom. 11:7).

HARD TRUTH

For centuries people have been puzzled by the nation of Israel. The Roman government recognized the Jewish religion, but it still called the nation *secta nefaria*—a "nefarious sect." The great historian Arnold Toynbee classified Israel as "a fossil civilization" and did not know what to do with it. For some reason, the nation did not fit into his historical theories.

Paul devoted all of Romans 11 to presenting proof that God is not through with Israel. Israel is God's elect nation; He foreknew them, or chose them, and they are His. The fact that most of the nation has rejected Christ is no proof that God has finished with His people. In his day, Elijah thought that the nation had totally departed from God. He thought he was the only faithful Jew left, but discovered that there were 7,000 more.

Paul referred to this "remnant" in 9:27. At no time has the entire nation of Israel been true to the Lord. If a remnant had been saved, thus proving that God was not through with His people, then what had happened to the rest of the nation? They had been *hardened*. But Paul made it clear that the hardening of Israel is neither total nor final, and this is proof that God has a future for the nation.

Applying God's Truth:

1. Do you think any nation has ever surpassed Israel as God's "elect" nation?

2. What can *you* learn from the example set by the "remnant" of Israel?

3. In what ways do supposedly godly people become "hardened" in today's society?

Scripture: Read Romans 11:16-36

"Just as you who were at one time disobedient to God have now received mercy as a result of their disobedience, so they too have now become disobedient in order that they too may now receive mercy as a result of God's mercy to you" (Rom. 11:30-31).

GOD'S REMARKABLE PLANS

We must remember that God chose the Jews so that the Gentiles might be saved. "All peoples on earth will be blessed through you" was God's promise to Abraham (Gen. 12:3). The tragedy was that Israel became exclusive and failed to share the truth with the Gentiles. They thought that the Gentiles had to become Jews in order to be saved. But God declared both Jews and Gentiles to be lost and condemned. This meant that He could have mercy on all because of the sacrifice of Christ on the cross.

Having contemplated God's great plan of salvation for Jews and Gentiles, all Paul could do was sing a hymn of praise. As someone has remarked, "Theology becomes doxology!" Only a God as wise as our God could take the fall of Israel and turn it into salvation for the world! His plans will not be aborted nor will His purposes lack fulfillment. No human being can fully know the mind of the Lord; and the more we study His ways, the more we offer Him praise. Are we to conclude that God does *not* know what He is doing, and that the nation of Israel completely ruined His plans? Of course not! God is too wise to make plans that will not be fulfilled. Israel did not allow Him to rule, so He overruled!

Applying God's Truth:

1. Israel "became exclusive" with God's truth. Do you ever tend to be exclusive with whom you discuss the Gospel?

2. Since God could turn the fall of Israel into the salvation of the world, can you think of one of your own "falls" that perhaps God will convert into good for a lot of people?

3. Has God "overruled" some of your plans lately? How do you feel when it happens?

Scripture: Read Romans 12:1-6

"Offer your bodies as living sacrifices. . . . Do not conform any longer to the pattern of this world, but be transformed by the renewing of your mind. Then you will be able to test and approve what God's will is" (Rom. 12:1-3).

FULL SURRENDER

Your mind controls your body, and your will controls your mind. Many people think they can control their will by "willpower," but usually they fail. (This was Paul's experience as recorded in 7:15-21.) It is only when we yield the will to God that His power can take over and give us the willpower (and the won't power!) that we need to be victorious Christians.

We surrender our wills to God through disciplined prayer. As we spend time in prayer, we surrender our will to God and pray, with the Lord, "Not my will, but Thy will be done." We must pray about everything, and let God have His way in everything.

For many years I have tried to begin each day by surrendering my body to the Lord. Then I spend time with His Word and let Him transform my mind and prepare my thinking for that new day. Then I pray, and I yield the plans of the day to Him and let Him work as He sees best. I especially pray about those tasks that upset or worry me—and He always sees me through. To have a right relationship with God, we must start the day by yielding to Him our bodies, minds, and wills.

Applying God's Truth:

1. What improvements would you like to make in your mind? Your will? Your body?

2. In what ways do you surrender each of these three areas to God? How might you be more completely surrendered in each case?

3. Can you think of specific ways that God has recently used your body, mind, and/or will to bring peace to your life and glory to Himself?

Scripture: Read Romans 12:17–13:14

"Do not be overcome by evil, but overcome evil with good" (Rom. 12:21).

RESPONDING TO EVIL

The Christian must not play God and try to avenge himself. Returning evil for evil, or good for good, is the way most people live. But the Christian must live on a higher level and return good for evil. Of course, this requires *love*, because our first inclination is to fight back. It also requires *faith*, believing that God can work and accomplish His will in our lives and the lives of those who hurt us.

A friend of mine once heard a preacher criticize him over the radio and tell things that were not only unkind, but also untrue. My friend became very angry and was planning to fight back, when a godly preacher said, "Don't do it. If you defend yourself, then the Lord can't defend you. Leave it in His hands." My friend followed that wise counsel, and the Lord vindicated him.

As children of God, we must live on the highest level—returning good for evil. Anyone can return good for good and evil for evil. The only way to overcome evil is with good. If we return evil for evil, we only add fuel to the fire. And even if our enemy is not converted, we have still experienced the love of God in our own hearts and have grown in grace.

Applying God's Truth:

1. When faced with evil, why are love *and* faith required to combat it?

2. Can you think of a personal example where you left an unjust situation in God's hands and allowed *Him* to defend you?

3. Is it possible to grow stronger and more mature even though you "lose" in conflicts with evil? If so, why do you think it's so rare to see people return good for evil?

Scripture: Read Romans 14:1-12

"Who are you to judge someone else's servant? To his own master he stands or falls. And he will stand, for the Lord is able to make him stand" (Rom. 14:4).

JESUS IS LORD OF OTHER PEOPLE TOO

Paul explained that his readers did not have to give an account for anyone else but themselves. So they were to make sure that their account would be a good one. He was stressing the principle of lordship—make Jesus Christ the Lord of your life, and let Him be the Lord in the lives of other Christians as well.

Two of the most famous Christians in the Victorian Era in England were Charles Spurgeon and Joseph Parker, both of them mighty preachers of the Gospel. Early in their ministries they fellowshipped and even exchanged pulpits. Then they had a disagreement, and the reports even got into the newspapers. Spurgeon accused Parker of being unspiritual because he attended the theater. Interestingly enough, Spurgeon smoked cigars, a practice many believers would condemn. Who was right? Who was wrong? Perhaps *both* of them were wrong!

When it comes to questionable matters in the Christian life, cannot dedicated believers disagree without being disagreeable? "I have learned that God blesses people I disagree with!" a friend of mine told me one day, and I have learned the same thing. When Jesus Christ is Lord, we permit Him to deal with His own servants as He wishes.

Applying God's Truth:

1. Do you think it's more difficult to allow Jesus to be Lord of *your* life, or of other peoples' lives? Why?

2. What activities do you think cause most disagreements among various groups of Christians? Why?

3. As the secular world views the Christian world, do you think they are more critical over our participation in the things we argue about, or the internal conflicts that arise over such participation? Explain.

Scripture: Read Romans 14:13-23

"Let us stop passing judgment on one another. Instead, make up your mind not to put any stumbling block or obstacle in your brother's way" (Rom. 14:13).

PREVENTING STUMBLING; ENCOURAGING GROWTH

When a child comes into a home, everything has to change. Mother and father are careful not to leave the scissors on the chair or anything dangerous within reach. But as the child matures, it is possible for the parents to adjust the rules of the house and deal with him in a more adult fashion. It is natural for a child to stumble when he is learning to walk. But if an adult constantly stumbles, we know something is wrong.

Young Christians need the kind of fellowship that will protect them and encourage them to grow. But we cannot treat them like "babies" all their lives! The older Christians must exercise love and patience and be careful not to cause them to stumble. But the younger Christians must "grow in the grace and knowledge of our Lord and Savior Jesus Christ" (2 Peter 3:18). As they mature in the faith, they can help other believers to grow. To gear the ministry of a Sunday School class or local church only to the baby Christians is to hinder their growth as well as the ministry of the more mature saints. The weak must learn from the strong, and the strong must love the weak. The result will be peace and maturity to the glory of God.

Applying God's Truth:

1. Who are some Christians you know whom you feel are still "weak" in certain areas? Are you giving them time to mature? What are you doing to help them?

2. Would you say your Sunday School class, church service, Bible study group, and so forth are geared for "baby" Christians, mature Christians, or somewhere between?

3. If you find that you are more (or less) mature than the others in most of the programs that are currently available to you, what do you think you should do?

Scripture: Read Romans 15

"It has always been my ambition to preach the gospel where Christ was not known, so that I would not be building on someone else's foundation" (Rom. 15:20).

TIME TO MOVE ON

The vast area of opportunity in other parts of the empire kept Paul from visiting Rome sooner. He was not hindered from going to Rome by satanic opposition or physical obstacles, but by the challenge of completing his work right where he was. He was so faithful in his evangelistic outreach that he was able to say that he had no more place to minister in those parts. This did not mean that Paul personally witnessed to every person in that area, but that he took the Gospel and left behind witnessing churches and Christians who would carry on the work. Paul finished one job before he started another one, a good example for our evangelistic ministry today.

Paul's desire for many years had been to visit Rome and then move on to Spain, but there is no record that he ever did. Tradition says that he did go to Spain, and to Britain, after he was released, but church tradition is not always to be trusted.

Applying God's Truth:

1. If Paul came to your country to spread the Gospel, where do you think he would start? Why?

2. How do you determine when it's time to "move on" from one Christian group (or project) to another?

3. Do you have any *long-term* spiritual goals or dreams? ("Someday I hope to . . .")

Scripture: Read Romans 16

"Now to him who is able to establish you by my gospel . . . so that all nations might believe and obey him—to the only wise God be glory forever through Jesus Christ! Amen" (Rom. 16:25-27).

SIGNING OFF

The closing benediction (vv. 25-27) is the longest one Paul ever wrote. It reflects his special ministry to the Gentiles. "The mystery" has to do with God's program of uniting believing Jews and Gentiles in the one body, the church (see Eph. 3). This was Paul's special message. It was because of this message that the Judaizers persecuted Paul, because they wanted to maintain Jewish privileges. Both Jews and Gentiles in the Roman churches needed to know what God's program was. Some of this Paul had explained in chapters 9 through 11.

Christians are established by the truth, which explains why Paul wrote this letter: to explain God's plan of salvation to Christians so they would be established, and so they would share the truth with the lost. After all, we cannot really share with others something we do not have ourselves.

This means that our own study of Romans should make us more stable in the faith and more excited to share Christ with others. And the result: "To the only wise God be glory forever through Jesus Christ!"

Applying God's Truth:

1. If you wanted to encourage your church with a benediction of what God is able to do, what would you say to them?

2. If you had been a Gentile in the predominantly Jewish church at this time, how do you think you would have felt after reading Paul's letter to the Romans? Why?

3. If a theme of Romans is to "Be Right," in what ways do you feel you can be more right *now* than when you began reading through it?

CONTENTMENT

30 Daily Readings from the Book of Ecclesiastes

P EOPLE ARE NEVER FREE OF TRYING TO BE CONTENT." ECOLOGIST MURRAY Brookchin wrote that in the June 1, 1992 issue of the *London Independent*; and more than a century earlier, the American naturalist Henry David Thoreau wrote, "The mass of men lead lives of quiet desperation."

Both men are right.

Today, we can go to the drugstore and buy mood elevators and even buy sleep, but we can't buy peace and contentment. If we want to escape the rat race, we can visit a theme park and purchase hours of entertainment; but the rat race will still be there when we walk out the gate. True contentment is a matter of the inner person: having the right priorities, measuring life by the right standards, focusing on the right goals, and exercising the right faith. It means taking God into every area of your life and letting Him have control.

If anybody knew the folly of living for the rat race (he called it chasing after the wind), it was King Solomon. He had everything and he tried everything, and he recorded his experiments and experiences for us to read in an ancient book we call Ecclesiastes—"The Preacher."

The most recent self-help manual in the bookstore doesn't begin to give you the insights that Solomon shares in this journal of a man who tried to catch the wind. Solomon writes about success, leadership, life goals, social injustice, sex and marriage, money, and even old age and death. He honestly records his own feelings and failures and the lessons he learned from these experiments in the laboratory of life. He paid the price—you get all the benefits of his wisdom!

He tells you the master secret of having contentment in a world that wants to rob you of peace. Solomon points the way to the kind of lifestyle that makes living worthwhile and saves you from the dead-end streets of modern civilization.

Jesus said, "I have come that they may have life, and have it to the full" (John 10:10).

Solomon knew about that abundant life centuries ago, and you can know about it today. As each day you learn from King Solomon, you'll discover that life can be satisfying and successful when you walk with God and trust Him.

Scripture: Read Ecclesiastes 1:1

"The words of the Teacher, son of David, king in Jerusalem" (Ecc. 1:1).

SOLOMON'S SEQUEL

N owhere in this book did the author give his name, but the descriptions he gave of himself and his experiences would indicate that the writer was King Solomon. Solomon began his reign as a humble servant of the Lord, seeking God's wisdom and help (1 Kings 3:5-15). As he grew older, his heart turned away from Jehovah to the false gods of the many wives he had taken from foreign lands (11:1ff). These marriages were motivated primarily by politics, not love, as Solomon sought alliances with the nations around Israel.

No amount of money or authority could stop the silent but sure ripening of divine judgment. The famous Scottish preacher Alexander Whyte said that "the secret worm . . . was gnawing all the time in the royal staff upon which Solomon leaned." The king's latter years were miserable because God removed His hand of blessing (1 Kings 11) and maintained Solomon's throne only because of His promise to David.

Ecclesiastes appears to be the kind of book a person would write near the close of life, reflecting on life's experiences and the lessons learned. Solomon probably wrote Proverbs and the Song of Solomon during the years he faithfully walked with God; and near the end of his life, he wrote Ecclesiastes. There is no record that King Solomon repented and turned to the Lord, but his message in Ecclesiastes suggests that he did.

Applying God's Truth:

1. What is the most foolish thing you've done out of love for someone?

2. If the wisest man who ever lived could not remain faithful to God, do you think its realistic to expect that you can? Explain.

3. Based on Solomon's experiences, what would you say might be more important than wisdom in regard to continual spiritual growth?

Scripture: Read Ecclesiastes 1:2

"'Meaningless! Meaningless!' says the Teacher. 'Utterly meaningless! Everything is meaningless'" *(Ecc. 1:2)*.

WHETHER VAIN

V anity of vanities," lamented Solomon, "all is vanity!" (according to the *King James Version* of v. 2). Solomon liked that word *vanity*; he used it thirty-eight times in Ecclesiastes as he wrote about life under the sun. The word means emptiness, futility, vapor, that which vanishes quickly and leaves nothing behind.

From the human point of view ("under the sun"), life does appear futile, and it is easy for us to get pessimistic. The Jewish writer Sholom Aleichem once described life as "a blister on top of a tumor, and a boil on top of that." You can almost feel that definition!

The American poet Carl Sandburg compared life to "an onion—you peel it off one layer at a time, and sometimes you weep." And British playwright George Bernard Shaw said that life was "a series of inspired follies."

What a relief to turn from these pessimistic views and hear Jesus Christ say, "I have come that they may have life, and have it to the full" (John 10:10). Or to read Paul's majestic declaration, "Therefore, my dear brothers, stand firm. Let nothing move you. Always give yourselves fully to the work of the Lord, because you know that your labor for the Lord is not in vain" (1 Cor. 15:58).

Life is not in vain if it is lived according to the will of God, and that is what Solomon teaches in this neglected and often misunderstood book.

Applying God's Truth:

1. Have you ever gone through periods when you considered your life and felt all was vanity (meaningless)?

2. How would you define your current philosophy of life in a couple of sentences?

3. What relationships and activities provide the most meaning in your life?

Scripture: Read Ecclesiastes 1:3

"What does man gain from all his labor at which he toils under the sun?" (Ecc. 1:3)

PROBLEMS THEN AND NOW

What is the practical application of this book for us today? Is Ecclesiastes nothing but an interesting exhibit in a religious museum, or does it have a message for people in the Space Age?

Its message is for today. After all, the society which Solomon investigated a millennium before the birth of Christ was not too different from our world today. Solomon saw injustice to the poor, crooked politics, incompetent leaders, guilty people allowed to commit more crime, materialism, and a desire for the good old days. It sounds up-to-date, doesn't it?

If you have never trusted Jesus Christ as your Savior, then this book urges you to do so without delay. Why? Because no matter how much wealth, education, or social prestige you may have, life without God is futile. You are only chasing after the wind if you expect to find satisfaction and personal fulfillment in the things of the world. "What good is it for a man to gain the whole world, yet forfeit his soul?" asked Jesus (Mark 8:36).

Solomon experimented with life and discovered that there was no lasting satisfaction in possessions, pleasures, power, or prestige. He had everything, yet his life was empty! There is no need for you and me to repeat these experiments. Let's accept Solomon's conclusions and avoid the heartache and pain that must be endured when you experiment in the laboratory of life.

Applying God's Truth:

1. What have you witnessed lately that caused you to question the fairness of life?

2. What are some of the things you've tried in an attempt to bring more meaning to life?

3. How would you contrast the quality of your life before a relationship with Jesus with life afterward?

Scripture: Read Ecclesiastes 1:4-8

"Generations come and generations go, but the earth remains forever" (Ecc. 1:4).

AS SURE AS THE WORLD

From the human point of view, nothing seems more permanent and durable than the planet on which we live. When we say that something is as sure as the world, we are echoing Solomon's confidence in the permanence of Planet Earth. With all of its diversity, nature is uniform enough in its operation that we can discover its laws and put them to work for us. In fact, it is this dependability that is the basis for modern science.

Nature is permanent, but man is transient, a mere pilgrim on earth. His pilgrimage is a brief one, for death finally claims him. At the very beginning of his book, Solomon introduced a topic frequently mentioned in Ecclesiastes: the brevity of life and the certainty of death.

Individuals and families come and go, nations and empires rise and fall, but nothing changes, for the world remains the same. Thomas Carlyle called history a mighty drama, enacted upon the theater of time, with suns for lamps and eternity for a background. Solomon would add that the costumes and sets may occasionally change, but the actors and the script remain pretty much the same; and that's as sure as the world.

Applying God's Truth:

1. How frequently do you think about your inevitable death? How does it make you feel?

2. How do you try to ensure that you're making the most of your life while you have the opportunity?

3. As a member of your generation, how well are you connected to the older generation(s) as well as the younger one(s)?

Scripture: Read Ecclesiastes 1:9-11

"Is there anything of which one can say, 'Look! This is something new? It was here already, long ago; it was here before our time" (Ecc. 1:10).

EVERYTHING OLD IS NEW AGAIN

A young man approached me at a conference and asked if he could share some new ideas for youth ministry. He was very enthusiastic as he outlined his program, but the longer I listened, the more familiar his ideas became. I encouraged him to put his ideas into practice, but then told him that we had done all of those things in Youth for Christ before he was born, and that YFC workers were still doing them. He was a bit stunned to discover that there was indeed nothing new under the sun.

Solomon wrote, of course, about the basic principles of life and not about methods. As the familiar couplet puts it: Methods are many, principles are few/methods always change, principles never do. The ancient thinkers knew this. The Stoic philosopher Marcus Aurelius wrote, "They that come after us will see nothing new, and they who went before us saw nothing more than we have seen." The only people who really think they have seen something new are those whose experience is limited or whose vision can't penetrate beneath the surface of things. Because something is recent, they think it is new; they mistake novelty for originality.

Applying God's Truth:

1. What are some of the principles you've held throughout your life that are identical to those of your parents and preceding generations?

2. How would you distinguish between novelty and originality?

3. If it's true that there is no new thing under the sun, why do you think people today put so much emphasis on new and improved, new and better, and other promises of hitherto undiscovered products and services?

Scripture: Read Ecclesiastes 1:12-18

"I applied myself to the understanding of wisdom, and also of madness and folly, but I learned that this, too, is a chasing after the wind. For with much wisdom comes much sorrow; the more knowledge, the more grief" (Ecc. 1:17-18).

LIVING IN CIRCLES

When Adam and Eve sinned, they did get an experiential knowledge of good and evil, but, since they were alienated from God, this knowledge only added to their sorrow. It has been that way with man ever since. Whether it be jet planes, insecticides, or television, each advance in human knowledge and achievement only creates a new set of problems for society.

For some people, life may be monotonous and meaningless; but it does not have to be. For the Christian believer, life is an open door, not a closed circle; there are daily experiences of new blessings from the Lord. True, we can't explain everything; but life is not built on explanations: it's built on promises—and we have plenty of promises in God's Word!

The scientist tells us that the world is a closed system and nothing is changed. The historian tells us that life is a closed book and nothing is new. The philosopher tells us that life is a deep problem and nothing is understood.

But Jesus Christ is the power of God and the wisdom of God (1 Cor. 1:24), and He has miraculously broken into history to bring new life to all who trust Him. If you are living in circles, then turn your life over to Him.

Applying God's Truth:

1. Do you think Solomon's observation that in much wisdom is much grief is the same as declaring that ignorance is bliss? Why?

2. Do you agree that in much wisdom is much grief? Give some specific examples to support your answer.

3. In what ways do you feel you may be living in circles?

Scripture: Read Ecclesiastes 2:1-11

"I denied myself nothing my eyes desired; I refused my heart no pleasure. . . . Yet when I surveyed all that my hands had done . . . everything was meaningless" *(Ecc. 2:10-11).*

WHEN PLEASURE IS TREASURED

Today's world is pleasure-mad. Millions of people will pay almost any amount of money to buy experiences and temporarily escape the burdens of life. While there is nothing wrong with innocent fun, the person who builds his or her life only on seeking pleasure is bound to be disappointed in the end.

Why? For one thing, pleasure-seeking usually becomes a selfish endeavor, and selfishness destroys true joy. People who live for pleasure often exploit others to get what they want, and they end up with broken relationships as well as empty hearts. People are more important than things and thrills. We are to be channels, not reservoirs; the greatest joy comes when we share God's pleasure with others.

If you live for pleasure alone, enjoyment will decrease unless the intensity of the pleasure increases. Then you reach a point of diminishing returns when there is little or no enjoyment at all, only bondage. For example, the more that people drink, the less enjoyment they get out of it. This means they must have more drinks and stronger drinks in order to have pleasure; the sad result is desire without satisfaction. Instead of alcohol, substitute drugs, gambling, promiscuous sex, money, fame, or any other pursuit, and the principle will hold true: when pleasure alone is the center of life, the result will ultimately be disappointment and emptiness.

Applying God's Truth:

1. On a scale of 1 (least) to 10 (most), to what extent would you say you are a pleasure-seeker?

2. In what ways do people you know try to use pleasure to find fulfillment in life?

3. How can you enjoy life to the fullest, without having your pleasurable experiences diminish in effectiveness?

Scripture: Read Ecclesiastes 2:12-23

"I hated all the things I had toiled for under the sun, because I must leave them to the one who comes after me. And who knows whether he will be a wise man or a fool?" (Ecc. 2:18-19)

MONEY MANAGEMENT

Solomon was born wealthy, and great wealth came to him because he was the king. But he was looking at life under the sun and speaking for the common people who were listening to his discussion. The day would come when Solomon would die and leave everything to his successor. This reminds us of our Lord's warning in the Parable of the Rich Fool (Luke 12:13-21) and Paul's words in 1 Timothy 6:7-10. A Jewish proverb says, "There are no pockets in shrouds."

Money is a medium of exchange. Unless it is spent, it can do little or nothing for you. You can't eat money, but you can use it to buy food. It will not keep you warm, but it will purchase fuel. A writer in *The Wall Street Journal* called money an article which may be used as a universal passport to everywhere except heaven, and as a universal provider of everything except happiness.

Of course, you and I are stewards of our wealth; God is the Provider (Deut. 8:18) and the Owner, and we have the privilege of enjoying it and using it for His glory. One day we will have to give an account of what we have done with His generous gifts. While we cannot take wealth with us when we die, we can send it ahead as we use it today according to God's will (Matt. 6:19-34).

Applying God's Truth:

1. To what extent would you say you are concerned about leaving a good inheritance for your children? Do you wonder if they will appreciate it as they should?

2. What is your philosophy of money? How much importance do you think it deserves?

3. What does it mean to you to be a steward of your wealth?

Scripture: Read Ecclesiastes 2:24-26

"A man can do nothing better than to eat and drink and find satisfaction in his work. This too, I see, is from the hand of God, for without him, who can eat or find enjoyment?" (Ecc. 2:24)

EAT, DRINK, AND BE THANKFUL

Solomon is not advocating "Eat, drink, and be merry, for tomorrow we die!" That is the philosophy of fatalism, not faith. Rather, he is saying, "Thank God for what you do have, and enjoy it to the glory of God." Paul gave his approval to this attitude when he exhorted us to trust in God, who richly provides us with everything for our enjoyment (1 Tim. 6:17).

Solomon made it clear that not only were the blessings from God, but even the enjoyment of the blessings was God's gift to us (Ecc. 2:24). He considered it evil if a person had all the blessings of life from God but could not enjoy them (6:1-5). It is easy to see why the Jewish people read Ecclesiastes at the Feast of Tabernacles, for Tabernacles is their great time of thanksgiving and rejoicing for God's abundant provision of their needs. The farmer who prayed at the table, "Thanks for food and for good digestion" knew what Solomon was writing about.

The important thing is that we seek to please the Lord (2:26) and trust Him to meet every need. God wants to give us wisdom, knowledge, and joy; these three gifts enable us to appreciate God's blessings and take pleasure in them. It is not enough to possess things; we must also possess the kind of character that enables us to use things wisely and enjoy them properly.

Applying God's Truth:

1. What are your Top Ten blessings from God?

2. For each of the things you've listed, are you experiencing the degree of enjoyment that you feel you should? If not, how can you enjoy them even more?

3. How can you develop the kind of character that enables you to use things wisely and enjoy them properly?

Scripture: Read Ecclesiastes 3:1-8

"There is a time for everything, and a season for every activity under heaven: a time to be born and a time to die" (Ecc. 3:1-2).

TIMES AND SEASONS

You don't have to be a philosopher or a scientist to know that times and seasons are a regular part of life, no matter where you live. Were it not for the dependability of God-ordained natural laws, both science and daily life would be chaotic, if not impossible. Not only are there times and seasons in this world, but there is also an overruling providence in our lives. From before our birth to the moment of our death, God is accomplishing His divine purposes, even though we may not always understand what He is doing.

Solomon affirmed that God is at work in our individual lives, seeking to accomplish His will. All of these events come from God and they are good in their time. The inference is plain: if we cooperate with God's timing, life will not be meaningless. Everything will be beautiful in its time (v. 11), even the most difficult experiences of life.

Things like abortion, birth control, mercy killing, and surrogate parenthood make it look as though man is in control of birth and death, but Solomon said otherwise. Birth and death are not human accidents; they are divine appointments, for God is in control. Psalm 139:13-16 states that God so wove us in the womb that our genetic structure is perfect for the work He has prepared for us to do (Eph. 2:10). We may foolishly hasten our death, but we cannot prevent it when our time comes, unless God so wills it.

Applying God's Truth:

1. Read Ecclesiastes 3:1-8 and identify any of the times and seasons you seem to be going through right now.

2. Can you think of an instance when recognizing God's timing brought meaning to your life? In what way?

3. How might you discover more meaning in life by letting go of certain things and turning to God instead?

Scripture: Read Ecclesiastes 3:9-22

"I know that there is nothing better for men than to be happy and do good while they live. That everyone may eat and drink, and find satisfaction in all his toil—this is the gift of God" (Ecc. 3:12-13).

ENJOYMENT AND ETERNITY

When the well-known British Methodist preacher William Sangster learned that he had progressive muscular atrophy and could not get well, he made four resolutions and kept them to the end: (1) I will never complain; (2) I will keep the home bright; (3) I will count my blessings; (4) I will try to turn it to gain. This is the approach to life that Solomon wants us to take.

However, we must note that Solomon is not saying, "Don't worry—be happy!" He is promoting faith in God, not "faith in faith" or "pie in the sky, by and by." Faith is only as good as the object of faith, and the greatest object of faith is the Lord. He can be trusted.

How can life be meaningless and monotonous for you when God has made you a part of His eternal plan? You are not an insignificant insect, crawling from one sad annihilation to another. If you have trusted Jesus Christ, you are a child of God being prepared for an eternal home. The Puritan pastor Thomas Watson said, "Eternity to the godly is a day that has no sunset; eternity to the wicked is a night that has no sunrise."

The proper attitude for us is fear of the Lord (v. 14), which is not the cringing of a slave before a cruel master, but the submission of an obedient child to a loving parent. If we fear God, we need not fear anything else for He is in control.

Applying God's Truth:

1. What are four resolutions you could make to help you better cope with the difficult periods of life?

2. In what ways do you feel God is preparing you now for your eternal home?

3. How would you define fear of the Lord to someone hearing the phrase for the first time?

Scripture: Read Ecclesiastes 4:1-6

"I saw the tears of the oppressed—and they have no comforter; power was on the side of their oppressors—and they have no comforter. And I declared that the dead, who had already died, are happier than the living, who are still alive" (Ecc. 4:1-2).

DISORDER IN THE COURT

Solomon went into a courtroom to watch a trial, and there he saw innocent people being oppressed by power-hungry officials. The victims wept, but their tears did no good. Nobody stood with them to comfort or assist them. The oppressors had all the power and the victims were helpless to protest or ask for redress.

Why didn't Solomon do something about this injustice? After all, he was the king. Alas, even the king couldn't do a great deal to solve the problem. For once Solomon started to interfere with his government and reorganize things, he would only create new problems and reveal more corruption. This is not to suggest that we today should despair of cleaning out political corruption. As Christian citizens, we must pray for all in authority and do what we can to see that just laws are passed and fairly enforced. But it's doubtful that a huge administrative body like the one in Israel would ever be free of corruption, or that a crusader could have improved the situation.

Edward Gibbon, celebrated author of *The Decline and Fall of the Roman Empire*, said that political corruption was "the most infallible symptom of constitutional liberty." Perhaps he was right; for where there is freedom to obey, there is also freedom to disobey. Some of Solomon's officials decided they were above the law, and the innocent suffered.

Applying God's Truth:

1. In what ways do you think our court system permits injustices?

2. How do you feel when you become the victim of an injustice by someone wealthier or more influential than you? What, if anything, do you try to do to right the scales of justice?

3. Do you regularly pray for people in authority—even if they misuse their authority to take advantage of you and others?

Scripture: Read Ecclesiastes 4:7-16

"Two are better than one, because they have a good return for their work" (Ecc. 4:9).

Two Threads Are Better Than One

Two are certainly better than one when it comes to working (v. 9) because two workers can get more done. Even when they divide the profits, they still get a better return for their efforts than if they had worked alone. Also, it's much easier to do difficult jobs together because one can be an encouragement to the other.

Two are better when it comes to walking (v. 10). Roads and paths in Palestine were not paved or even leveled, and there were many hidden rocks in the fields. It was not uncommon for even the most experienced traveler to stumble and fall, perhaps break a bone, or even fall into a hidden pit (Ex. 21:33-34). How wonderful to have a friend who can help you up (or out).

Two are better than one when it comes to warmth (Ecc. 4:11). Two travelers camping out, or even staying in the courtyard of a public inn, would feel the cold of the Palestinian night and need one another's warmth for comfort. The only way to be warm alone is to carry extra blankets and add to your load.

Finally, two are better than one when it comes to their watchcare, especially at night (v. 12). It was dangerous for anyone to travel alone, day or night; most people traveled in groups for fellowship and for safety.

If two travelers are better than one, then three would fare even better. Solomon had more than numbers in mind; he was also thinking of the unity involved in three cords woven together—what a beautiful picture of friendship!

Applying God's Truth:

1. What have you done lately to help someone's work go a little easier?

2. What have you done lately to assist someone who has stumbled in his or her spiritual walk and could use some help?

3. What kind of help could you use at this point in your life? Who might be able to help if you alerted that person to your need?

Scripture: Read Ecclesiastes 5:1-7

"Guard your steps when you go to the house of God. Go near to listen rather than to offer the sacrifice of fools, who do not know that they do wrong" (Ecc. 5:1).

THE SACRIFICE OF FOOLS

Solomon had visited the courtroom, the marketplace, the highway, and the palace. Now he paid a visit to the temple, that magnificent building whose construction he had supervised. He watched the worshipers come and go, praising God, praying, sacrificing, and making vows. He noted that many of them were not at all sincere in their worship, and they left the sacred precincts in worse spiritual condition than when they had entered. What was their sin? They were robbing God of the reverence and honor that He deserved. Their acts of worship were perfunctory, insincere, and hypocritical.

Even though God's glorious presence doesn't dwell in our church buildings as it did in the temple, believers today still need to heed this warning. The worship of God is the highest ministry of the church and must come from devoted hearts and yielded wills. For God's people to participate in public worship while harboring unconfessed sin, is to ask for God's rebuke and judgment.

The important thing is that the worshiper go near to listen, that is, to obey the Word of God. Sacrifices are not substitutes for obedience. Offerings in the hands without obedient faith in the heart become the sacrifice of fools, because only a fool thinks he can deceive God. The fool thinks he is doing good, but he or she is only doing evil. And God knows it.

Applying God's Truth:

1. What kinds of sacrifices do people offer today that may be a substitute for genuine obedience to God?

2. What other forms of insincere worship take place in the church today?

3. How can you ensure that your own worship remains pure and sincere?

Scripture: Read Ecclesiastes 5:8-20

"Whoever loves money never has money enough; whoever loves wealth is never satisfied with his income" (Ecc. 5:10).

MATTERS OF WEALTH AND HEALTH

There is no escaping the fact that we need a certain amount of money in order to live in this world, but money of itself is not the magic cure-all for every problem. John Wesley, cofounder of the Methodist Church, told his people, "Make all you can, save all you can, give all you can." Wesley himself could have been a very wealthy man, but he chose to live simply and give generously.

The late Joe Louis, world heavyweight boxing champion, used to say, "I don't like money, actually, but it quiets my nerves." But Solomon said that possessing wealth is no guarantee that your nerves will be calm and your sleep sound. According to him, the common laborer sleeps better than the rich man. *The Living Bible* expresses verse 12 perfectly: "The man who works hard sleeps well whether he eats little or much, but the rich must worry and suffer insomnia."

More than one preacher has mentioned John D. Rockefeller in his sermons as an example of a man whose life was almost ruined by wealth. At the age of fifty-three, Rockefeller was the world's only billionaire, earning about a million dollars a week. But he was a sick man who lived on crackers and milk and could not sleep because of worry. When he started giving his money away, his health changed radically, and he lived to celebrate his ninety-eighth birthday!

Yes, it's good to have the things that money can buy, provided you don't lose the things money can't buy.

Applying God's Truth:

1. Do you think there is a direct correlation between having an abundance of money and an abundance of peace? Why?

2. What do you think of Wesley's command to "Make all you can, save all you can, give all you can"?

3. To what extent do you think that worrying about money is a source of other problems in your life? In what ways?

Scripture: Read Ecclesiastes 6:1-9

"All man's efforts are for his mouth, yet his appetite is never satisfied" (Ecc. 6:7).

LIVING VERSUS EXISTING

Rich and poor alike labor to stay alive. We must either produce food or earn money to buy it. The rich man can let his money work for him, but the poor man has to use his muscles if he and his family are going to eat. But even after all this labor, the appetite of neither one is fully satisfied.

Why does a person eat? So that he can add years to his life. But what good is it for me to add years to my life if I don't add life to my years? I'm like the birds that I watch in the backyard. They spend all their waking hours either looking for food or escaping from enemies. (We have cats in our neighborhood.) These birds are not really living; they are only existing. Yet they are fulfilling the purposes for which the Creator made them—and they even sing about it!

Solomon is not suggesting that it's wrong either to work or to eat. Many people enjoy doing both. But if life consists only in working and eating, then we are being controlled by our appetites and that almost puts us on the same level as animals. As far as nature is concerned, self-preservation may be the first law of life, but we who are made in the image of God must live for something higher.

Applying God's Truth:

1. Is your work a fulfilling activity for you? How might it become more fulfilling?

2. How much enjoyment do you get out of eating? Do you make the most out of your meals?

3. What things can you do to keep from letting routine activities (like working and eating) take control and prevent you from enjoying what is truly important in life?

Scripture: Read Ecclesiastes 6:10

"Better what the eye sees than the roving of the appetite. . . . Whatever exists has already been named, and what man is has been known" (Ecc. 6:9-10a).

IT'S YOUR CHOICE

Since what's going to be is going to be, why bother to make decisions? Isn't it all predestined anyway? Whatever exists has already been named, and what man is has been known (v. 10a). To the Jewish mind, giving a name to something is the same as fixing its character and stating what the thing really is. During the time of creation, God named the things that He made; and nobody changed those designations. Light is light and not darkness; day is day and not night.

Our name is "man"—Adam, "from the earth" (Gen. 2:7). Nobody can change that: we came from the earth and we will return to the earth (3:19). Man by any other name would still be man, made from the dust and eventually returning to the dust.

The fact that God has named everything does not mean that our world is a prison and we have no freedom to act. Certainly God can accomplish His divine purposes with or without our cooperation, but He invites us to work with Him. We cooperate with God as we accept the names He has given to things: sin is sin; obedience is obedience; truth is truth. If we alter these names, we move into a world of illusion and lose touch with reality. This is where many people are living today.

We are free to decide and choose our world, but we are not free to change the consequences. If we choose a world of illusion, we start living on substitutes, and there can be no satisfaction in a world of substitutes.

Applying God's Truth:

1. Does the fact that you serve an omniscient God make you feel that your life has less spontaneity and choice than it should have? Why?

2. What are some of the changes you would like to make in your life?

3. How do you think you might begin to cooperate with God to bring about some of the changes you have listed?

Scripture: Read Ecclesiastes 6:10b-12

"No man can contend with one who is stronger than he" (Ecc. 6:10b).

QUESTIONING GOD

Solomon seems to say, "It just doesn't pay to argue with God or to fight God. This is the way life is, so just accept it and let God have His way. You can't win, and even if you do think you win, you ultimately lose."

But his is a negative view of the will of God. It gives the impression that God's will is a difficult and painful thing that should be avoided at all cost. Jesus said that God's will was the food that nourished and satisfied Him (John 4:32-34). It was meat, not medicine. The will of God comes from the heart of God and is an expression of the love of God. (See Ps. 33:11.) What God wills for us is best for us because He knows far more about us than we do.

Why would anyone want to have his or her own way just for the privilege of exercising freedom? Insisting on having our own way isn't freedom at all; it's the worst kind of bondage. In fact, the most terrible judgment we could experience in this life would be to have God give us up and let us have our own way (Rom. 1:24, 26, 28).

God is free to act as He sees best. He is not a prisoner of His attributes, His creation, or His eternal purposes. You and I may not understand how God exercises His freedom, but it isn't necessary for us to know all. Our greatest freedom comes when we are lovingly lost in the will of God. Our Father in heaven doesn't feel threatened when we question Him, debate with Him, or even wrestle with Him, so long as we love His will and want to please Him.

Applying God's Truth:

1. What kind of emotions does the thought of God's will bring to your heart?

2. Do you think God is displeased when you question His will for you? Why?

3. Is it easy for you to trust that God knows best and leave things in His hands? Or do you want to understand everything that's going on as it is happening?

Scripture: Read Ecclesiastes 7:1-8

"A good name is better than fine perfume, and the day of death better than the day of birth" (Ecc. 7:1).

LOOKING DEATH IN THE FACE

Solomon was not contrasting birth and death, nor was he suggesting that it is better to die than to be born because you can't die unless you have been born. He was contrasting two significant days in human experience: the day a person receives his or her name and the day when that name shows up in the obituary column. The life lived between those two events will determine whether that name leaves behind a lovely fragrance or a foul stench.

Solomon advised the people to look death in the face and learn from it. He did not say that we should be preoccupied with death because that could be abnormal. But there is a danger that we might try to avoid confrontations with the reality of death and, as a result, not take life as seriously as we should. "Teach us to number our days aright, that we may gain a heart of wisdom" (Ps. 90:12).

The late Dr. Ernest Becker wrote in his Pulitzer-Prize-winning book *The Denial of Death*: ". . . the idea of death, the fear of it, haunts the human animal like nothing else; it is a mainspring of human activity—activity designed largely to avoid the fatality of death, to overcome it by denying in some way that it is the final destiny for man" (Free Press, 1975, p. ix). King Solomon knew this truth centuries ago!

Applying God's Truth:

1. In what ways does thinking about death help you take life more seriously?

2. Would you say you spend more time thinking back about the things you've done since you were born, or thinking about what you hope to do before you die? Are you satisfied that your balance of the two is what is should be?

3. Would you say you are haunted by the fear of death, or is your eventual death something that inspires you to a greater faith in God? Explain.

Scripture: Read Ecclesiastes 7:9-12

"Do not say, 'Why were the old days better than these?' For it is not wise to ask such questions" (Ecc. 7:10).

SEIZE THE DAY

An Arab proverb says, "Watch your beginnings." Good beginnings will usually mean good endings. The Prodigal Son started with happiness and wealth, but ended with suffering and poverty (Luke 15:11-24). Joseph began as a slave but ended up a sovereign! God always saves the best wine until the last (John 2:10), but Satan starts with his best and then leads the sinner into suffering and perhaps even death.

When life is difficult and we are impatient for change, it is easy to long for the good old days when things were better. When the foundation was laid for the second temple, the old men wept for the good old days and the young men sang because the work had begun (Ezra 3:12-13). It has been said that the good old days are the combination of a bad memory and a good imagination, and often this is true.

Yesterday is past and cannot be changed, and tomorrow may not come; so make the most of today. *Carpe diem!* wrote the Roman poet Horace. "Seize the day!" This does not mean we shouldn't learn from the past or prepare for the future, because both are important. It means that we must live today in the will of God and not be paralyzed by yesterday or hypnotized by tomorrow. The Victorian essayist Hilaire Belloc wrote, "While you are dreaming of the future or regretting the past, the present, which is all you have, slips from you and is gone."

Applying God's Truth:

1. In what ways do you try to watch your beginnings? Do you keep God's will in mind as you make plans?

2. When times are difficult, what are some things you can do to maintain a focus on the future rather than drifting into a longing for the past?

3. What can you do right now to seize today?

Scripture: Read Ecclesiastes 7:13-29

"When times are good, be happy; but when times are bad, consider: God has made the one as well as the other. Therefore, a man cannot discover anything about his future" (Ecc. 7:14).

The Best of Times, the Worst of Times

Wisdom gives us perspective so that we aren't discouraged when times are difficult, or arrogant when things are going well. It takes a good deal of spirituality to be able to accept prosperity as well as adversity, for often prosperity does greater damage.

God balances our lives by giving us enough blessings to keep us happy and enough burdens to keep us humble. If all we had were blessings in our hands, we would fall right over, so the Lord balances the blessing in our hands with burdens on our backs. That helps to keep us steady, and as we yield to Him, He can even turn the burdens into blessings.

Why does God constitute our lives in this way? The answer is simple: to keep us from thinking we know it all and that we can manage our lives by ourselves. A man cannot discover anything about his future (v. 14). Just about the time we think we have an explanation for things, God changes the situation and we have to throw out our formula. This is where Job's friends went wrong: they tried to use an old road map to guide Job on a brand-new journey, and the map didn't fit. No matter how much experience we have in the Christian life, or how many books we read, we must still walk by faith.

Applying God's Truth:

1. Can you think of a recent time when you became discouraged during difficult times? Or when you were arrogant when things were going well?

2. Do you feel you have a level of wisdom adequate enough to allow you to accept both adversity and prosperity? If not, what do you think you need to do?

3. During times of adversity do you try to see what God might be trying to teach you? Or are you usually too busy complaining?

Scripture: Read Ecclesiastes 8:1-13

"Although a wicked man commits a hundred crimes and still lives a long time, I know that it will go better with God-fearing men, who are reverent before God" (Ecc. 8:12).

IT JUST ISN'T FAIR

If there is no God, then we have nobody to blame but ourselves (or fate) for what happens in the world. But if we believe in a good and loving God, we must face the difficult question of why there is so much suffering in the world. Does God know about it and yet not care? Or does He know and care but lack the power to do anything about it?

Some people ponder this question and end up becoming either agnostics or atheists, but in so doing, they create a whole new problem: Where does all the good come from in the world? It's difficult to believe that matter alone produced the beautiful and enjoyable things we have in our world, even in the midst of so much evil.

Other people solve the problem by saying that evil is only an illusion and we shouldn't worry about it, or that God is in the process of evolving and can't do much about the tragedies of life. They assure us that God will get stronger and things will improve as the process of evolution goes on.

Solomon didn't deny the existence of God or the reality of evil, nor did he limit the power of God. Solomon solved the problem of evil by affirming these factors and seeing them in their proper perspective.

During the darkest days of World War II, somebody asked a friend of mine, "Why doesn't God stop the war?" My friend wisely replied, "Because He didn't start it in the first place." Solomon would have agreed with that answer.

Applying God's Truth:

1. When people ask your opinion, how do you explain the existence of suffering?

2. Do you think God's power or His love are limited in any way? Explain.

3. Are you suffering in some way in which you need to apply what you believe?

Scripture: Read Ecclesiastes 8:14-17

"No one can comprehend what goes on under the sun. Despite all his efforts to search it out, man cannot discover its meaning" (Ecc. 8:17).

THE FIRST STEP TOWARD KNOWLEDGE

The person who has to know everything, or who thinks he knows every-thing, is destined for disappointment in this world. Through many difficult days and sleepless nights, the Preacher applied himself diligently to the mysteries of life. He came to the conclusion that no one can comprehend what goes on under the sun (v. 17). Perhaps we can solve a puzzle here and there, but no man or woman can comprehend the totality of things or explain all that God is doing.

Historian Will Durant surveyed human history in his multivolume *Story of Civilization* and came to the conclusion that "our knowledge is a receding mirage in an expanding desert of ignorance." Of course, this fact must not be used as an excuse for stupidity. "The secret things belong to the LORD our God, but the things revealed belong to us and to our children forever, that we may follow all the words of this law" (Deut. 29:29). God doesn't expect us to know the unknowable, but He does expect us to learn all that we can and obey what He teaches us. In fact, the more we obey, the more He will teach us (John 7:17).

A confession of ignorance is the first step toward true knowledge. "The man who thinks he knows something does not yet know as he ought to know" (1 Cor. 8:2). The person who wants to learn God's truth must possess honesty and humility.

Applying God's Truth:

1. What are some of the mysteries of life that you frequently ponder?

2. How is your faith affected when you struggle with something you can't figure out?

3. Do you think there are things God doesn't want us to know, or should we keep struggling to understand the mysteries of life?

Scripture: Read Ecclesiastes 9:1-4

"Anyone who is among the living has hope—even a live dog is better off than a dead lion!" (Ecc. 9:4)

A FINAL APPOINTMENT

I'm not afraid to die;" quipped Woody Allen, "I just don't want to be there when it happens." But he will be there when it happens, as must every human being, because there is no escaping death when your time has come. Death is not an accident, it's an appointment (Heb. 9:27), a destiny that nobody but God can cancel or change.

Life and death are in the hand of God (Ecc. 9:1), and only He knows our future, whether it will bring blessing (love) or sorrow (hatred). Solomon was not suggesting that we are passive actors in a cosmic drama, following an unchangeable script handed to us by an uncaring director. Throughout this book, Solomon has emphasized our freedom of discernment and decision. But only God knows what the future holds for us and what will happen tomorrow because of the decision we make today.

"As it is with the good man, so with the sinner" (v. 2). "If so, why bother to live a godly life?" someone may ask. "After all, whether we obey the Law or disobey, bring sacrifices or neglect them, make or break promises, we will die just the same." Yes, we share a common destiny on earth—death and the grave—*but we do not share a common destiny in eternity.* For that reason, everybody must honestly face the last enemy (1 Cor. 15:26) and decide how to deal with it. How people deal with the reality of death reveals itself in the way they deal with the realities of life.

Applying God's Truth:

1. Have you placed your life in the hand of God? How about your death?

2. Is there anything you feel you need to do before you die? If so, are you working toward getting it done?

3. Does thinking about death inspire you to greater action, or frighten you into passivity?

Scripture: Read Ecclesiastes 9:5-10

"The living know that they will die, but the dead know nothing; they have no further reward, and even the memory of them is forgotten" (Ecc. 9:5).

WHEN HOPE BECOMES HOPELESS

What Solomon wrote about the dead can be reversed and applied to the living. The dead do not know what is happening on earth, but the living know and can respond to it. The dead cannot add anything to their reward or their reputation, but the living can. The dead cannot relate to people on earth by loving, hating, or envying, but the living can. Solomon was emphasizing the importance of seizing opportunities while we live, rather than blindly hoping for something better in the future, because death will end our opportunities on this earth.

"The human body experiences a powerful gravitational pull in the direction of hope," wrote journalist Norman Cousins, who himself survived a near-fatal illness and a massive heart attack. "That is why the patient's hopes are the physician's secret weapon. They are the hidden ingredients in any prescription."

We endure because we hope, but "hope in hope" (like "faith in faith") is too often only a kind of self-hypnosis that keeps us from facing life honestly. While a patient may be better off with an optimistic attitude, it is dangerous for him to follow a false hope that may keep him from preparing for death. That kind of hope is hopeless. When the end comes, the patient's outlook may be cheerful, but the outcome will be tragic.

Applying God's Truth:

1. If you knew you were to die soon, would your plans for today change in any way? How?

2. What are some opportunities you need to seize while you still have the opportunity?

3. What is your definition of hope? Does your hope keep your faith strong?

Scripture: Read Ecclesiastes 9:11-18

"The race is not to the swift or the battle to the strong, nor does food come to the wise or wealth to the brilliant or favor to the learned; but time and chance happen to them all" (Ecc. 9:11).

NO GUARANTEES

Anticipating the response of his listeners (and his readers), Solomon turned from his discussion of death and began to discuss life. If death is unavoidable, somebody would argue, then the smartest thing we can do is major on our strengths and concentrate on life. When death comes, at least we'll have the satisfaction of knowing we worked hard and achieved some success.

Dont be too sure of that! was Solomon's reply. You can't guarantee what will happen in life, because life is unpredictable.

Our abilities are no guarantee of success (vv. 11-12). While it is generally true that the fastest runners win the races, the strongest soldiers win the battles, and the smartest and most skillful workers win the best jobs, it is also true that these same gifted people can fail miserably because of factors out of their control. The successful person knows how to make the most of time and procedure (8:5), but only the Lord can control time and chance (9:11).

Of course, Christians don't depend on such things as luck or chance because their confidence is in the loving providence of God. A dedicated Christian doesn't carry a rabbit's foot or trust in lucky days or numbers. Canadian humorist Stephen Leacock said, "I'm a great believer in luck. I find that the harder I work, the more I have of it." Christians trust God to guide them and help them in making decisions, and they believe that His will is best. They leave time and chance in His capable hands.

Applying God's Truth:

1. What would you say are your most significant strengths? In what ways do you try to count on those strengths for success?

2. Do you have any personal superstitions? To what extent do you tend to rely on luck or chance?

3. From this point on, how can you better leave time and chance completely in God's hands?

Scripture: Read Ecclesiastes 10:1-10

"Fools are put in many high positions, while the rich occupy the low ones. I have seen slaves on horseback, while princes go on foot like slaves" (Ecc. 10:6-7).

FOOLISH RULERS

If there is one person who needs wisdom, it is the ruler of a nation. When God asked Solomon what gift he especially wanted, the king asked for wisdom (1 Kings 3:3-28). Lyndon B. Johnson said, "A president's hardest task is not to do what's right, but to know what's right." That requires wisdom.

If a ruler is proud, he may say and do foolish things that cause him to lose the respect of his associates (Ecc. 10:4). The picture here is of a proud ruler who easily becomes angry and takes out his anger on the attendants around him. Of course, if a man has no control over himself, how can he hope to have control over his people?

To be sure, there is a righteous anger that sometimes needs to be displayed (Eph. 4:26), but not everything we call righteous indignation is really righteous. It is so easy to give vent to jealousy and malice by disguising them as holy zeal for God. Not every religious crusader is motivated by love for God or obedience to the Word. His or her zeal could be a mask that is covering hidden anger or jealousy.

But if a ruler is too pliable, he is also a fool (Ecc. 10:5-7). If he lacks character and courage, he will put fools in the high offices and qualified people in the low offices. The servants will ride on horses while the noblemen will walk. If a ruler has incompetent people advising him, he is almost certain to govern the nation unwisely.

The best rulers (and leaders) are men and women who are tough-minded but tenderhearted, who put the best people on the horses and don't apologize for it.

Applying God's Truth:

1. What bosses have you most respected? Which have you least respected? What caused the differences in your opinions?

2. Do you feel that you have sufficient control over yourself so that you can help control others? If not, what areas do you need to work on?

3. Would you say you are too proud? Too pliable? Or do you feel you are achieving an appropriate balance?

Scripture: Read Ecclesiastes 10:11-20

"Do not revile the king even in your thoughts, or curse the rich in your bedroom, because a bird of the air may carry your words, and a bird on the wing may report what you say" (Ecc. 10:20).

LOOKING OUT FOR NUMBER ONE

In recent years, various developing nations have seen how easy it is for unscrupulous leaders to steal government funds in order to build their own kingdoms. Unfortunately, it has also happened recently to some religious organizations. The courts might not catch up with all the unscrupulous politicians, but God will eventually judge them, and His judgment will be just.

The familiar saying "A little bird told me" probably originated from verse 20. You can imagine the group of these officers having a party in one of their private rooms and, instead of toasting the king, they are cursing [making light of] him. Of course, they wouldn't do this if any of the king's friends were present, but they were sure that the company would faithfully keep the secret. Alas, somebody told the king what was said, and this gave him reason to punish them or dismiss them from their offices.

Even if we can't respect the person in the office, we must respect the office (Rom. 13:1-7; 1 Peter 2:13-17). "You shall not revile God, nor curse a ruler of your people" (Ex. 22:28). These hirelings were certainly indiscreet when they cursed the king, for they should have known that one of their number would use this event either to intimidate his friends or to ingratiate himself with the ruler. A statesman asks, "What is best for my country?" A politician asks, "What is best for my party?" But a mere officeholder, a hireling, asks, "What is safest and most profitable for me?"

Applying God's Truth:

1. Do you know of any ministries or religious organizations that have been shaken by scandals concerning their leaders? What was the root of the problem? What were the results?

2. Can you think of anything you've said today that might embarrass you if a little bird passed it along to someone else?

3. Think of some leaders you don't particularly respect. What can you do to at least respect the office, if not the person?

Scripture: Read Ecclesiastes 11

"Cast your bread upon the waters, for after many days you will find it again" (Ecc. 11:1).

A QUEST FOR ADVENTURE

When I was a boy, I practically lived in the public library during the summer months. I loved books, the building was cool, and the librarians gave me the run of the place since I was one of their best customers. One summer I read nothing but true adventure stories written by real heroes like Frank Buck and Martin Johnson. These men knew the African jungles better than I knew my hometown! I was fascinated by *I Married Adventure*, the autobiography of Martin Johnson's wife Osa. When Clyde Beatty brought his circus to town, I was in the front row watching him tame the lions.

Since those boyhood days, life has become a lot calmer for me, but I trust I haven't lost that sense of adventure. In fact, as I get older, I'm asking God to keep me from getting set in my ways in a life that is routine, boring, and predictable. "I don't want my life to end in a swamp," said British expositor F.B. Meyer. I agree with him. When I trusted Jesus Christ as my Savior, I married adventure; and that meant living by faith and expecting the unexpected.

Solomon used two activities to illustrate his point: the merchant sending out his ships (vv. 1-2) and the farmer sowing his seed (vv. 3-6). In both activities, a great deal of faith is required because neither the merchant nor the farmer can control the circumstances. If the merchant and the farmer waited until the circumstances were ideal, they would never get anything done! Life has a certain amount of risk to it, and that's where faith comes in.

Applying God's Truth:

1. What was the last adventurous thing you did?

2. If you had a bit more faith in God, what new adventure might you like to try?

3. What is your usual attitude toward risk? Are you satisfied with it, or would you like to become more (or less) a risk-taker? How might you make any desired changes?

Scripture: Read Ecclesiastes 12

"Fear God and keep his commandments, for this is the whole duty of man. For God will bring every deed into judgment, including every hidden thing, whether it is good or evil" *(Ecc. 12:13-14).*

SATISFACTION GUARANTEED

People may seem to get away with sin (8:11), but their sins will eventually be exposed and judged righteously. Those who have not trusted the Lord Jesus Christ will be doomed forever. "The eternity of punishment is a thought which crushes the heart," said Charles Spurgeon. "The Lord God is slow to anger, but when He is once aroused to it, as He will be against those who finally reject His Son, He will put forth all His omnipotence to crush His enemies."

Six times in his discourse, Solomon told us to enjoy life while we can; but at no time did he advise us to enjoy sin. The joys of the present depend on the security of the future. If you know Jesus Christ as your Savior, then your sins have already been judged on the cross; and there is now no condemnation for those who are in Christ Jesus (Rom. 8:1 and see John 5:24). But if you die having never trusted Christ, you will face judgment at His throne and be lost forever (Rev. 20:11-15).

Is life worth living? Yes, if you are truly alive through faith in Jesus Christ. Then you can be satisfied, no matter what God may permit to come to your life.

"He who has the Son has life; he who does not have the Son of God does not have life" (1 John 5:12).

You can receive life in Christ and be satisfied.

Applying God's Truth:

1. Do you know of someone who truly seems to think he or she will get by with his or her sinful actions? What can you learn from this person?

2. Do you feel more satisfied with life now than you did when you began these readings? In what ways? What areas of life do you still need to work on?

3. What are three things you can do from now on that are likely to bring you a greater degree of satisfaction with life?

WHOLENESS

30 Daily Readings from the Book of Colossians

TODAY WE LIVE IN A WORLD THAT LACKS INTEGRITY, AND ONE WORD describes the lives and experiences of many people: *fragmented.*

Some people's lives are in pieces because they can't handle the pressures that come their way. Problems arise and these people fall apart. Other people are fragmented because they don't know who they are and they lack a foundation on which to build their lives. Still others aren't whole because they're trying to please too many people and reach too many goals, not all of them worthy goals.

In other words, some people are blown apart, some are pulled apart, and some are just quietly falling apart.

Which are you?

Fragmented people are unhappy people. They try to keep up a bold front, but even that pretense becomes another part of their disintegrated lives. Pretending only makes thing worse.

Paul's letter to the Christians in Colosse explains that Jesus Christ is holding this universe together *and can hold our lives together if we'll trust Him.* "In Him all things hold together" (1:17) is one of the main messages of this important letter, a message that can make a difference in your life today.

But let me give a word of warning: this isn't a theological ABC book for amateurs. It's a book of solid theology for people who are serious about putting their lives together and making them amount to something in the will of God. It's for Christians who will read and meditate and think. If you take this book seriously, Jesus Christ will help you integrate your life; and the God who runs the universe will help manage your life and keep it together.

You'll move from *fragmentation* to *integration* as Jesus Christ exercises His lordship and power in your daily life.

You'll be a whole person in a broken world, and you'll help others to find this wholeness through faith in Jesus Christ.

Scripture: Read Colossians 1:1-2

"To the holy and faithful brothers in Christ at Colosse: Grace and peace to you from God our Father" (Col. 1:2).

GOOD BEGINNINGS

Colosse probably would never have been mentioned in the New Testament had it not been for the church there. The city is never named in the Book of Acts because Paul did not start the Colossian church nor did he ever visit it. Paul had *heard* of their faith (Col. 1:4, 9), but he had never seen these believers personally (2:1). Here was a church of unknown people, in a small town, receiving an inspired letter from the great Apostle Paul!

How did the Colossian church begin? It was the outgrowth of Paul's three-year ministry in Ephesus (Acts 19; 20:17-38). So effective was the witness of the church at Ephesus that "all the Jews and Greeks who lived in the province of Asia heard the word of the Lord" (19:10).

There is a good lesson for us here: God does not always need an apostle, or a "full-time Christian worker" to get a ministry established. Nor does He need elaborate buildings and extensive organizations. Here laymen were used of God to start ministries. It is God's plan that the Christians in the large urban areas, like Ephesus, reach out into the smaller towns and share the Gospel. Is your church helping to evangelize "small-town" mission fields?

Applying God's Truth:

1. On a scale of 1 (least) to 10 (most), how sensitive do you think your church is in recognizing the spiritual needs of its surrounding communities?

2. On the same scale, how sensitive are you personally to the needs of others around you?

3. What is one thing you can do this week to increase your own or your church's awareness of surrounding needs?

Scripture: Read Colossians 1:3-4

"We always thank God, the Father of our Lord Jesus Christ, when we pray for you, because we have heard of your faith in Christ Jesus and of the love you have for all the saints" (Col. 1:3-4).

A NOTE OF ENCOURAGEMENT

The famous Scottish preacher, Alexander Whyte, was known as an appreciator. He loved to write postcards to people, thanking them for some kindness or blessing they had brought to his life. Those messages often brought a touch of encouragement to a heart just when it was needed most. Appreciation is great medicine for the soul.

The Apostle Paul was a great encourager, and this epistle is a good example of the grace of thanksgiving. In this section he gives thanks for what Christ has done in the lives of the Colossian Christians. But he also mentions thanksgiving in five other places in this letter. When you recall that Paul wrote this letter in prison, his attitude of thanksgiving is even more wonderful.

Like Paul, we should be grateful for what God is doing in the lives of others. As Christians, we are all members of one body. If one member of the body is strengthened, this helps to strengthen the entire body. If one church experiences a revival touch from God, it will help all the churches.

Applying God's Truth:

1. When other people receive praise or recognition, are you usually glad for them, or a bit jealous? Why?

2. How do you tend to respond when you do something nice for someone and he or she shows no appreciation?

3. Can you think of people for whom you should show appreciation? If so, what are some specific ways to do so?

Scripture: Read Colossians 1:5-6a

"The faith and love that spring from the hope that is stored up for you in heaven and that you have already heard about in the word of truth, the gospel that has come to you" (Col. 1:5-6a).

THE GOSPEL TRUTH

There are many messages and ideas that can be called true, but only God's Word can be called truth. Satan is the liar; to believe his lies is to be led astray into death. Jesus is the Truth; when we trust Him, we experience life. Men have tried to destroy God's truth, but they have failed. The Word of truth still stands!

Everybody has faith in something. But faith is only as good as the object in which a person puts his trust. The jungle pagan worships a god of stone; the educated city pagan worships money or possessions or status. In both cases, faith is empty. The true Christian believer has faith in Jesus Christ, and that faith is based on the Word of truth. Any other kind of faith is but superstition—it cannot save.

John Selden (1584–1654) was a leading historian and legal authority in England. He had a library of 8,000 volumes and was recognized for his learning. When he was dying, he said to Archbishop Ussher: "I have surveyed most of the learning that is among the sons of men, and my study is filled with books and manuscripts on various subjects. But at present, I cannot recollect any passage out of all my books and papers whereon I can rest my soul, save this from the sacred Scriptures: 'The grace of God that bringeth salvation hath appeared to all men'" (Titus 2:11, KJV).

Applying God's Truth:

1. What are some of the subtle lies you've heard others promote in regard to Christianity?

2. In what things do you tend to put your faith? To what extent do these things affect your faith in Christ?

3. What is one verse or passage from God's truth that might help you keep your faith strong today?

Scripture: Read Colossians 1:6b-8

"All over the world this gospel is producing fruit and growing, just as it has been doing among you since the day you heard it and understood God's grace in all its truth" (Col. 1:6).

SEED POWER

The Word of God is seed. This means the Word has life in it. When it is planted in the heart, it can produce fruit.

Near King's Cross station in London, England, there is a cemetery containing a unique grave, that of the agnostic Lady Ann Grimston. She is buried in a marble tomb, marked by a marble slab. Before she died, she said sarcastically to a friend, "I shall live again as surely as a tree will grow from my body."

An unbeliever, Lady Ann Grimston did not believe that there was life after death. However, *a tree did grow from her grave!* A tiny seed took root, and as it grew, it cracked the marble and even tore the metal railing out of the ground! There is life and power in a seed, and there is life and power in the Word of God.

When God's Word is planted and cultivated, it produces fruit. Faith, hope, and love are among the firstfruits in the spiritual harvest. These spiritual graces are among the evidences that a person has truly been born again.

Applying God's Truth:

1. What are you reaping as a result of God's Word sown in your heart?

2. What do you do to help sow the Word in the hearts of others?

3. Based on the amount of growth of God's Word in your life, would you describe yourself as: (a) still a seed; (b) a sprout; (c) a sapling; (d) a growing tree; or (e) a mighty oak?

Scripture: Read Colossians 1:9

"Since the day we heard about you, we have not stopped praying for you and asking God to fill you with the knowledge of his will through all spiritual wisdom and understanding" (Col. 1:9).

COMPLETE!

When a person is born into God's family by faith in Jesus Christ, he is born with all that he needs for growth and maturity. This is the theme of Colossians: "You have been given fullness in Christ" (2:10). No other experience is needed than the new birth. "Do not look for something new," Paul warned the church. "Continue to grow in that which you received at the beginning" (author's paraphrase).

Every believer needs to have the "knowledge of His will." The Greek word translated *knowledge* in this verse carries the meaning of "full knowledge." There is always more to learn about God and His will for our lives. No Christian would ever dare to say that he had "arrived" and needed to learn nothing more. Like the college freshman who handed in a 10-page report on "The History of the Universe," that Christian would only declare his ignorance.

The will of God is an important part of a successful Christian life. God wants us to *know* His will and *understand* it. God is not a distant dictator who issues orders and never explains. Because we are His friends, we can know what He is doing and why He is doing it. As we study His Word and pray, we discover new and exciting truths about God's will for His people.

Applying God's Truth:

1. If your sense of feeling complete in Jesus were represented by a gasoline gauge on a car, would your reading be "Full," "Empty," or somewhere in between?

2. If you believe you are complete in Christ, but don't *feel* complete, what could you do?

3. What steps might you take in order to better know and understand God's will for your life by, say, this time next week?

Scripture: Read Colossians 1:10

"We pray this in order that you may live a life worthy of the Lord and may please him in every way" (Col. 1:10).

WALKING AND WORKING

The false teachers in Colosse attracted people through their offer of "spiritual knowledge," but they did not relate this knowledge to life. In the Christian life, knowledge and obedience go together. There is no separation between *learning* and *living*. The wisdom about which Paul prayed was not simply a head knowledge of deep spiritual truths. True spiritual wisdom must affect the daily life. Wisdom and practical intelligence must go together.

In my pastoral ministry, I have met people who have become intoxicated with "studying the deeper truths of the Bible." Usually they have been given a book or introduced to some teacher's tapes. Before long, they get so smart they become dumb! All biblical truths are practical, not theoretical. If we are growing in knowledge, we should also be growing in grace.

Three words summarize the practicality of the Christian life: *wisdom, walk,* and *work*. The sequence is important: first, wisdom; then walk; then work. I cannot work for God unless I am walking with Him; but I cannot walk with Him if I am ignorant of His will. The believer who spends time daily in the Word and prayer will know God's will and be able to walk with Him and work for Him.

Applying God's Truth:

1. On a scale where 1 = "Knowledge of Scripture and No Application," 10 = "Lots of 'Christian' Activity with No Real Depth," and 5 = "An Ideal Balance of Knowledge and Action," where would you be?

2. What are you doing to improve your walk with God?

3. What are you doing to improve your work for Him?

Scripture: Read Colossians 1:11-14

"Bearing fruit in every good work, growing in the knowledge of God, being strengthened with all power . . . and joyfully giving thanks to the Father" (Col. 1:10b-12).

FOUR FACTORS

Wisdom and conduct should always be related to moral character. One of the great problems in our evangelical world today is the emphasis on "spiritual knowledge" and "Christian service," without connecting these important matters to personal character.

For example, some teachers and preachers claim to have God's wisdom—yet they lack love and kindness and the other basic qualities that make the Christian life beautiful and distinctive. Even some "soul-winning Christians" are so busy serving God that they cannot take time to check facts—so they publish lies about other Christians. For some months, I read a certain religious publication. But when I discovered that they had no "Letters to the Editor" column (except for praise), and that they had never published a correction or apologized for an error, I stopped reading the magazine.

Knowledge, conduct, service, and character must always go together. We know God's will that we might obey it; and, in obeying it, we serve Him and grow in Christian character. While none of us is perfectly balanced in these four factors, we ought to strive for that balance.

Applying God's Truth:

1. If you never told other people you were a Christian, how long do you think it would take them to notice? Why?

2. Can you take constructive criticism as well as you receive praise? Why or why not?

3. If you made a pie chart to graphically represent the characteristics of knowledge, conduct, service, and character in your life, what would the individual percentages be? (The total should be 100 percent.)

Scripture: Read Colossians 1:15

"[Jesus] is the image of the invisible God, the firstborn over all creation" (Col. 1:15).

ALL YOU NEED

Paul's main theme in Colossians is the preeminence of Jesus Christ. There is no need for us to worry about angelic mediators or spiritual emanations. God has sent His Son to die for us! Every person who believes on Jesus Christ is saved and is a part of His body, the church, of which He is the Head. We are united to Christ in a wonderful, living relationship!

While in an airport waiting for my plane to be called, I was approached by a young man who wanted to sell me a book. One look at the garish cover told me the book was filled with Oriental myths and philosophies.

"I have a book here that meets all my needs," I told the young man, and I reached into my briefcase and took out my Bible.

"Oh, we aren't against the Bible!" he assured me. "It's just that we have something more, and it makes our faith even better."

"Nobody can give me more than Jesus Christ has already given me," I replied. Sad to say, there are many Christians who actually believe that some person, religious system, or discipline can add something to their spiritual experience. But they already have everything they will ever need in the person and work of Jesus Christ.

Applying God's Truth:

1. During the past 24 hours, what are some of the things you've seen other people put before Christ?

2. What are some things that you—currently or in times past—might tend to let interfere with your relationship with Jesus?

3. How do people you know sometimes try to add to the Gospel? Why do you think they do so?

Scripture: Read Colossians 1:16-17

"[Jesus] is before all things, and in him all things hold together" (Col. 1:17).

HOLDING IT TOGETHER

A guide took a group of people through an atomic laboratory and explained how all matter was composed of rapidly moving particles. The tourists studied models of molecules and were amazed to learn that matter is made up primarily of space. During the question period, one visitor asked, "If this is the way matter works, what holds it all together?" For that, the guide had no answer.

But the Christian has an answer: Jesus Christ! Because "He is before all things," He can hold all things together. This is another affirmation that Jesus Christ is God. Only God existed before all of creation, and only God can make creation cohere. To make Jesus Christ less than God is to dethrone Him.

It used to bother me to sing the familiar song, "This Is My Father's World." I thought Satan and sin were in control of this world. I have since changed my mind, and now I sing the song with joy and victory. Jesus Christ made all things, He controls all things, and by Him all things hold together. Indeed this is my Father's world!

Applying God's Truth:

1. If you increasingly believe that Jesus holds all things together, what are some situations you are currently facing in which you should trust Him more?

2. Have you yielded every area of your life to God's wise control? If not, what else do you need to trust Him to handle?

3. Believing that Jesus is before all things, what are some potentially stressful things you expect to face in the future that you should leave in His hands?

Scripture: Read Colossians 1:18-20

"And He is the head of the body, the church; he is the beginning and the firstborn from among the dead, so that in everything he might have the supremacy" (Col. 1:18).

THE GREATEST ATTRACTION

In 1893, the World's Columbian Exposition was held in Chicago, and more than 21 million people visited the exhibits. Among the features was a "World Parliament of Religions," with representatives of the world's religions meeting to share their "best points" and perhaps come up with a new religion for the world.

Evangelist D.L. Moody saw this as a great opportunity for evangelism. He used churches, rented theaters, and even rented a circus tent (when the show was not on) to present the Gospel of Jesus Christ. His friends wanted Moody to attack the "Parliament of Religions," but he refused. "I am going to make Jesus Christ so attractive," he said, "that men will turn to Him." Moody knew that Jesus Christ was the preeminent Savior, not just one of many "religious leaders" of history.

But the false teachers of Colosse could never give Jesus Christ the place of preeminence; for, according to their philosophy, Jesus Christ was only one of the many "emanations" from God. He was not the only way to God (John 14:6); rather, He was but one rung on the ladder! It has well been said, "If Jesus Christ is not Lord of all, He cannot be Lord at all."

Applying God's Truth:

1. How do you usually respond when confronted by people of other religions?

2. What do cults and other religions promise in order to recruit followers? How might you respond to their claims based on Colossians 1:18?

3. What are three specific things you can do this week to try to "make Jesus [more] attractive" to others?

Scripture: Read Colossians 1:21-23

"Now [God] has reconciled you by Christ's physical body through death to present you holy in his sight, without blemish and free from accusation—if you continue in your faith, established and firm, not moved from the hope held out in the gospel" (Col. 1:22-23).

HOW FIRM YOUR FOUNDATION?

Paul's statement to the Colossians seems to cast a shadow on the assurance of our future glory (v. 13). Is it possible for a believer to lose his salvation? No, the *if* clause does not suggest doubt or lay down a condition by which we "continue in our faith."

Paul used an architectural image in this verse—a house, firmly set on the foundation. The town of Colosse was located in a region known for earthquakes, and the word translated *moved from* can mean "earthquake stricken." Paul was saying, "If you are truly saved, and built on the solid foundation, Jesus Christ, then you will continue in the faith and nothing will move you. You have heard the Gospel and trusted Jesus Christ, and He has saved you."

In other words, we are not saved by continuing in the faith. But we continue in the faith and thus prove that we are saved. It behooves each professing Christian to test his own faith and examine his own heart to be sure he is a child of God.

Applying God's Truth:

1. What tends to make Christians question their assurance of salvation?

2. What are some of the "earthquakes" you have faced that threatened to shake your spiritual foundation?

3. What can you learn from these verses that will help you face future "earthquakes"?

Scripture: Read Colossians 1:24-27

"To them God has chosen to make known among the Gentiles the glorious riches of this mystery, which is Christ in you, the hope of glory" (Col. 1:27).

EVERYBODY IN!

God had initiated a new program—His *mystery*—that was not explained by the Old Testament prophets. The mystery is that today God is uniting Jews and Gentiles in the church. Imagine what this message meant to the Gentiles. They were no longer excluded from the glory and riches of God's grace! During the Old Testament dispensation, a Gentile had to become a Jewish proselyte in order to share in the blessings of Israel. But in the new dispensation, Jews and Gentiles alike are saved by faith in Jesus Christ (Rom. 10:12-13).

We who have grown up in somewhat Christian surroundings have a tendency to take all this for granted. But think of the excitement this message must have generated in a church composed of new believers who had no background in the church.

I was privileged to minister in Africa for three weeks, and there I was introduced to some of the finest Christians I have ever met. I taught the Word to over 500 national pastors in Kenya for almost a week, and each service was a challenge and blessing to me. Many of the pastors still had the marks of paganism and idolatry on their bodies; yet their faces were aglow with the joy of the Lord. I went to Africa to minister to them, *but they ministered to me!* They reminded me not to take for granted the glorious riches I have in Jesus Christ.

Applying God's Truth:

1. Do you ever feel "left out" at church or in other Christian groups? In what ways?

2. Put yourself in the place of a Gentile believer hearing Paul's words for the first time. Describe your feelings.

3. What are some ways you can minister to people who usually minister to you?

Scripture: Read Colossians 1:28-29

"We proclaim him, admonishing and teaching everyone with all wisdom, so that we may present everyone perfect in Christ. To this end I labor, struggling with all his energy, which so powerfully works in me" (Col. 1:28-29).

PRAYER AT WORK

A more literal translation of the first part of Colossians 1:29 is "For this I labor to the point of exhaustion, agonizing." What a picture of prayer! So much of our praying is calm and comfortable, and yet Paul exerted his spiritual muscles the way a Greek runner would exert himself in the Olympic games.

This does not mean that our prayers are more effective if we exert all kinds of fleshly energy. Nor does it mean that we must "wrestle with God" and wear Him out before He will meet our needs. Paul described a *spiritual striving*: it was God's power at work in his life.

Prayer is not our trying to change God's mind. It is learning what is the mind of God and asking accordingly (1 John 5:14-15). The Holy Spirit constantly intercedes for us even though we do not hear His voice (Rom. 8:26-27). He knows the Father's will and He helps us pray in that will.

There are times when we simply do not feel like praying—and that is when we must pray the most! The Spirit gives us divine energy for prayer, in spite of the way we feel. The resurrection power of Jesus Christ is made available to us.

Applying God's Truth:

1. As a pray-er, would you say you are more like an Olympic marathoner, a good distance runner, an occasional sprinter, or a couch potato?

2. In what ways do you motivate yourself to pray when you don't feel like it?

3. When could you set aside time and "labor to the point of exhaustion" in prayer?

Scripture: Read Colossians 2:1-7

"Just as you received Christ Jesus as Lord, continue to live in him, rooted and built up in him, strengthened in the faith as you were taught, and overflowing with thankfulness" (Col. 2:6-7).

FIGHTING THE WOLVES

I recall a story about a pastor who was concerned about some unsavory businesses that had opened near a school. His protests finally led to a court case, and the defense attorney did all he could to embarrass the Gospel minister.

"Are you not a pastor?" the lawyer asked. "And doesn't the word *pastor* mean 'shepherd'?" To this definition the minister agreed.

"Well, if you are a shepherd, why aren't you out taking care of the sheep?"

"Because today I'm fighting the wolves!" was the pastor's quick reply, and a good answer it was.

Knowing that there were enemies already attacking the church in Colosse, Paul offered encouragement. By heeding his admonitions, the Colossians would overcome their enemies.

In the Christian life, we never stand still: we either go forward or gradually slip backward. "Let us go on to maturity!" is the call we must obey (Heb. 6:1). The Christian who is not making spiritual progress is an open target for the enemy to attack and destroy.

Applying God's Truth:

1. What are some of the current "wolves" in your life?

2. In your spiritual life, would you say you have been gradually slipping backward, making occasional progress, or making regular progress? How might you "pick up the pace"?

3. As you go forward, are you "overflowing with thankfulness"? If not, what are some things you might try?

Scripture: Read Colossians 2:8-15

"In Christ all the fullness of the Deity lives in bodily form, and you have been given fullness in Christ, who is the head over every power and authority" (Col. 2:9-10).

SHARING THE FULLNESS

When Jesus Christ ascended to heaven, He went in a human body. It was a glorified body, to be sure, but it was real. After His resurrection, our Lord was careful to assure His disciples that He was the same Person in the same body; He was not a ghost or a spirit. (See John 20:19-29.) There is a glorified Man in heaven! The God-Man, Jesus Christ, embodies the fullness of God!

Now, the remarkable thing is this: *every believer shares that fullness!* "You have been given fullness in Christ" (Col. 2:10). The tense of the Greek verb indicated that this fullness is a permanent experience. Dr. Kenneth Wuest's very literal *Expanded Translation* reads, "And you are in Him, having been completely filled full with the present result that you are in a state of fullness."

When a person is born again into the family of God, he is born complete in Christ. His spiritual growth is not by *addition*, but by *nutrition*. He grows from the inside out. Nothing needs to be added to Christ because He already is the very fullness of God. As the believer draws on Christ's fullness, he is "filled to the measure of all the fullness of God" (Eph. 3:19). What more does he need?

Applying God's Truth:

1. What does it mean to you that Jesus ascended to heaven in a real body?

2. If someone saw you on an average day, do you think he or she could tell that "you have been given fullness in Christ"? Why or why not?

3. Since nothing needs to be added to what you are, how can you continue to mature as a Christian?

Scripture: Read Colossians 2:16-19

"Do not let anyone who delights in false humility and the worship of angels dis-qualify you for the prize. Such a person goes into great detail about what he has seen, and his unspiritual mind puffs him up with idle notions" (Col. 2:18).

PLAYING BY THE RULES

The word translated *disqualify* means "to declare unworthy of a prize." It is an athletic term: the umpire disqualifies the contestant because he has not obeyed the rules. The contestant does not cease to be a citizen of the land, but he forfeits the honor of winning a prize. A Christian who fails to obey God's directions does not lose his salvation. But he does lose the approval of the Lord and the rewards He has promised to those who are faithful (1 Cor. 3:8).

It is a gracious act of God that He has promised reward to those who serve Him. Certainly He does not owe us anything! We ought to be so grateful that he has saved us from judgment that we would serve Him whether or not we received a reward. Most of God's servants probably obey Him out of love and devotion and never think about rewards. Just as there are degrees of punishment in hell (Matt. 23:15), so there will be degrees of glory in heaven—even though all believers will be like Christ in their glorified bodies.

The old Puritan Thomas Watson said it perfectly: "Though every vessel of mercy shall be full [in heaven], yet one may hold more than another."

Applying God's Truth:

1. How do you feel when you're in a competition where lots of people are cheating? How does this apply to today's verse?

2. Which of God's rules do you tend to break or "stretch" from time to time?

3. In addition to eternal rewards you might miss if you are misled by others in regard to God's truth, what might you be missing out on *now*?

Scripture: Read Colossians 2:20-23

"Since you died with Christ to the basic principles of this world, why, as though you still belonged to it, do you submit to its rules: 'Do not handle! Do not taste! Do not touch!'?" *(Col. 2:20-21)*

TOO MUCH SELF-DENIAL

P aul first condemned legalism and mysticism; next he attacked and condemned *asceticism*. An ascetic practices rigorous self-denial and even self-mortification in order to become more spiritual. Ascetic practices were popular during the Middle Ages: wearing hair shirts next to the skin, sleeping on hard beds, whipping oneself, not speaking for days (maybe years), going without food or sleep, etc.

There is a definitely a relationship between legalism and asceticism, for the ascetic often subjects himself to rules and regulations. As Christians, we admit that physical discipline is needed in our lives. Many of us eat too much and are overweight. Some of us drink too much coffee or cola drinks and are nervous and upset. We believe that our bodies are temples of the Holy Spirit, yet sometimes we do not care for our bodies as we should. There is a place in our Christian lives for proper care of our bodies.

But the ascetic hopes to sanctify the soul by his discipline of the body, and it is this heresy that Paul attacked. Just as days and diets have no sanctifying value, neither does fleshly discipline.

Applying God's Truth:

1. While we may not wear hair shirts or whip ourselves, can you think of any somewhat ascetic practices of certain Christians today?

2. What do you think are the benefits of incorporating physical disciplines into spiritual maturity?

3. What are the potential drawbacks?

Scripture: Read Colossians 3:1-2

"Since, then, you have been raised with Christ, set your hearts on things above, where Christ is seated at the right hand of God. Set your minds on things above, not on earthly things" (Col. 3:1-2).

LOOKING UP

How do we set our hearts on things above? The secret is found in a literal translation of verse 2: "Habitually set your mind—your attention—on things above, not on things on the earth." Our feet must be on earth, but our minds must be in heaven. This is not to suggest that (as D.L. Moody used to say) we become "so heavenly minded that we are no earthly good." It means that the practical everyday affairs of life get their direction from Christ in heaven. It means further that we look at earth from heaven's point of view.

While attending a convention in Washington, D.C. I watched a Senate committee hearing over television. I believe they were considering a new ambassador to the United Nations. The late Senator Hubert Humphrey was making a comment as I turned on the television set: "You must remember that in politics, how you stand depends on where you sit." He was referring, of course, to the political party seating arrangement in the Senate, but I immediately applied it to my position in Christ. How I stand—and walk—depends on where I sit; *and I am seated with Christ in the heavenlies!*

Applying God's Truth:

1. What are three things that are currently interfering with your ability to "seek those things which are above"?

2. How can you be "heavenly minded" more frequently and still be "earthly good"?

3. Envision yourself seated with Christ right now. What would you want to ask or tell Him?

Scripture: Read Colossians 3:3-4

"For you died, and your life is now hidden with Christ in God. When Christ, who is your life, appears, then you also will appear with him in glory" (Col. 3:3-4).

A MATTER OF LIFE AND DEATH

Christ not only died *for* us (substitution), but we died *with* him (identification). Christ not only died *for* sin, bearing its penalty; but He died *unto* sin, breaking its power. Because we are "in Christ" through the work of the Holy Spirit (1 Cor. 12:13), we died with Christ. This means that we can have victory over the old sin nature that wants to control us.

Someone has said, "Life is what you are alive to." A child may come alive when you talk about a baseball game or an ice-cream cone. A teenager may come alive when you mention cars or dates. Paul wrote, "For me, to live is Christ" (Phil. 1:21). Christ was Paul's life and he was alive to anything that related to Christ. So should it be with every believer.

Years ago I heard a story about two sisters who enjoyed attending dances and wild parties. Then they were converted and found new life in Christ. They received an invitation to a party and sent their RSVP in these words: "We regret that we cannot attend because we recently died."

Applying God's Truth:

1. How do you feel when you think of how Christ died for you?

2. Do you feel the same way when you think of how you died with Him? Explain.

3. What makes you "come alive"? Do any of these things interfere with your being able to exclaim, "For me, to live is Christ"?

Scripture: Read Colossians 3:5-11

"Put to death, therefore, whatever belongs to your earthly nature: sexual immorality, impurity, lust, evil desires, and greed, which is idolatry" (Col. 3:5).

IDOL TIME

Greed (or *covetousness* in the *King James Version*) is the sin of always wanting more, whether it be more things or more pleasures. The covetous person is never satisfied with what he has, and he is usually envious of what other people have. This is idolatry, for covetousness puts things in the place of God. "You shall not covet" is the last of the Ten Commandments (Ex. 20:17). Yet this sin can make us break all of the other nine! A greedy person will dishonor God, take God's name in vain, lie, steal, and commit every other sin in order to satisfy his sinful desires.

Do believers in local churches commit such sins? Unfortunately, they sometimes do. Each of the New Testament epistles sent to local churches makes mention of these sins and warns against them.

I am reminded of a pastor who preached a series of sermons against the sins of the saints. A member of his congregation challenged him one day and said that it would be better if the pastor preached those messages to the lost. "After all," said the church member, "sin in the life of a Christian is different from sin in the lives of other people."

"Yes," replied the pastor, "it's *worse!*"

Applying God's Truth:

1. On a scale of 1 (least) to 10 (most), how covetous (greedy) would you say you are?

2. In your own experiences, what are some additional sins you've witnessed among people who are basically greedy?

3. What things do you do to prevent covetousness from getting out of control and hindering your spiritual maturity?

Scripture: Read Colossians 3:12-14

"As God's chosen people, holy and dearly loved, clothe yourselves with compassion, kindness, humility, gentleness, and patience" (Col. 3:12).

AN EXCLUSIVE RELATIONSHIP

Because we have trusted Christ, we have been "set apart" from the world, unto the Lord. That is the meaning of the word *holy*. We are not our own; we belong completely to Him (1 Cor. 6:19-20). Just as the marriage ceremony sets apart a man and a woman for each other exclusively, so salvation sets the believer apart exclusively for Jesus Christ. Would it not be a horrible thing, at the end of a wedding, to see the groom run off with the maid of honor? It is just as horrible to contemplate the Christian living for the world and the flesh.

When an unbeliever sins, he is a creature breaking the laws of the holy Creator and Judge. But when a Christian sins, he is a child of God breaking the loving heart of his Father. Love is the strongest motivating power in the world. As the believer grows in his love for God, he will grow in his desire to obey Him and walk in the newness of life that he has in Christ.

Applying God's Truth:

1. In what ways are you "set apart" from the world?

2. Can you think of any additional ways that you need to be set apart in order to show more devotion to Christ than to worldly concerns?

3. If your relationship with Jesus were a marriage, what kind of shape would it be in? If it were a physical parent/child relationship, do you think it would be a good one overall? Explain.

Scripture: Read Colossians 3:15

"Let the peace of Christ rule in your hearts, since as members of one body you were called to peace. And be thankful" (Col. 3:15).

LET PEACE RULE

In the Greek games there were judges (we would call them *umpires*) who rejected contestants who were not qualified, and who disqualified those who broke the rules. The peace of God is the "umpire" in our believing hearts. When we obey the will of God, we have His peace within; but when we step out of His will (even unintentionally), we lose His peace.

If we have peace in our hearts, we will be at peace with others in the church. We are called to one body, and our relationship in that body must be one of harmony and peace. If we are out of the will of God, we are certain to bring discord and disharmony to the church. Jonah thought he was at peace, when actually his sins created a storm!

When a Christian loses the peace of God, he begins to go off in directions that are out of the will of God. He turns to the things of the world and the flesh to compensate for his lack of peace within. He tries to escape, but he cannot escape *himself*! It is only when he confesses his sins, claims God's forgiveness, and does God's will that he experiences God's peace within.

Applying God's Truth:

1. How do you feel when an umpire makes what you feel is a bad call against your favorite team? How do you feel when God expects something from you that you don't feel is fair?

2. Have you ever experienced a false peace (like Jonah)? How long did it last? What were the results?

3. What situations are you facing today for which you need to experience God's peace?

Scripture: Read Colossians 3:16-17

"Let the word of Christ dwell in you richly as you teach and admonish one another with all wisdom, and as you sing psalms, hymns and spiritual songs with gratitude in your hearts to God" (Col. 3:16).

SING ALONG

Psalms were the songs taken from the Old Testament. For centuries, the churches in the English-speaking world sang only metrical versions of the Psalms. I am glad to see today a return to the singing of Scripture, especially the Psalms. Hymns were songs of praise to God written by believers but not taken from the Psalms. The church today has a rich heritage of hymnody which, I fear, is being neglected. Spiritual songs were expressions of biblical truth other than in psalms and hymns. When we sing a hymn, we address the Lord; when we sing a spiritual song, we address each other.

Someone has said that a successful Christian life involves attention to three books: God's Book, the Bible; the pocketbook; and the hymnbook. I agree. I often use a hymnal in my devotional time, to help express my praise to God. As a believer grows in his knowledge of the Word, he will want to grow in his expression of praise. He will learn to appreciate the great hymns of the church, the Gospel songs, and the spiritual songs that teach spiritual truths. To sing only the elementary songs of the faith is to rob himself of spiritual enrichment.

Applying God's Truth:

1 What are some of your favorite hymns and spiritual songs? Why?

2. How important is singing in your church worship?

3. How important are hymns and spiritual songs in your personal worship?

Scripture: Read Colossians 3:18-19

"Wives, submit to your husbands, as is fitting in the Lord. Husbands, love your wives and do not be harsh with them" (Col. 3:18-19).

LOVE AND SUBMISSION

Paul did not address the wives first because they were neediest! The Gospel radically changed the position of women in the Roman world. It gave them a new freedom and stature that some of them were unable to handle, and for this reason Paul admonished them.

We must not think of *submission* as "slavery" or "subjugation." The word comes from the military vocabulary and simply means "to arrange under rank." The fact that one soldier is a private and another is a colonel does not mean that one man is necessarily *better* than the other. It only means that they have different ranks.

God does all things "in a fitting and orderly way" (1 Cor. 14:40). If He did not have a chain of command in society, we would have chaos. The fact that the woman is to submit to her husband does not suggest that the man is better than the woman. It only means that the man has the responsibility of headship and leadership in the home.

Headship is not dictatorship or lordship. It is loving leadership. In fact, both the husband and the wife must be submitted to the *Lord* and to *each other* (Eph. 5:21). It is a mutual respect under the lordship of Jesus Christ.

Applying God's Truth:

1. Do you think there are ever times when it is appropriate for a wife to refuse to submit to her husband? Explain.

2. Of the two commands Paul gives in Colossians 3:18-19, which do you think is harder to obey? Why?

3. In what area(s) do you find it hardest to submit to someone else, or to God? When is it easiest?

Scripture: Read Colossians 3:20–4:1

"Children, obey your parents in everything, for this pleases the Lord" (Col. 3:20).

KID STUFF

John H. Starkey was a violent British criminal. He murdered his own wife, then was convicted for the crime and executed. The officials asked General William Booth, founder of the Salvation Army, to conduct Starkey's funeral. Booth faced as ugly and mean a crowd as he had ever seen in his life, but his first words stopped them and held them: "John H. Starkey never had a praying mother!"

Children have rights, but they also have responsibilities; and their foremost responsibility is to obey. They are to obey "in everything" and not simply in those things that please themselves. Will their parents ever ask them to do something that is wrong? Not if the parents are submitted to the Lord and to one another, and not if they love each other and their children.

The child who does not learn to obey his parents is not likely to grow up obeying any authority. He will defy his teachers, the police, his employers, and anyone else who tries to exercise authority over him. The breakdown in authority in our society reflects the breakdown of authority in the home.

Applying God's Truth:

1. How is a child's obedience to parents significant in regard to his or her eventual obedience to God?

2. Do you have ways of telling whether a child (who is a stranger to you) is obedient or not? If so, how?

3. When people observe you, do you think they can tell whether or not you're an obedient child of God? How?

Scripture: Read Colossians 4:2

"Devote yourselves to prayer, being watchful and thankful" (Col. 4:2).

DEVOTED TO DEVOTIONS

Prayer and worship are perhaps the highest uses of the gift of speech. It has well been said that the purpose of prayer is not to get man's will done in heaven, but to get God's will done on earth. Prayer is not telling God what to do or what to give. Prayer is asking God for that which He wants to do and give, according to His will (1 John 5:14-15).

As we read the Word and fellowship with our Father, we discover His will and then boldly ask Him to do what He has planned. Richard Trench (1807–1886), archbishop of Dublin, said it perfectly: "Prayer is not overcoming God's reluctance; it is laying hold of His willingness."

Of course, it is possible to pray in our hearts and never use the gift of speech; but we are using words even if we don't say them audibly. True prayer must first come from the heart, whether the words are spoken or not.

Applying God's Truth:

1. On a scale of 1 (least) to 10 (most), how intently would you say you "devote yourself to prayer"?

2. What is one portion of God's will for your life that you've recently determined? Have you verbally affirmed it in prayer?

3. As you pray, in what ways are you "watchful"? In what ways are you "thankful"?

Scripture: Read Colossians 4:3-4

"Pray for us, too, that God may open a door for our message, so that we may proclaim the mystery of Christ, for which I am in chains. Pray that I may proclaim it clearly, as I should" (Col. 4:3-4).

A CLEAR PROCLAMATION

A visitor at Spurgeon's Tabernacle in London was being shown around the building by the pastor, Charles Spurgeon.

"Would you like to see the powerhouse of this ministry?" Spurgeon asked, as he showed the man into a lower auditorium. "It is here that we get our power, for while I am preaching upstairs, hundreds of my people are in this room praying." Is it any wonder that God blessed Spurgeon's preaching of the Word?

You, as a church member, can assist your pastor in the preaching of the Word by praying for him. Never say to your pastor, "Well, the least I can do is to pray for you." The *most* you can do is to pray! Pray for your pastor as he prepares the Word, studies, and meditates. Pray that the Holy Spirit will give deeper insights into the truths of the Word. Pray too that your pastor will practice the Word that he preaches so that it will be real in his own life. As he preaches the message, pray that the Spirit will give him freedom of utterance, and that the Word will reach into hearts and minds in a powerful way. (And it wouldn't hurt to pray for other church leaders too.)

Applying God's Truth:

1. What are some specific ways that you can more effectively pray for your pastor?

2. In addition to the pastor, who are some other people in your church who need your prayers today?

3. What things may interfere with the "clear" presentation of the Gospel? How can prayer help deal with such interferences?

Scripture: Read Colossians 4:5-6

"Let your conversation be always full of grace, seasoned with salt, so that you may know how to answer everyone" *(Col. 4:6).*

SALTY TALK

Christians in general, and Christian leaders in particular, must have "a good reputation with outsiders" (1 Tim. 3:7). When members of a church are calling a new pastor, they ought to investigate his testimony among his neighbors and the businessmen who know him. Even though unsaved people are in the dark spiritually, they have a great deal of discernment when it comes to the things of this life. It is unfortunate when members of a church call a pastor who has not paid his bills and has left behind a bad witness to unsaved people.

It is not enough simply to walk wisely and carefully before unbelievers. We must also *talk* with them and share the Gospel message with them. But we must take care that our speech is controlled by *grace*, so that it points to Christ and glorifies the Lord. This means we must have grace in our hearts (Col. 3:16) because it is from the heart that the mouth speaks. With grace in our hearts and on our lips, we will be faithful witnesses and not judges or prosecuting attorneys!

Applying God's Truth:

1. Can you think of a recent scandal involving a prominent Christian figure? What was the response of the non-Christians in your area?

2. What do you think it means to let your speech be "seasoned with salt"?

3. What people can you think of whose Christian testimony is one of "faithful witness"? Do you know any "judges"? "Prosecuting attorneys"?

Scripture: Read Colossians 4:7-13

"My fellow prisoner Aristarchus sends you his greetings" (Col. 4:10).

NAME RECOGNITION

Aristarchus was identified as Paul's fellow prisoner, and also as Paul's fellow worker (v. 11). Aristarchus was from Macedonia and was one of Paul's traveling companions (Acts 19:29). He was originally from Thessalonica (20:4) and willingly risked his life in the Ephesian riot (19:28-41). He sailed with Paul to Rome (27:2), which meant he also experienced the storm and shipwreck that Luke so graphically described in Acts 27.

Aristarchus stayed with Paul no matter what the circumstances were—a riot in Ephesus, a voyage, a storm, or even a prison. It is not likely that Aristarchus was an official Roman prisoner. "Fellow prisoner" probably means the Aristarchus shared Paul's confinement with him so that he could be a help and comfort to the apostle. He was a voluntary prisoner for the sake of Jesus Christ and the Gospel.

Paul could not have accomplished all that he did apart from the assistance of his friends. Aristarchus stands out as one of the greatest of Paul's helpers. He did not look for an easy task. He did not run when the going got tough. He suffered with Paul and labored with Paul.

Applying God's Truth:

1. Since Aristarchus was so supportive of Paul, why do you think he isn't better known?

2. Can you think of people who serve God faithfully, yet whose efforts frequently go unnoticed?

3. What might you do to recognize the work of the Aristarchus-like people in your church or ministry?

Scripture: Read Colossians 4:14-18

"Our dear friend Luke, the doctor, and Demas send greetings" (Col. 4:14).

GOING DOWN?

D emas is mentioned only three times in Paul's letters, and these three references tell a sad story. First he is called "Demas . . . my fellow worker" and is linked with three good men—Mark, Aristarchus, and Luke (Phile. 24). Then he is simply called "Demas," and there is no special word of identification or commendation (Col. 4:14). But the third reference tells what became of Demas: "Demas, because he loved this world, has deserted me" (2 Tim. 4:10).

At one point in his life, John Mark had forsaken Paul: but he was reclaimed and restored. Demas forsook Paul and apparently was never reclaimed. His sin was that he loved this present world. The word *world* refers to the whole system of things that runs this world, or "society without God."

Christians today can succumb to the world just as Demas did. How easy it is to maintain a religious veneer, while all the time we are living for the things of this world. Demas thought that he could serve two masters, but eventually he had to make a decision; unfortunately, he made the wrong decision.

It must have hurt Paul greatly when Demas forsook him. It also hurt the work of the Lord, for there never has been a time when the laborers were many. This decision hurt Demas most of all, for he wasted his life on that which could never last.

Applying God's Truth:

1. Do you know anyone who, like Demas, seems in danger of forsaking his spiritual commitments? If so, is there any way for you to help this person?

2. What tends to lure *you* away from the faith—if you aren't careful?

3. Based on what you've read in Colossians, what can you do to stay faithful when you're tempted to wander away from God?

COMFORT

30 Daily Readings from the Book of Isaiah

IT'S TOO BAD THAT OUR ENGLISH WORD COMFORT HAS LOST ITS ORIGINAL meaning of "with strength." The purpose of comfort isn't to pamper and protect us but to strengthen us and enable us to carry the burdens of life and serve the Lord effectively.

God isn't a doting grandparent who shelters us from problems and "kisses" our bruises to "make them well." He's a loving Father who wants us to mature and become more like Jesus Christ; and for that, we must face new challenges and depend on new strength from above.

"O, do not pray for easy lives," said Phillip Brooks. "Pray to be stronger men! Do not pray for tasks equal to your powers. Pray for powers equal to your tasks!" (The Rt. Rev. William Scarlett, D.D., *Phillips Brooks: Selected Sermons*, E.P. Dutton & Company, Inc., p. 352). That's what God's comfort is all about: power from God to meet the demands of life and to grow because of them. If we don't grow, we can't tackle bigger tasks and serve God in harder places.

The Prophet Isaiah lived in a day similar to our own. The nations were frequently at war; political schemes and alliances changed from day to day; the economy was frequently threatened; the people practiced a routine religion that covered up their hidden idolatry; and few people really wanted to hear the Word of the Lord.

Into this discouraging scene came Isaiah, sharing the comfort—the strength—of the Lord. His major theme was salvation. His major purpose was to give strength to a people who were prone to drift with the current and depend on everything but the Lord.

As you walk with Isaiah, learn to receive God's comfort, *and learn to share it with others*. They need it too.

Scripture: Read Isaiah 40:1

"Comfort, comfort my people, says your God" (Isa. 40:1).

MUCH UPHEAVAL; MUCH COMFORT

I saiah is great for two reasons," wrote William Sanford LaSor in his fascinating book *Great Personalities of the Old Testament* (Revell, p. 136): "He lived in momentous days, in critical days of international upheaval, and he wrote what many consider to be the greatest book in the Old Testament." "We see Isaiah move with fearless dignity through the chaos of his day," wrote E.M. Blaiklock, "firm in his quiet faith, sure in his God" (*Handbook of Bible People*, Scripture Union, p. 329).

Isaiah is the prophet we need to hear today as he cries out God's message above the din of world upheaval, "Comfort, comfort my people." The English word *comfort* comes from two Latin words that together mean "with strength." When Isaiah says to us, "Be comforted!" it is not a word of pity but of power. God's comfort does not weaken us; it strengthens us. God is not indulging us but empowering us. "In quietness and confidence shall be your strength."

As we study Isaiah's book, we shall meet not only this outstanding prophet, but also some mighty kings and rulers; and we shall witness the rise and fall of magnificent kingdoms. We shall see God's people chastened and then restored. But above all else, we shall see the Lord Jesus Christ, God's "Suffering Servant," as He does the will of God and suffers and dies for the sins of the world.

Applying God's Truth:

1. Can you think back to a time when God's comfort gave you much strength? What did you learn from that experience?

2. What situation(s) are you currently facing where you are in great need of God's comfort?

3. What are your goals (or hopes) as you read through the Book of Isaiah?

Scripture: Read Isaiah 1:1

"The vision concerning Judah and Jerusalem that Isaiah son of Amoz saw" (Isa. 1:1).

A PROPHECY YOU CAN COUNT ON

The name *Isaiah* means "salvation of the Lord," and salvation (deliverance) is the key theme of his book. He wrote concerning *five different acts of deliverance* that God would perform: (1) the deliverance of Judah from Assyrian invasion (chaps. 36–37); (2) the deliverance of the nation from Babylonian Captivity (chap. 40); (3) the future deliverance of the Jews from worldwide dispersion among the Gentiles (chaps. 11–12); (4) the deliverance of lost sinners from judgment (chap. 53); and (5) the final deliverance of creation from the bondage of sin when the kingdom is established (chaps. 60; 66:17).

Sir Winston Churchill was once asked to give the qualifications a person needed in order to succeed in politics, and he replied: "It is the ability to foretell what is going to happen tomorrow, next week, next month, and next year. And to have the ability afterwards to explain why it didn't happen."

Because God's prophets were correct *all of the time*, they didn't have to explain away their mistakes. "If what a prophet proclaims in the name of the Lord does not take place or come true," wrote Moses, "that is a message the Lord has not spoken" (Deut. 18:22). Isaiah wrote: "To the law and to the testimony! If they do not speak according to this word, they have no light of dawn" (Isa. 8:20). Isaiah was a man who had God's light, and he was not afraid to let it shine.

Applying God's Truth:

1. Isaiah's name meant "salvation of the Lord." If you were given a name to reflect your spiritual goals or mission, what do you think it might be?

2. In what ways do you think others see God's light shine from your life?

3. What are five "acts of deliverance" that you wish God would perform in your life?

Scripture: Read Isaiah 1:2-4

"The ox knows his master, the donkey his owner's manger, but Israel does not know, my people do not understand" (Isa. 1:3).

ISAIAH: A PERSONALITY PROFILE

W hat kind of man was Isaiah the prophet? As you read his prophecy, you will discover that he was *a man in touch with God.* He saw God's Son and God's glory, he heard God's message, and he sought to bring the nation back to God before it was too late.

Isaiah was a man who *loved his nation.* He was a patriot with a true love for his country, pleading with Judah to return to God and warning kings when their foreign policy was contrary to God's will.

He was also a man who *hated sin and sham religion.* His favorite name for God is "the Holy One of Israel," and he uses it twenty-five times in his book. (It is used only five times in the rest of the Old Testament.) He looked at the crowded courts of the temple and cried out, "They have forsaken the Lord; they have spurned the Holy One of Israel and turned their backs on him" (v. 4). Jehovah was holy, but the nation was sinful; and Isaiah called the people to repent.

Isaiah was certainly a *courageous man.* Unafraid to denounce kings and priests, and unwavering when public opinion went against him, he boldly declared the Word of God.

He was a man *skilled in communicating God's truth.* Not content with merely declaring facts, Isaiah clothed those facts in striking language that would catch the attention of a people blind and deaf to spiritual truth. Like our Lord Jesus Christ, Isaiah knew how to stir the imagination of his listeners so that he might arouse their interest and teach them God's truth (Matt. 13:10-17).

Applying God's Truth:

1. Of all Isaiah's qualities described here, which would you say is most important for a prophet of God? Why?

2. Which of these qualities best describes *you?*

3. How do you think a person with these characteristics would fit in a nation that has "turned their backs" on God?

Scripture: Read Isaiah 1:5–3:26

"Your hands are full of blood; wash and make yourselves clean. Take your evil deeds out of my sight! Stop doing wrong, learn to do right!" (Isa. 1:15-17)

RELIGION GONE WRONG

The disgusting thing about Isaiah's rebellious nation is that they were a *religious people* (vv. 10-15). They attended temple services and brought a multitude of sacrifices to the Lord; but their hearts were far from God, and their worship was hypocritical. Judah's worship of Jehovah was iniquity, not piety; and God was sick of it!

But before passing judgment on worshipers in a bygone era, perhaps we should confess the sins of the "worshiping church" today. According to researcher George Barna, 93 percent of the households in the United States contain a Bible and more than 60 percent of the people surveyed claim to be religious; but we would never know this from the way people act. One Protestant church exists for every 550 adults in America, but does all this "religion" make much difference in our sinful society?

The average church allocates about 5 percent of its budget for reaching others with the Gospel, but 30 percent for buildings and maintenance. Where churches have life and growth, such construction may be needed; but too often the building becomes "a millstone instead of a milestone," to quote Vance Havner. At least 62 percent of the people Barna surveyed said that the church was not relevant to today's world and is losing its influence on society. (See *The Frog in the Kettle* by George Barna, published by Regal Books.) It may be that, like the worshipers in the ancient Jewish temple, we are only going through the motions.

Applying God's Truth:

1. In what ways are many Christians today "religious," yet with their hearts "far from God"?

2. Would you say you live in "a Christian nation"? Explain.

3. What do you think is the #1 problem in the church today?

Scripture: Read Isaiah 4–6

"Then I heard the voice of the Lord saying, 'Whom shall I send? And who will go for us?' And I said, 'Here am I. Send me!'" (Isa. 6:8)

ISAIAH'S VISION

Anyone reading the first few chapters of Isaiah's book might be inclined to ask, "What right does this man have to pronounce judgment on the leaders of our land and the many worshipers in the temple?" The answer is in chapter 6: Isaiah's account of his call to ministry. Before he announced any "woes" on others, he first confessed his own sin and said, "Woe is me!" He saw the Holy One of Israel, and he could not keep silent.

The sight of a holy God, and the sound of the holy hymn of worship, brought great conviction to Isaiah's heart; and he confessed that he was a sinner. Unclean lips are caused by an unclean heart (Matt. 12:34-35). Isaiah cried out to be cleansed inwardly, and God met his need. If this scene had been on earth, the coals would have come from the brazen altar where the sacrificial blood had been shed, or perhaps from the censer of the high priest on the Day of Atonement (Lev. 16:12). Isaiah's cleansing came by blood and fire, and it was verified by the word of the Lord.

Before we can minister to others, we must permit God to minister to us. Before we pronounce "woe" upon others, we must sincerely say, "Woe is me!" Isaiah's conviction led to confession, and confession led to cleansing (1 John 1:9).

"Go and tell" is still God's command to His people. He is waiting for us to reply, "Here am I; send me."

Applying God's Truth:

1. Do you think today's servants of God are "called" as clearly as Isaiah was? If not, how can they be as sure as Isaiah was that they're doing God's will?

2. Do you feel fully equipped and qualified to "go" wherever God sends you? If not, what would need to be done first?

3. Aside from feeling qualified, are you *willing* to say, "Here am I. Send me"? Explain.

Scripture: Read Isaiah 7–8

"The Lord himself will give you a sign: The virgin will be with child and will give birth to a son, and will call him Immanuel" (Isa. 7:14).

A SURE SIGN

These were perilous days for the nation of Judah. Assyria was growing stronger and threatening the smaller nations whose security depended on a very delicate political balance. Syria and Ephraim (the Northern Kingdom) tried to pressure Judah into an alliance against Assyria, but Ahaz refused to join them. Why? Because he had secretly made a treaty with Assyria! (2 Kings 16:5-9)

If Ahaz had believed God's promise, he would have broken his alliance and called the nation to prayer and praise; but the king continued in his unbelief. Realizing the weakness of the king's faith, Isaiah offered to give a sign to encourage him. But knowing that he was secretly allied with Assyria, how could Ahaz honestly ask the Lord for a special sign? So, instead of speaking only to the king, Isaiah addressed the whole "house of David" and gave the prophecy concerning "Immanuel."

Of course, the *ultimate* fulfillment of this prophecy is in our Lord Jesus Christ, who is "God with us." The virgin birth of Christ is a key doctrine; for if Jesus Christ is not God come in sinless human flesh, then we have no Savior. However, this "sign" had an *immediate* significance to Ahaz and the people of Judah. A woman who was then a virgin would get married, conceive, and bear a son whose name would be "Immanuel." This son would be a reminder that God was with His people and would care for them. It is likely that this virgin was Isaiah's second wife, his first wife having died after his first son was born; and that Isaiah's second son was named both "Immanuel" and "Maher-shalal-hash-baz."

Applying God's Truth:

1. Do you identify with any of the weaknesses of King Ahaz? In what ways?

2. What changes might you make in your life if you more fully believed God's promise(s)?

3. What are some clear "signs" that God is active in your life?

Scripture: Read Isaiah 9–12

"For to us a child is born, to us a son is given, and the government will be on his shoulders. And he will be called Wonderful Counselor, Mighty God, Everlasting Father, Prince of Peace" (Isa. 9:6).

COME AGAIN

The Redeemer will come and bring to the world the dawning of a new day. We know that this prophecy refers to Christ because of the way it is quoted in Matthew 4:15-16. But Isaiah looked beyond the first coming of Christ to His second coming and the establishing of His righteous kingdom.

Isaiah 9:6 declares both the *humanity* ("A child is born") and the *deity* ("A son is given") of the Lord Jesus Christ. The prophet then leaps ahead to the Kingdom Age when Messiah will reign in righteousness and justice from David's throne. God had promised David that his dynasty and throne would be established forever, and this is fulfilled literally in Jesus Christ who will one day reign from Jerusalem.

If His name is "Wonderful," then there will be nothing dull about His reign! As Counselor, He has the wisdom to rule justly, and as the Mighty God, He has the power to execute His wise plans. "Everlasting Father" does not suggest that the Son is also the Father, for each person in the Godhead is distinct. "Father of Eternity" is a better translation. Among the Jews, the word *father* means "originator" or "source." For example, Satan is the "father [originator] of lies" (John 8:44). If you want anything eternal, you must get it from Jesus Christ; He is the "Father of eternity."

Applying God's Truth:

1. Isaiah saw not only the *coming* of Christ, but His *second coming* as well. How might your spiritual life change if you focused more on the future?

2. What do you most appreciate about the *humanity* of Jesus? What do you appreciate about His *deity*?

3. Of the titles given the Messiah, which gives you most encouragement? Why?

Scripture: Read Isaiah 13–18

"How you have fallen from heaven, O morning star, son of the dawn! You have been cast down to the earth, you who once laid low the nations!" (Isa. 14:12)

THE MIGHTY KEEP FALLING

I saiah warned that the kingdom of Judah would be taken into captivity by Babylon, and this happened in 586 B.C. Jeremiah prophesied that the Captivity would last for seventy years. Then Babylon would be judged and the Jews permitted to go home. So, the capture of Babylon by Darius would be good news to the Jews; for it would mean the end of their exile and bondage.

The picture in Isaiah 14:1-23 is that of a mighty monarch whose pride brought him to destruction. This is what happened to Belshazzar when Darius the Mede captured Babylon in 539 B.C. Isaiah described the king's arrival in sheol, the world of the dead, where the king's wealth, glory, and power vanished. The dead kings already in sheol stood in tribute to him (v. 9), but it was all a mockery. Death is the great leveler; there are no kings in the world of the dead. *Lucifer* (v. 12) is Latin for "morning star" and suggests that this king's glory did not last very long. The morning star shines but is soon swallowed up by the light of the sun.

The name *Lucifer* also indicates that Satan tries to imitate Jesus Christ, who is "the bright and morning star" (Rev. 22:16). "I will be like the Most High" reveals his basic strategy, for he is an imitator. Like the king of Babylon, Satan will one day be humiliated and defeated. He will be cast out of heaven and finally cast into hell. Whether God is dealing with kings or angels, Proverbs 16:18 is still true: "Pride goes before destruction, a haughty spirit before a fall."

Applying God's Truth:

1. What was the difference between the "fall" of Judah (God's people) and the "falls" of the surrounding Gentile nations?

2. In what ways do some people today sinfully strive to "be like the Most High"?

3. What's the difference between the desire to "be like the Most High" and a Christian's attempt to be more "Christlike"?

Scripture: Read Isaiah 19–23

"In that day Israel will be the third, along with Egypt and Assyria, a blessing on the earth" (Isa. 19:24).

INTERNATIONAL NEWS

Chapters 13 through 23 of Isaiah teach us some important lessons. First, *God is in control of the nations of the world, and He can do with them what He pleases.* "Though the mills of God grind slowly, yet they grind exceeding small" (Friedrich von Logau, translated by Henry Wadsworth Longfellow). Second, *God especially hates the sin of pride.* (See Isa. 13:11; 16:6; 23:9; and Prov. 8:13.) When nations turn from the living God to trust their wealth and their armaments, God must show them that He is the only sure refuge. Third, *God judges the nations for the way they treat each other.* Judah was the only nation mentioned that had God's Law, yet God held the other ten Gentile nations accountable for what they did. Finally, *God always gives a word of promise and hope to His people.* Babylon will fall, but God will care for Judah (Isa. 14:1-3, 32). Moab will not accept sanctuary from Jerusalem, but God will one day establish Messiah's throne there (16:5). Assyria and Egypt may be avowed enemies of the Jews, but one day the three nations will together glorify God (19:23-25).

Therefore, no matter how frightening the national or international situation may become, God's children can have peace because they know Almighty God is on His throne. The nations may rage and plot against God, but "The One enthroned in heaven laughs" (Ps. 2:4). When the Lord of heaven and earth is your Father, and you gladly wear Christ's yoke, you have nothing to fear.

Applying God's Truth:

1. When you consider the turmoil around the world, what are some of your biggest fears?

2. What difference does it make in your personal life to believe that "God is in control of the nations of the world"?

3. In spite of national and international problems, what would you say is God's "word of promise and hope" to His people today?

Scripture: Read Isaiah 24–25

"You have been a refuge for the poor, a refuge for the needy in his distress, a shelter from the storm and a shade from the heat" (Isa. 25:4).

SEEKING REFUGE

Isaiah paints two pictures: the buffeting of a storm and the beating down of a burning sun in the desert. Where can travelers go for refuge? They see a huge rock and find refuge in it. God is that Rock, and He will be a refuge for His believing people during that terrible "Day of the Lord." The victory shouts of the enemy will disappear the way heat vanishes when a cloud covers the sea.

God cares for His own in times of trial and judgment. He kept Noah and his family alive through the Flood and guarded Israel when His judgments fell on Egypt. He protected believing Rahab and her family when Jericho fell and preserved a faithful remnant when Judah was taken into Babylonian Captivity. Throughout the centuries, He has kept His church in spite of the attacks of Satan and will deliver His church from the wrath to come. When "the Day of the Lord" comes to this godless world, God will see to it that the Jewish remnant will be preserved. "Hide yourselves for a little while until his wrath has passed by. See, the Lord is coming out of his dwelling to punish the people of the earth for their sins" (26:20-21).

Applying God's Truth:

1. What are some of the current "storms" in your life—the emotionally upsetting situations you face?

2. What are your current sources of "heat"—stress, pressure, and so forth?

3. In what ways is God a refuge for each of the situations you've listed? How can you more fully experience His loving protection?

Scripture: Read Isaiah 26–27

"Sing about a fruitful vineyard: I, the Lord, watch over it; I water it continually. I guard it day and night so that no one may harm it. I am not angry" (Isa. 27:2-4).

THE GRAPES OF RESISTANCE

I saiah sees both the Israel of his day and the Israel of the future day when God's kingdom will be established. God was not angry with His people; He just yearned for them to return to Him and fervently trust Him. He used war (Assyria) to punish the Northern Kingdom and captivity (Babylon) to discipline the Southern Kingdom, but He did this in love and not in anger.

In "the Day of the Lord," God will use suffering to purge His people and prepare them for their kingdom. Isaiah 27:9 does not suggest that personal suffering can atone for sin, for only the sacrifice of Jesus Christ can do that. God uses suffering as a discipline to bring us to submission so that we will seek Him and His holiness (Heb. 12:1-11). The Babylonian Captivity cured the Jews of their idolatry once and for all.

In Isaiah's day, the vineyard was producing wild grapes, but in the future kingdom, Israel will be fruitful and flourishing. God will guard His people and give them all that they need to bring glory to His name. The nation will "bud and blossom and fill all the world with fruit" (Isa. 27:6).

The Bible speaks of three vines: the people of Israel (vv. 5, 27), Christ and His church (John 15), and godless Gentile society, "the vine of the earth" (Rev. 14:18). The vineyard of Israel is not bearing fruit, the "vine of the earth" is filling the world with poisonous fruit, and God's people must be faithful branches in the Vine and produce fruit that glorifies God's name.

Applying God's Truth:

1. How would you describe your current spiritual life in terms of a vineyard?

2. What are some evidences of "fruit" due to God's involvement in your life?

3. Looking back, can you see how God has worked to make you more productive for Him? Can you cite specific instances?

Scripture: Read Isaiah 28

"Priests and prophets stagger from beer and are befuddled with wine; they reel from beer, they stagger when seeing visions, they stumble when rendering decisions" (Isa. 28:7).

MISUSING A GOOD GIFT

Like all devout Jews, Isaiah loved Jerusalem, the holy city, the city of David, the place of God's dwelling. But Isaiah saw storm clouds gathering over the city and announced that trouble was coming. He began his message announcing God's judgment on Ephraim (vv. 1-6). Their arrogance was detestable to God, for they thought their fortress city of Samaria was impregnable. Samaria reigned in luxury and pleasure and had no fear of her enemies.

The Lord was also appalled by their drunkenness. To the Jews, wine was a gift from God and a source of joy. The Law did not demand total abstinence, but it did warn against drunkenness.

A government official in Washington, D.C. once quipped, "We have three parties in this city: the Democratic Party, the Republican Party, and the cocktail party." Indeed, Washington, D.C. ranks high on the list of cities noted for alcohol consumption. Many people don't realize that alcohol and nicotine, America's favorite legal narcotics, do far more damage than all the illegal drugs combined. According to Dr. Arnold Washton, alcohol and nicotine kill 450,000 people annually, while illegal drugs kill about 6,000 (*Willpower's Not Enough*, Harper & Row, 1989, p. 13). What hope is there for our affluent, pleasure-loving society that gives lip service to religion and ignores the tragic consequences of sin and the judgment that is sure to come?

Applying God's Truth:

1. What would you say if a non-Christian friend asked, "What does the Bible say about drinking?"

2. Drunkenness was related to arrogance for the people of Ephraim. Do you think the two traits are still related? In what ways?

3. What advice and/or warning would you give a young person just beginning to start drinking on a regular basis? What would you tell an adult who seems to be addicted?

Scripture: Read Isaiah 29

"Once more the humble will rejoice in the Lord; the needy will rejoice in the Holy One of Israel. The ruthless will vanish, the mockers will disappear" (Isa. 29:19-20).

AWAITING GOD'S BALANCE

I saiah asked the people to look ahead and consider what God had planned for them. In their political strategy, they had turned things upside down, but God would one day turn everything around by establishing His glorious kingdom on earth. The devastated land would become a paradise, the disabled would be healed, and the outcasts would be enriched and rejoice in the Lord. There would be no more scoffers or ruthless people practicing injustice in the courts. The founders of the nation, Abraham and Jacob, would see their many descendants all glorifying the Lord.

In light of this glorious future, why should Judah turn to feeble nations like Egypt for help? God is on their side, and they can trust Him! God cared for Jacob during all of his years of trial, and surely He could care for Jacob's children. It is tragic when a nation forgets its great spiritual heritage and turns from trusting the Lord to trusting the plans and promises of men.

At the Constitutional Convention in Philadelphia in 1787, Benjamin Franklin said, "I have lived, Sir, a long time, and the longer I live, the more convincing the proofs I see of this truth—*that God governs in the affairs of men*. I therefore beg leave to move that henceforth prayers imploring the assistance of heaven and its blessings on our deliberations be held in this Assembly every morning. . . ."

Isaiah sought that attitude in Jerusalem, but instead, he found only scoffing and unbelief.

Applying God's Truth:

1. Have you ever gotten yourself in trouble by making a bad alliance with a person or group rather than seeking God's help? What were the circumstances?

2. Are you currently in any cumbersome situations that you would like to be free of? What do you think God would have you do?

3. How can you ensure that your future decisions will reflect God's will for your life rather than someone else's?

Scripture: Read Isaiah 30–31

"Assyria will fall by a sword that is not of man; a sword, not of mortals, will devour them" (Isa. 31:8).

WHOM DO YOU TRUST?

Judah's faith was in men, not in God. They trusted in the legs of horses and the wheels of chariots, not in the hand of the Lord. Why should the Lord fear the Assyrians? Does a lion fear a flock of sheep and their shepherds? Do the eagles fear as they hover over their young in the nest? God will pounce on Assyria like a lion and swoop down like an eagle, and that will be the end! In one night, the Assyrian army was wiped out (37:36).

Think of the money Judah would have saved and the distress they would have avoided had they only rested in the Lord their God and obeyed His will. All their political negotiations were futile and their treaties worthless. They could trust the words of the Egyptians but not the Word of God!

As God's church today faces enemies and challenges, it is always a temptation to turn to the world or the flesh for help. But our first response must be to examine our hearts to see if there is something we need to confess and make right. Then we must turn to the Lord in faith and obedience and surrender to His will alone. We must trust Him to protect us and fight for us.

A friend of mine kept a card on his office desk that read: Faith Is Living Without Scheming. In one statement, that is what Isaiah was saying to Judah and Jerusalem; and that is what he is saying to us today.

Applying God's Truth:

1. Do you agree that "Faith is living without scheming"? What, exactly, do you think that means?

2. What can you do to remain patient and faithful while waiting for God to act on your behalf?

3. What are some sources of help that even good people tend to turn to rather than trusting God?

Scripture: Read Isaiah 32–33

"The Lord is our judge, the Lord is our lawgiver, the Lord is our king; it is he who will save us" (Isa. 33:22).

A HOPEFUL FORECAST

In 1919, American writer Lincoln Steffens visited the Soviet Union to see what the Communist revolution was accomplishing; and in a letter to a friend, he wrote, "I have seen the future, and it works." If he were alive today, he would probably be less optimistic; but in those days, "the Russian experiment" seemed to be dramatically successful.

A university professor posted a sign on his study wall that read, "The future is not what it used to be." Since the advent of atomic energy, many people wonder if there is any future at all. Albert Einstein said that he never thought about the future because it came soon enough!

In Isaiah 32–35, the prophet invites us to look at future events to see what God has planned for His people and His world. In Isaiah 32:1, Isaiah writes about "*a* king"; but in 33:17, he calls him "*the* king." By the time you get to verse 22, He is "*our king*." It is not enough to say that Jesus Christ is "*a* king" or even "*the* King." We must confess our faith in Him and say with assurance that He is "our King."

In contrast to the evil rulers of Isaiah's day, Messiah will reign in *righteousness* and *justice*. In addition, the King will be like a rock of refuge for the people and like a refreshing river in the desert.

Isaiah ministered to spiritually blind, deaf, and ignorant people; but in the kingdom, all will see and hear God's truth as well as understand and obey it. This will happen because the nation will have a new heart and enter into a New Covenant with the Lord.

Applying God's Truth:

1. What people do you know who would agree that Jesus is *a* king? *The* King? *Our* King?

2. Right this minute, what are some of your worries about the future? If you *really* trust God, why do you think you're still worried?

3. In what ways has God been like "a refreshing river in the desert" for you in the past? What does that suggest about your future?

Scripture: Read Isaiah 34–35

"A highway will be there; it will be called the Way of Holiness. The unclean will not journey on it; it will be for those who walk in that Way" (Isa. 35:8).

THE ROAD LESS TRAVELED

Isaiah 35:8 expresses one of Isaiah's favorite themes: the highway (11:16; 19:23; 40:3; 62:10). During the Assyrian invasion, the highways were not safe (33:8), but during the Kingdom Age it will be safe to travel. There will be one special highway: "The Way of Holiness." In ancient cities, there were often special roads that only kings and priests could use; but when Messiah reigns, *all of His people* will be invited to use this highway. Isaiah pictures God's redeemed, ransomed, and rejoicing Jewish families going up to the yearly feasts in Jerusalem to praise their Lord.

When Isaiah spoke and wrote these words, it is likely that the Assyrians had ravaged the land, destroyed the crops, and made the highways unsafe for travel. The people were cooped up in Jerusalem, wondering what would happen next. The remnant was trusting God's promises and praying for God's help, and God answered their prayers. If God kept His promises to His people centuries ago and delivered them, will He not keep His promises in the future and establish His glorious kingdom for His chosen people? Of course He will!

The future is your friend when Jesus Christ is your Savior.

Applying God's Truth:

1. In what way is your spiritual journey like going down a highway?

2. Do you feel completely safe as you travel the "Way of Holiness"? If not, how could you feel safer?

3. How can you be sure you stay on the right highway without taking any wrong turns?

Scripture: Read Isaiah 36

"In the fourteenth year of King Hezekiah's reign, Sennacherib king of Assyria attacked all the fortified cities of Judah and captured them" (Isa. 36:1).

A KING TO RELATE TO

Except for David and Solomon, no king of Judah is given more attention or commendation in Scripture than Hezekiah. "Hezekiah trusted in the Lord, the God of Israel. There was no one like him among all the kings of Judah, either before him or after him" (2 Kings 18:5).

He began his reign about 715 B.C., though he may have been coregent with his father as early as 729 B.C. He restored the temple facilities and services of worship, destroyed the idols and the hill shrines where the people falsely worshiped Jehovah, and sought to bring the people back to vital faith in the Lord. He led the people in a nationwide two-week celebration of Passover and invited Jews from the Northern Kingdom to participate.

After the fall of the Northern Kingdom in 722 B.C., Judah had constant problems with Assyria. Hezekiah finally rebelled against Assyria (2 Kings 18:7); and when Sennacherib threatened to attack, Hezekiah tried to bribe him with tribute (vv. 13-16). It was a lapse of faith on Hezekiah's part that God could not bless. Sennacherib accepted the treasures but broke the treaty (Isa. 33:1) and invaded Judah in 701 B.C. The account of God's miraculous deliverance of His people is given in Isaiah 36–37.

Chapters 36–39 teach us some valuable lessons about faith, prayer, and the dangers of pride. Though the setting today may be different, the problems and temptations are still the same; for Hezekiah's history is our history, and Hezekiah's God is our God.

Applying God's Truth:

1. Prior to this reading, how much did you know about King Hezekiah? (For further research, see 2 Kings 18–20; 2 Chron. 29–32; and Isa. 36–39.)

2. When you, like Hezekiah, "inherit" something that all your predecessors have made a mess of, do you tend to do what's easy and go with the flow, or do what's hard and correct the situation? What are some examples?

3. What do you think made Hezekiah so different from the kings who preceded him? What can you learn from his example?

Scripture: Read Isaiah 37

"The angel of the Lord went out and put to death a hundred and eighty-five thousand men in the Assyrian camp. . . . So Sennacherib king of Assyria broke camp and withdrew" (Isa. 37:36-37).

NO PROBLEM TOO BIG

Sennacherib boasted of his military might and his great conquests, for no obstacle stood in his way. If he so desired, like a god, he could even dry up the rivers! But the king of Assyria forgot that he was only God's tool for accomplishing His purposes on the earth, and the tool must not boast against the Maker (10:5-19). God would humble Sennacherib and his army by treating them like cattle and leading them away from Jerusalem (37:7, 29).

The Assyrian commander had joked that one Assyrian junior officer was stronger than 2,000 Jewish charioteers (36:8-9), but it took *only one* of God's angels to destroy 185,000 Assyrian soldiers! Isaiah had prophesied the destruction of the Assyrian army. God would mow them down like a forest (10:33-34), devastate them with a storm (30:27-30), and throw them into the fire like garbage on the city dump (vv. 31-33).

But that was not all. After Sennacherib left Judah, a defeated man, he returned to his capital city of Nineveh. Twenty years later, as a result of a power struggle among his sons, Sennacherib was assassinated by two of his sons in fulfillment of Isaiah's prophecy (37:7); and it happened in the temple of his god! The field commander had ridiculed the gods of the nations, but Sennacherib's own god could not protect him.

Applying God's Truth:

1. Do you know bullies like Sennacherib? How do you handle such abusive people?

2. How do you feel when you seem tremendously outnumbered? Why?

3. What can you learn from this story to apply to stressful situations you're currently facing?

Scripture: Read Isaiah 38–39

"In those days Hezekiah became ill and was at the point of death. The prophet Isaiah son of Amoz went to him and said, 'This is what the Lord says: Put your house in order, because you are going to die; you will not recover'" (Isa. 38:1).

MIRACLE RECOVERY

Hezekiah was an author of psalms (38:20) and supervised a group of scholars who copied the Old Testament Scriptures (Prov. 25:1). In the beautiful meditation in Isaiah 38, the king tell us how he felt during his experience of illness and recovery. He had some new experiences that made him a better person.

For one thing, God gave him *a new appreciation of life* (vv. 9-12). We take life for granted till it is about to be taken from us, and then we cling to it as long as we can. Hezekiah pictured death as the end of a journey, a tent taken down, and a weaving cut from the loom. Life was hanging by a thread!

He also had *a new appreciation of prayer* (vv. 13-14). Were it not for prayer, Hezekiah could not have made it. At night, the king felt like a frail animal being attacked by a fierce lion; and in the daytime, he felt like a helpless bird. During this time of suffering, Hezekiah examined his own heart and confessed his sins, and God forgave him.

The king ended with *a new appreciation of opportunities for service* (vv. 15-20). There was a new humility in his walk, a deeper love for the Lord in his heart, and a new song of praise on his lips. He had a new determination to praise God all the days of his life, for now those days were very important to him.

Applying God's Truth:

1. Since Isaiah was God's prophet, and God's prophets were always correct, why do you think Hezekiah prayed for more time after God said he would not recover?

2. Do you think this is a case where God actually changed His mind? Explain.

3. What can you remember from this story the next time you're facing a seemingly hopeless and final situation?

Scripture: Read Isaiah 40:1-26

"Comfort, comfort my people, says your God. . . . The grass withers and the flow-ers fall, but the word of our God stands forever" *(Isa. 40:1, 8)*.

READING THE IBV (ISAIAH BIBLE VERSION)

The Book of Isaiah can be called "a Bible in miniature." There are sixty-six chapters in Isaiah and sixty-six books in the Bible. The thirty-nine chapters in the first part of Isaiah may be compared to the Old Testament with its thirty-nine books, and both focus primarily on God's judgment of sin. The twenty-seven chapters of the second part may be seen to parallel the twenty-seven books of the New Testament, and both emphasize the grace of God.

The "New Testament" section of Isaiah opens with the ministry of John the Baptist (40:3-5; Mark 1:1-4) and closes with the new heavens and the new earth (Isa. 65:17; 66:22). At the heart of the "New Testament" section of Isaiah's book is our Lord Jesus Christ and His sacrifice on the cross for our sins. No wonder Isaiah has been called "the evangelical prophet."

As you study Isaiah 40–66, keep in mind that it was originally addressed to a group of discouraged Jewish refugees who faced a long journey home and a difficult task when they got there. Note how often God says to them, "Fear not!" and how frequently He assures them of His pardon and His pres-ence. It is no surprise that God's people for centuries have turned to these chapters to find assurance and encouragement in the difficult days of life; for in these messages, God says to all of His people, "Be comforted!"

Applying God's Truth:

1. Isaiah's message was that something better was coming in the future. Do God's people still need that message? Why?

2. In what ways do you relate with people who are discouraged and have difficult tasks?

3. How many circumstances can you think of where you long to hear God say, "Fear not! Be comforted"?

Scripture: Read Isaiah 40:27–44:28

"Those who hope in the Lord will renew their strength. They will soar on wings like eagles; they will run and not grow weary, they will walk and not be faint" (Isa. 40:31).

PLOD WHILE YOU WAIT

God knows how we feel and what we fear, and He is adequate to meet our every need. We can never obey God in our own strength, but we can always trust Him to provide the strength we need (Phil. 4:13). If we trust ourselves, we will faint and fall; but if we wait on the Lord by faith, we will receive strength for the journey. The word *wait* (KJV) does not suggest that we sit around and do nothing. It means "to hope," to look to God for all that we need. This involves meditating on His character and His promises, praying, and seeking to glorify Him.

The word *renew* means "to exchange," as taking off old clothes and putting on new. We exchange our weakness for His power (2 Cor. 12:1-10). As we wait before Him, God enables us to soar when there is a crisis, to run when the challenges are many, and to walk faithfully in the day-by-day demands of life. *It is much harder to walk in the ordinary pressures of life than to fly like the eagle in a time of crisis.*

"I can plod," said William Carey, the father of modern missions. "That is my only genius. I can persevere in any definite pursuit. To this I owe everything."

The greatest heroes of faith are not always those who seem to be soaring; often they are the ones who are patiently plodding. As we wait on the Lord, He enables us not only to fly higher and run faster, but also to *walk longer.* Blessed are the plodders, for they eventually arrive at their destination!

Applying God's Truth:

1. What do you find most difficult about waiting upon and hoping in the Lord? Why?

2. When are some times you have flown like an eagle during a crisis?

3. What are three things you can do to be sure you keep plodding ahead *every* day?

Scripture: Read Isaiah 45–48

"See, I have refined you, though not as silver; I have tested you in the furnace of affliction" *(Isa. 48:10).*

GET OUT OF BABYLON!

The Jews had become comfortable and complacent in their Captivity and did not want to leave. They had followed the counsel of Jeremiah (Jer. 29:4-7) and had houses, gardens, and families; and it would not be easy for them to pack up and go to the Holy Land. *But that was where they belonged and where God had a work for them to do.* God told them that they were hypocritical in using His name and identifying with His city but not obeying His will (Isa. 48:1-2). They were stubborn and were not excited about the new things God was doing for them.

Had they obeyed the Lord in the first place, they would have experienced peace and not war (vv. 18-19), but it was not too late. He had put them into the furnace to refine them and prepare them for their future work. "Leave Babylon" was God's command (v. 20). God would go before them and prepare the way, and they had nothing to fear.

One would think that the Jews would have been eager to leave their "prison" and return to their land to see God do new and great things for them. They had grown accustomed to the security of bondage and had forgotten the challenges of freedom. The church today can easily grow complacent with its comfort and affluence. God may have to put us into the furnace to remind us that we are here to be *servants* and not *consumers* or *spectators.*

Applying God's Truth:

1. How do Christians today become complacent with the "captivity" of sin?

2. When were some times you could have avoided a lot of trouble if you had obeyed God "in the first place"?

3. How is your character refined in the "furnace of affliction"?

Scripture: Read Isaiah 49

"I will also make you a light for the Gentiles, that you may bring my salvation to the ends of the earth" (Isa. 49:6).

GENTILE LIGHT

Messiah came as both a servant and a warrior, serving those who trust Him and ultimately judging those who resist Him. All of God's servants should be like prepared weapons. "It is not great talents God blesses so much as great likeness to Jesus," wrote Robert Murray McCheyne. "A holy minister [servant] is an awful weapon in the hand of God."

The Jewish nation was called to glorify God and be a light to the Gentiles, but they failed in their mission. This is why Messiah is called "Israel" in verse 3: He did the work that Israel was supposed to do. Today, the church is God's light in this dark world, and like Israel, we seem to be failing in our mission to take the Good News to the ends of the earth. We cannot do the job very effectively when only 5 percent of the average local church budget is devoted to evangelism!

As Jesus Christ ministered on earth, especially to His own people Israel, there were times when His work seemed in vain (v. 4). The religious leaders opposed Him, the disciples did not always understand Him, and those He helped did not always thank Him. He lived and labored by faith, and God gave Him success.

Our Lord could not minister to the Gentiles until first He ministered to the Jews (vv. 5-6). He was despised by both Jews and Gentiles, but He did God's work and was glorified.

Applying God's Truth:

1. Can you think of any groups of people whom you tend to overlook as potential recipients of the Gospel?

2. In what ways might the "light" of the church shine brighter in today's world?

3. How could your own light brighten a little more gloom than usual today?

Scripture: Read Isaiah 50–51

"Because the Sovereign Lord helps me, I will not be disgraced. Therefore have I set my face like flint, and I know I will not be put to shame" (Isa. 50:7).

COMPLETE SUBMISSION

The emphasis in this portion of Isaiah is on the servant's submission to the Lord God in every area of His life and service. His *mind* was submitted to the Lord God so that He could learn His Word and His will (v. 4). Everything Jesus said and did was taught to Him by His Father. He prayed to the Father for guidance and meditated on the Word. What God taught the servant, the servant shared with those who needed encouragement and help. The servant sets a good example here for all who know the importance of a daily "quiet time" with the Lord.

The servant's *will* was also yielded to the Lord God. A "wakened ear" (v. 4) is one that hears and obeys the voice of the master. The people to whom Isaiah ministered were neither "willing" nor "obedient" (1:19), but the servant did gladly the will of the Lord God. This was not easy, for it meant yielding His body to wicked men who mocked Him, whipped Him, spat on Him, and then nailed Him to a cross.

The servant did all of this *by faith* in the Lord God. He was determined to do God's will even if it meant going to a cross, for He knew that the Lord God would help Him. The servant was falsely accused, but He knew that God would vindicate Him and eventually put His enemies to shame. Keep in mind that when Jesus Christ was ministering here on earth, He had to live by faith even as we must today. He did not use His divine powers selfishly for Himself but trusted God and depended on the power of the Spirit.

Applying God's Truth:

1. Do you need to more fully submit your mind to God? Your will? Your body? How can you make any needed changes?

2. What connections do you detect between faith and submission?

3. How does feeling disgrace or shame affect your spiritual growth? How can you deal with any problems in these areas?

Scripture: Read Isaiah 52

"So will he sprinkle many nations, and kings will shut their mouths because of him" (Isa. 52:15).

SOUNDS OF SILENCE

The people whose mouths dropped open with astonishment at the servant's humiliation and exaltation will shut their mouths in guilt when they hear His proclamation. Paul interprets this as the preaching of the Gospel to the Gentile nations (Rom. 15:20-21). "So that every mouth may be silenced and the whole world held accountable to God" (3:19).

Many people have been tortured and killed in an inhumane way, but knowing about their suffering does not touch our conscience, though it might arouse our sympathy. Our Lord's sufferings and death were different, because *they involved everybody in the world.* The Gospel message is not "Christ died," for that is only a fact in history, like "Napoleon died." The Gospel message is that "Christ died *for our sins*" (1 Cor. 15:1-4, italics mine). You and I are as guilty of Christ's death as Annas, Caiaphas, Herod Antipas, and Pilate.

Now we see why people are astonished when they understand the message of the Gospel: This man whom they condemned has declared that *they are condemned* unless they turn from sin and trust Him. *You cannot rejoice in the Good News of salvation until first you face the bad news of condemnation.* Jesus did not suffer and die because He was guilty, but because *we* were guilty. People are astonished at this fact; it shuts their mouths.

Applying God's Truth:

1. Can you recall a time when you received news that left you completely speechless?

2. What are some problems that you know about, yet that haven't really touched your conscience?

3. How do you feel when you dwell on the fact that Christ died for *your* sins?

Scripture: Read Isaiah 53

"He was oppressed and afflicted, yet he did not open his mouth; he was led like a lamb to the slaughter, and as a sheep before her shearers is silent, so he did not open his mouth" (Isa. 53:7).

SINLESS AND SILENT

Isaiah 53:7 speaks of Jesus' silence under suffering and verse 8 of His silence when illegally tried and condemned to death. In today's courts, a person can be found guilty of terrible crimes; but if it can be proved that something in the trial was illegal, the case must be tried again. *Everything* about Jesus' trials was illegal, but He did not appeal for another trial.

The servant is compared to a lamb, which is one of the frequent symbols of the Savior in Scripture. A lamb died for each Jewish household at Passover, and the servant died for His people, the nation of Israel. Jesus is "the Lamb of God, who takes away the sin of the world" (John 1:29); and twenty-eight times in the Book of Revelation, Jesus is referred to as "the Lamb."

Since Jesus Christ was crucified *with* criminals *as* a criminal, it was logical that His dead body would be left unburied, but God had other plans. The burial of Jesus Christ is as much a part of the Gospel as is His death, for the burial is proof that He actually died. The Roman authorities would not have released the body to Joseph and Nicodemus if the victim were not dead. A wealthy man like Joseph would never carve out a tomb for himself so near to a place of execution, particularly when his home was miles away. He prepared it for Jesus and had the spices and graveclothes ready for the burial. How wonderfully God fulfilled Isaiah's prophecy!

Applying God's Truth:

1. Many times Jesus' words had silenced His opponents. Why do you think He remained silent at His trial?

2. In what ways is a lamb a good symbol for Jesus? In each case, can you make the same application to *yourself*?

3. How do you feel when you are condemned for something you didn't do? What can you learn from Jesus' response in the same situation?

Scripture: Read Isaiah 54–56

"Come, all you who are thirsty, come to the waters. . . . Come, buy wine and milk without money and without cost" *(Isa. 55:1)*.

THE #1 THIRST QUENCHER

The invitation to come to the waters is extended to "everyone" and not just to the Jews. Anyone who is thirsting for that which really satisfies is welcome to come. As in Isaiah 25:6, the prophet pictures God's blessings in terms of a great feast, where God is the host.

In the East, water is a precious ingredient, and an abundance of water is a special blessing. Wine, milk, and bread were staples of a Middle Eastern diet. The people were living on substitutes that did not nourish them. They needed "the real thing" which only the Lord could give. In Scripture, both water and wine are pictures of the Holy Spirit (John 7:37-39; Eph. 5:18). Jesus is the "bread of life" (John 6:32-35), and His living Word is like milk (1 Peter 2:2). Our Lord probably had Isaiah 55:2 in mind when He said, "Do not work for food that spoils, but for food that endures to eternal life" (John 6:27).

People have to work hard to dig wells, care for flocks and herds, plant seed, and tend to the vineyards. But the Lord offered to them *free* everything they were laboring for. If they listen to His Word, they will be inclined to come; for God draws sinners to Himself through the Word (John 5:24). Note the emphasis on *hearing* in Isaiah 55:2-3. Jesus Christ is God's covenant to the Gentiles ("peoples"), and His promises will stand as long as His Son lives, which is forever.

Applying God's Truth:

1. What is something you have recently been "thirsting" for?

2. How does intense thirst affect your mood and productivity? How might this be true in a spiritual sense as well?

3. What are the "waters" that will eliminate your spiritual thirst? Explain.

Scripture: Read Isaiah 57–59

"Justice is far from us, and righteousness does not reach us. We look for light, but all is darkness; for brightness, but we walk in deep shadows" (Isa. 59:9).

TRUTH VERSUS LIES

There was a great deal of injustice in the land, with the rich exploiting the poor and the rulers using their authority only to make themselves rich. The people lifted their hands to worship God, but their hands were stained with blood (1:15, 21). God could not answer their prayers because their sins hid His face from them.

It was a conflict between *truth* and *lies*, just as it is today. When people live on lies, they live in a "twilight zone" and do not know where they are going. When truth falls, it creates a "traffic jam"; and justice and honesty cannot make progress. God is displeased with injustice, and He wonders that none of His people will intercede or intervene. So the Lord Himself intervened and brought the Babylonians to destroy Judah and Jerusalem and to teach His people that they cannot despise His Law and get away with it.

God's judgment on His people was a foreshadowing of that final Day of the Lord when all the nations will be judged. When it is ended, Israel will be not only God's *chosen* people but God's *cleansed* people, and the glory of the Lord will radiate from Mt. Zion.

The glory of the Lord in the promised kingdom is the theme of the closing chapters of Isaiah. While we are waiting and praying, "Thy kingdom come," perhaps we should also be interceding and intervening. We are the salt of the earth and the light of the world, and God expects us to make a difference.

Applying God's Truth:

1. What would you say are the primary injustices in today's society?

2. What lies still influence God's people? How do *you* avoid being taken in by them?

3. In what ways are you "interceding and intervening" as you await God's kingdom?

Scripture: Read Isaiah 60–62

"I, the Lord, love justice; I hate robbery and iniquity. In my faithfulness I will reward them and make an everlasting covenant with them" (Isa. 61:8).

JUBILEE!

The background of Isaiah 61 is the "Year of Jubilee" described in Leviticus 25:7ff. Every seven years, the Jews were to observe a "sabbatical year" and allow the land to rest. After seven sabbaticals, or forty-nine years, they were to celebrate the fiftieth year as the "Year of Jubilee." During that year, all debts were canceled, all land was returned to the original owners, the slaves were freed, and everybody was given a fresh new beginning. This was the Lord's way of balancing the economy and keeping the rich from exploiting the poor.

If you have trusted Christ as your Savior, you are living today in a spiritual "Year of Jubilee." You have been set free from bondage; your spiritual debt to the Lord has been paid; you are living in "the acceptable year of the Lord." Instead of the ashes of mourning, you have a crown on your head; for He has made you a king (Rev. 1:6). You have been anointed with the oil of the Holy Spirit, and you wear a garment of righteousness.

In her days of rebellion, Israel was like a fading oak and a waterless garden (Isa. 1:30); but in the kingdom, she will be like a watered garden (58:11) and a tree (oak) of righteousness (61:3). In their kingdom "Year of Jubilee," the Jewish people will rebuild, repair, and restore their land; and the Gentiles will shepherd Israel's flocks and herds and tend to their crops. Instead of being farmers and shepherds, the Jews will be priests and ministers! God will acknowledge them as His firstborn (Ex. 4:22) and give them a double portion of His blessing.

Applying God's Truth:

1. Do you have any kind of system that ensures rest, canceled debts, and settled accounts for others on a regular basis? If not, what are some potential consequences?

2. In what ways do you demonstrate your freedom from bondage, release from spiritual debt, and so forth?

3. Can you think of a person or group you could provide with an unexpected gift of freedom and/or peace?

Scripture: Read Isaiah 63–66

"This is the one I esteem: he who is humble and contrite in spirit, and trembles at my word" (Isa. 66:2).

COMFORT KING

Throughout his book, Isaiah has presented us with alternatives: Trust the Lord and live, or rebel against the Lord and die. He has explained the grace and mercy of God and offered His forgiveness. He has also explained the holiness and wrath of God and warned of His judgment. He has promised glory for those who will believe and judgment for those who scoff. He has explained the foolishness of trusting man's wisdom and the world's resources.

The prophet calls the professing people of God back to spiritual reality. He warns against hypocrisy and empty worship. He pleads for faith, obedience, a heart that delights in God, and a life that glorifies God. "There is no peace," says my God, "for the wicked" (57:21); for in order to have peace, you must have righteousness. The only way to have righteousness is through faith in Jesus Christ (Rom. 3:19-31).

Isaiah's message has been, "Be comforted by the Lord!" *But God cannot comfort rebels!* If we are sinning against God and comfortable about it, something is radically wrong. That false comfort will lead to false confidence, and that will lead to the chastening hand of God. "Seek the Lord while He may be found" (55:6).

"I will praise you, O Lord. Although you were angry with me, your anger has turned away and you have comforted me" (12:1).

Applying God's Truth:

1. What are some clear alternatives you're currently facing in your life?

2. In what ways do you still tend to be a rebel in God's kingdom?

3. What three things has Isaiah taught you (or reminded you of) that you feel will be most significant in your near future?

JOY

30 Daily Readings from the Book of Philippians

T HE WORLD USES THE WORD *HAPPINESS*, BUT GOD TALKS ABOUT JOY. There's a difference, and when you learn what that difference is, your life will be different.

Happiness depends on happenings, what goes on around you. When your plans work out right, when you feel good, when problems are at a minimum, then you're happy. But when you wake up with a headache, or the boss rearranges your schedule, or somebody you love is hurting, then that happiness fades, and you're left feeling discouraged and defeated. You feel like quitting.

But life doesn't have to be like that. You can substitute joy for happiness and experience a whole new kind of life.

Joy doesn't depend on what goes on *around* you. It depends on what goes on *within* you. It is the result of a right relationship with God, a right attitude toward life, and a right faith in the power of Christ. Happiness says, "I am the captain of my fate!" and courts disaster.

Joy says, "I can do everything through him who gives me strength" (Phil. 4:13) and marches to victory.

Paul didn't write the Epistle to the Philippians from a comfortable library or an ivory tower. When he wrote it, he was a prisoner in Rome *and in danger of being executed any day*. Yet this letter is saturated with joy and rejoicing. Why? Because Paul was a man who knew Christ, a single-minded man with a mission to fulfill and a God to serve.

Outlook helps to determine outcome, and in this letter, Paul tells you how to have the kind of outlook that produces joy. He shares the "open secret" of having joy in spite of circumstances, people, things, or worry. He explains the basic principles of Christian experience that can turn your life into a daily celebration of the joy of the Lord.

Yes, you'll still have problems and battles and burdens, but you'll find yourself overcoming instead of being overcome.

You'll find yourself joyfully saying with Paul, "I can do everything through Him who gives me strength."

Scripture: Read Philippians 1:1-5

"I thank God every time I remember you. In all my prayers for all of you, I always pray with joy because of your partnership in the gospel from the first day until now" (Phil. 1:3-5).

THE SECRET OF JOY

Paul's letter to the Philippian church is something of a missionary thank-you letter, but it is much more than that. It is the sharing of Paul's secret of Christian joy. At least nineteen times in these four chapters, Paul mentions joy, rejoicing, or gladness!

The unusual thing about the letter is this: Paul's situation was such that there appeared to be no reason for him to be rejoicing. He was a Roman prisoner and his case was coming up shortly. He might be acquitted, or he might be beheaded! And, unfortunately, the believers at Rome (where he was being held) were divided: some were for Paul and some were against him. In fact, some of the Christians even wanted to make things more difficult for the apostle!

Yet, in spite of his danger and discomfort, Paul overflowed with joy. The secret of Christian joy is found in the way the believer thinks—his attitudes. After all, outlook determines outcome. As we think, so we are (Prov. 23:7).

Philippians, then, is a Christian psychology book, based solidly on biblical doctrine. It is a book that explains the mind the believer must have if he is going to experience Christian joy in a world filled with trouble.

Applying God's Truth:

1. Can you recall a time or times when you experienced joy even under threatening or adverse situations?

2. What are some current situations that tend to keep you from experiencing joy? How might you keep from letting such situations rob you of joy?

3. As you go through these devotional readings, what are some things you hope to accomplish?

Scripture: Read Philippians 1:6-7

"Being confident of this, that he who began a good work in you will carry it on to completion until the day of Christ Jesus" (Phil. 1:6).

REDUCING FRICTION

Isn't it remarkable that Paul is thinking of others and not of himself? As he awaits his trial in Rome, Paul's mind goes back to the believers in Philippi, and every recollection he has brings him joy. Read Acts 16; you may discover that some things happened to Paul at Philippi, the memory of which could produce sorrow. He was illegally arrested and beaten, was placed in the stocks, and was humiliated before the people. But even those memories brought joy to Paul. It was a source of joy to Paul to know that God was still working in the lives of his fellow believers in Philippi. The basis for joyful Christian fellowship is to have God at work in our lives day by day.

"There seems to be friction in our home," a concerned wife said to a marriage counselor. "I really don't know what the trouble is."

"Friction is caused by one of two things," said the counselor, and to illustrate he picked up two blocks of wood from his desk. "If one block is moving, and one is standing still, there's friction. Or, if both are moving but in opposite directions, there's friction. Now, which is it?"

"I'll have to admit that I've been going backward in my Christian life, and Joe has really been growing," the wife admitted. "What I need is to get back to fellowship with the Lord."

Applying God's Truth:

1. Does your spiritual growth seem to be an occasional thing, or do you see it as an ongoing process with God in control? Explain.

2. What are some things that cause friction in your spiritual development?

3. When did God begin a good work in you? How has your life changed since that time? What additional changes do you anticipate?

Scripture: Read Philippians 1:8-10

"This is my prayer: that your love may abound more and more in knowledge and depth of insight, so that you may be able to discern what is best and may be pure and blameless until the day of Christ" (Phil. 1:9-10).

A MARK OF MATURITY

Paul found joy in his memories of the friends at Philippi and in his growing love for them. He also found joy in remembering them before the throne of grace in prayer. This is a prayer for maturity, and Paul begins with *love*. After all, if our Christian love is what it ought to be, everything else should follow. He prays that they might experience *abounding* love and *discerning* love. Christian love is not blind! The heart and mind work together so that we have discerning love and love discernment. Paul wants his friends to grow in discernment.

The ability to distinguish is a mark of maturity. When a baby learns to speak, it may call every four-legged animal a "bow-wow." But then the child discovers that there are cats, dogs, white mice, cows, and other four-legged creatures. To a little child, one automobile is just like another, but not to a car-crazy teenager. He can spot the differences between models faster than his parents can even name the cars!

One of the sure marks of maturity is discerning love.

Applying God's Truth:

1. Think of ten close friends. How frequently do you pray for each one of them?

2. What do you think it means to have "discerning love"? In what ways is your love for others a discerning kind of love?

3. In your life do you seek what is good, or do you try to discern what is truly *best* for you?

Scripture: Read Philippians 1:11

"Filled with the fruit of righteousness that comes through Jesus Christ—to the glory and praise of God" (Phil. 1:11).

FRUITFULNESS VERSUS BUSYNESS

The difference between spiritual fruit and human "religious activity" is that fruit brings glory to Jesus Christ. Whenever we do anything in our own strength, we have a tendency to boast about it. True spiritual fruit is so beautiful and wonderful that no man can claim credit for it; the glory must go to God alone. This, then, is true Christian fellowship—a having-in-common that is much deeper than mere friendship.

Jerry had to go to New York City for special surgery, and he hated to go. "Why can't we have it done at home?" he asked his doctor. "I don't know a soul in that big, unfriendly city!" But when he and his wife arrived at the hospital, there was a pastor to meet them and invite them to stay at his home until they got settled. The operation was serious, and the wait in the hospital was long and difficult; but the fellowship of the pastor and his wife brought new joy to Jerry and his wife. They learned that circumstances need not rob us of joy if we will but permit these circumstances to strengthen the fellowship of the Gospel.

Applying God's Truth:

1. What are some characteristics you would consider "the fruit of righteousness"?

2. In contrast, what are some of the things you would classify as only "religious activity"?

3. In which of your relationships would you say you experience genuine Christian fellowship? In which ones do you settle for "mere friendship"?

Scripture: Read Philippians 1:12-13

"It has become clear throughout the whole palace guard and to everyone else that I am in chains for Christ" (Phil. 1:13).

ONWARD, PIONEERS

E veryone has heard of Charles Haddon Spurgeon, the famous British preacher, but few know the story of his wife, Susannah. Early in their married life, Mrs. Spurgeon became an invalid. It looked as though her only ministry would be encouraging her husband and praying for his work. But God gave her a burden to share her husband's books with pastors who were unable to purchase them. This burden soon led to the founding of the "Book Fund." As a work of faith, the "Book Fund" provided thousands of pastors with tools for their work. All this was supervised by Mrs. Spurgeon from her home. It was a pioneer ministry.

God still wants His children to take the Gospel into new areas. He wants us to be pioneers, and sometimes He arranges circumstances so that we can be nothing else but pioneers. In fact, that is how the Gospel originally came to Philippi! Paul had tried to enter other territory, but God had repeatedly shut the door (Acts 16:6-10). Paul wanted to take the message eastward into Asia, but God directed him to take it westward into Europe. What a difference it would have made in the history of mankind if Paul had been permitted to follow his plan!

Applying God's Truth:

1. Who are some people you know who aren't in prominent leadership roles, yet who have a lot of impact on others for advancing the Gospel? What can you learn from such people?

2. What are some "new areas" where you might be able to carry the Gospel?

3. Envision yourself as a spiritual "pioneer." What are some of the potential risks you need to be aware of? What are some of the potential benefits?

Scripture: Read Philippians 1:14-17

"Because of my chains, most of the brothers in the Lord have been encouraged to speak the word of God more courageously and fearlessly" (Phil. 1:14).

CHAINS AND CHANGE

Sometimes God has to put "chains" on His people to get them to accomplish a "pioneer advance" that could never happen any other way. Young mothers may feel chained to the home as they care for their children, but God can use those "chains" to reach people with the message of salvation. Susannah Wesley was the mother of nineteen children, before the days of labor-saving devices and disposable diapers! Out of that large family came John and Charles Wesley, whose combined ministries shook the British Isles.

At six weeks of age, Fanny Crosby was blinded, but even as a youngster she determined not to be confined by the chains of darkness. In time, she became a mighty force for God through her hymns and Gospel songs.

The secret is this: when you have the single mind (see Day 8), you look upon your circumstances as God-given opportunities for the furtherance of the Gospel, and you rejoice at *what God is going to do* instead of complaining about *what God did not do.*

Applying God's Truth:

1. What are some ways in which you feel "chained"?

2. Do you have any regrets—or perhaps complaints—of times when you hoped God would work in a certain way, yet He didn't?

3. What are some ways that you might overcome your chains and become a better witness for God?

Scripture: Read Philippians 1:18-20

"I eagerly expect and hope that I will in no way be ashamed, but will have suffi-cient courage so that now as always Christ will be exalted in my body, whether by life or by death" (Phil. 1:20).

LARGER THAN LIFE

D oes Christ need to be magnified? After all, how can a mere human being ever magnify the Son of God? Well, the stars are much bigger than the telescope, and yet the telescope magnifies them and brings them closer. The believer's body is to be a telescope that brings Jesus Christ closer to people. To the average person, Christ is a misty figure in history who lived centuries ago. But as the unsaved watch the believer go through a crisis, they can see Jesus magnified and brought so much closer. To the Christian with the sin-gle mind (see Day 8), Christ is with us here and now.

The telescope brings distant things closer, and the microscope makes tiny things look big. To the unbeliever, Jesus is not very big. Other people and other things are far more important. But as the unbeliever watches the Christian go through a crisis experience, he ought to be able to see how big Jesus Christ really is. The believer's body is a "lens" that makes a "little Christ" look very big, and a "distant Christ" come very close.

Paul was not afraid of life or death! Either way, he wanted to magnify Christ in his body. No wonder he had joy!

Applying God's Truth:

1. Can you think of any recent ways in which you have magnified (exalted) God? If so, how?

2. Do you ever feel embarrassed when presenting the Gospel to others? How do you muster "sufficient courage" to maintain an effective personal min-istry?

3. What kind of "lens" do you provide through which friends and acquain-tances see Christ? Do you magnify Him or tend to obscure the view in some way?

Scripture: Read Philippians 1:21-24

"To me, to live is Christ and to die is gain" (Phil. 1:21).

THE SINGLE MIND

James tells us that a double-minded man is unstable in all he does (James 1:8). Or, to use the old Latin proverb: "When the pilot does not know what port he is heading for, no wind is the right wind." The reason many Christians are upset by circumstances is because they do not cultivate "the single mind." Paul expresses this attitude of single-hearted devotion to Christ thus: "For to me, to live is Christ and to die is gain."

Paul discusses his difficult circumstances and faces them honestly. But his circumstances cannot rob him of his joy because he is not living to enjoy circumstances; he is living to serve Jesus Christ. He is a man with purpose. He did not look at Christ through his circumstances; rather, he looked at his circumstances through Christ—and this changed everything.

Paul rejoiced in his difficult circumstances because they helped to strengthen his fellowship with other Christians, gave him opportunity to lead others to Christ, and enabled him to defend the Gospel before the courts of Rome. When you have the single mind, your circumstances work *for* you and not *against* you.

Applying God's Truth:

1. What do you think it means to be "single minded," or to "have a single mind"?

2. What dominates your thoughts more than anything else?

3. Would you say your circumstances seem to influence your attitude about Jesus? Or does your relationship with Jesus tend to influence all your circumstances? Explain.

Scripture: Read Philippians 1:25-28

"Whatever happens, conduct yourselves in a manner worthy of the gospel of Christ" (Phil. 1:27).

PEOPLE MAY BE WATCHING

My wife and I were visiting in London and one day decided to go to the zoo. We boarded the bus and sat back to enjoy the ride, but it was impossible to enjoy it because of the loud, coarse conversation of the passengers at the front of the bus. Unfortunately, they were Americans, and we could see the Britishers around us raising their eyebrows and shaking their heads, as though to say, "Oh, yes, they're from America!" We were embarrassed because we knew that these people did not really represent the best of American citizens.

Paul is suggesting that we Christians are the citizens of heaven, and while we are on earth we ought to behave like heaven's citizens. He brings this concept up again in 3:20. It would be a very meaningful expression to the people in Philippi because Philippi was a Roman colony, and its citizens were actually Roman citizens, protected by Roman law. The church of Jesus Christ is a colony of heaven on earth! And we ought to behave like the citizens of heaven.

Applying God's Truth:

1. Why do you think Paul introduces his command with the phrase, "Whatever happens"?

2. Are you ever embarrassed by God? Are you ever embarrassed by other Christians? What's the difference?

3. How does your conduct relate to your expressions of faith? Try to think of some specific examples.

Scripture: Read Philippians 1:29-30

"It has been granted to you on behalf of Christ not only to believe on him, but also to suffer for him" (Phil. 1:29).

BROTHERS IN ARMS

Satan wants us to think we are alone in the battle, that our difficulties are unique, but such is not the case. Paul reminds the Philippians that he is going through the same difficulties they are experiencing hundreds of miles from Rome! A change in geography is usually no solution to spiritual problems because human nature is the same wherever you go, and the enemy is everywhere. Knowing that my fellow believers are also sharing in the battle is an encouragement for me to keep going and to pray for them as I pray for myself.

Actually, going through spiritual conflict is one way we have to *grow in Christ*. God gives us the strength we need to stand firm against the enemy, and this confidence is proof to him that he will lose and we are on the winning side. As we face the enemy and depend on the Lord, He gives us all that we need for battle. When the enemy sees our God-given confidence, it makes him fear.

So, the single mind enables us to have joy in the midst of battle because it produces in us consistency, cooperation, and confidence. We experience the joy of "spiritual teamwork" as we strive together for the faith of the Gospel.

Applying God's Truth:

1. War buddies grow particularly close because of the sufferings they share. Can you think of some past trials that drew you close to other people?

2. How does it make you feel during times of stress to know that others have suffered—and continue to suffer—in similar ways?

3. How can being "single minded" be an advantage during times of suffering?

Scripture: Read Philippians 2:1-6

"Your attitude should be the same as that of Christ Jesus: Who, being in very nature God, did not consider equality with God something to be grasped" (Phil. 2:5-6).

THE POTENTIAL OF PRIVILEGES

C ertainly, as God, Jesus Christ did not need anything! He had all the glory and praise of heaven. With the Father and the Spirit, He reigned over the universe. But verse 6 states an amazing fact: He did not consider His equality with God as "something to be grasped." Jesus did not think of Himself; He thought of others. His outlook (or attitude) was that of unselfish concern for others. This is "the mind of Christ," an attitude that says, "I cannot keep my privileges for myself, I must use them for others; and to do this, I will gladly lay them aside and pay whatever price is necessary."

A reporter was interviewing a successful job counselor who had placed hundreds of workers in their vocations quite happily. When asked the secret of his success, the man replied: "If you want to find out what a worker is really like, don't give him responsibilities—give him *privileges*. Most people can handle responsibilities if you pay them enough, but it takes a real leader to handle privileges. A leader will use his privileges to help others and build the organization; a lesser man will use privileges to promote himself." Jesus used His heavenly privileges for the sake of others—for *our* sake.

Applying God's Truth:

1. Do you ever wish for fame and recognition? What are some of your specific desires? What do you think motivates such dreams?

2. When you've worked hard to earn certain privileges, how hard do you try to hold on to them? Can you think of recent instances when you willingly gave up your hard-earned privileges to help out someone else?

3. What does it mean to you that Jesus "did not consider equality with God something to be grasped"?

Scripture: Read Philippians 2:7-8

"But [Jesus] made himself nothing, taking the very nature of a servant, being made in human likeness. And being found in appearance as a man, he humbled himself and became obedient to death—even death on a cross!" (Phil. 2:7-8)

CHOOSING SERVANTHOOD

Thinking of "others" in an abstract sense only is insufficient; we must get down to the nitty-gritty of true service. Jesus thought of others *and became a servant!* When Christ was born at Bethlehem, He entered into a *permanent* union with humanity from which there could be no escape. He willingly humbled Himself that He might lift us up! Jesus did not pretend to be a servant; He was not an actor playing a role. *He actually was a servant!* This was the true expression of His innermost nature. He was the God-Man, deity and humanity united in one, and He came as a servant.

Have you noticed as you read the four Gospels that it is Jesus who serves others, not others who serve Jesus? He is at the beck and call of all kinds of people—fishermen, harlots, tax collectors, the sick, the sorrowing. In the Upper Room, when His disciples apparently refused to minister, Jesus arose, laid aside His outer garments, put on the long linen towel, and *washed their feet!* (John 13) He took the place of a menial slave! This was the submissive mind in action—and no wonder Jesus experienced such joy!

Applying God's Truth:

1. Think of your acts of service to others. What percentage of them would you say are absolutely genuine? What percent might be considered "acting" or obligation?

2. What do you think was Jesus' secret to being such a good servant?

3. Do you believe there is a direct connection between serving others and receiving personal joy? Do your actions reflect your knowledge of this connection?

Scripture: Read Philippians 2:9-11

"Therefore God exalted him . . . that at the name of Jesus every knee should bow . . . and every tongue confess that Jesus Christ is Lord, to the glory of God the Father" (Phil. 2:9-11).

A SUBMISSIVE MIND

Our Lord's exaltation began with His resurrection. When men buried the body of Jesus, that was the last thing any human hand did to Him. From that point on, it was God who worked. Men had done their worst to the Savior, but God exalted Him and honored Him. Men gave Him names of ridicule and slander, but the Father gave Him a glorious name!

The person with the submissive mind, as he lives for others, must expect sacrifice and service; but in the end, it is going to lead to glory. Joseph suffered and served for thirteen years, but then God exalted him and made him the second ruler of Egypt. David was anointed king when he was but a youth. He experienced years of hardship and suffering, but at the right time, God exalted him as king of Israel.

The joy of the submissive mind comes not only from helping others, and sharing in the fellowship of Christ's sufferings, but primarily from the knowledge that we are glorifying God. We are letting our light shine through our good works, and this glorifies the Father in heaven. We may not see the glory today, but we shall see it when Jesus comes and rewards His faithful servants.

Applying God's Truth:

1. On a scale of 1 (least) to 10 (most), how impatient do you feel when you serve others and don't receive an immediate reward or acknowledgment?

2. Is it enough for you to know that God will reward your good works eventually? Or is it still hard to keep doing good for people who don't seem to appreciate it?

3. How can you stay focused on God's promised rewards and not so disappointed when your good deeds go unrecognized?

Scripture: Read Philippians 2:12-13

"Continue to work out your salvation with fear and trembling, for it is God who works in you to will and to act according to his good purpose" (Phil. 2:12-13).

A Spiritual "Workout"

W ork out your salvation" does not suggest "Work for your own salvation." To begin with, Paul is writing to people who are already "saints" (1:1), which means they have trusted Christ and have been set apart for Him. The verb *work out* carries the meaning of "work to full completion," such as working out a problem in mathematics. In Paul's day it was also used for "working a mine," that is, getting out of the mine all the valuable ore possible; or "working a field" so as to get the greatest harvest possible. The purpose God wants us to achieve is Christlikeness, "to be conformed to the likeness of his Son" (Rom. 8:29). There are problems in life, but God will help us to "work them out." Our lives have tremendous potential, like a mine or a field, and He wants to help us fulfill that potential.

The phrase "work out your own salvation" probably has reference particularly to the special problems in the church at Philippi, but the statement also applies to the individual Christian. We are not to be "cheap imitations" of other people, especially "great Christians." We are to follow only what we see of Christ in their lives!

Applying God's Truth:

1. On a scale of 1 (least) to 10 (most), how hard would you say you try to "work out your own salvation"?

2. Does your relationship with God still involve a degree of "fear and trembling," or have you begun to take some of your spiritual privileges for granted? Explain.

3. List some ways that God has worked in your life during the past few months, and thank Him for each one.

Scripture: Read Philippians 2:14-18

"Even if I am being poured out like a drink offering on the sacrifice and service coming from your faith, I am glad and rejoice with all of you" (Phil. 2:17).

VICTORY THROUGH SURRENDER

The world's philosophy is that joy comes from aggression: fight everybody to get what you want, and you will get it and be happy. The example of Jesus is proof enough that the world's philosophy is wrong. He never used a sword or any other weapon; yet He won the greatest battle in history—the battle against sin and death and hell. He defeated hatred by manifesting love; He overcame lies with truth. Because He surrendered, He was victorious!

There is a twofold joy that comes to the person who possesses and practices the submissive mind: a joy hereafter and a joy here and now. In the day of Christ, God is going to reward those who have been faithful to Him. The faithful Christian will discover that his sufferings on earth have been transformed into glory in heaven! He will see that his work was not in vain. It was this same kind of promise of future joy that helped our Savior in His sufferings on the cross (Heb. 12:1-2).

But we do not have to wait for the return of Christ to start experiencing the joy of the submissive mind. That joy is a present reality, and it comes through sacrifice and service.

Applying God's Truth:

1. Do you ever experience joy because of submission to others? In what specific ways?

2. What are some of the here-and-now joys you experience on a regular basis? How might you increase this level of joy?

3. What are some future joys you look forward to?

Scripture: Read Philippians 2:20-21

"I have no one else like [Timothy], who takes a genuine interest in your welfare. For everyone looks out for his own interests, not those of Jesus Christ" (Phil. 2:20-21).

IN SEARCH OF GOOD SAMARITANS

A reporter in San Bernardino, California arranged for a man to lie in the gutter on a busy street. Hundreds of people passed the man, but not one stopped to help him or even show sympathy!

Newspapers across the country a few years ago told how thirty-eight people watched a man stalk a young lady and finally attack her—and none of the spectators even picked up a phone to call the police!

A Kentucky doctor was driving down the highway to visit a patient when he saw an accident take place. He stopped and gave aid to the injured and then made his visit. One of the drivers he helped sued him!

Is it possible to be a "Good Samaritan" today? Must everybody harden his heart in order to protect himself? Perhaps sacrifice and service are ancient virtues that somehow do not fit into our so-called modern civilization. It is worth noting that even in Paul's day mutual concern was not a popular virtue. The Christians at Rome were not too interested in the problems at Philippi; Paul could not find *one person* among them willing to go to Philippi. Times have not changed too much.

Applying God's Truth:

1. Try to recall one time when you needed help but no one was willing to assist you in any way. How did you feel?

2. What are some of the jobs in your church that are hardest to fill? Why do you think it's so tough to find volunteers for certain jobs?

3. What are some ways that people you know "look out for [their] own interests, not those of Jesus Christ"?

Scripture: Read Philippians 2:22-30

"Timothy has proved himself, because as a son with his father he has served with me in the work of the gospel. I hope, therefore, to send him as soon as I see how things go with me" (Phil. 2:22-23).

A SERVANT'S REWARD

Timothy knew the meaning of sacrifice and service, and God rewarded him for his faithfulness. To begin with, Timothy had the joy of helping others. To be sure, there were hardships and difficulties, but there were also victories and blessings. He had the joy of serving with the great Apostle Paul and assisting him in some of his most difficult assignments.

But perhaps the greatest reward God gave to Timothy was to choose him to be Paul's replacement when the great apostle was called home. Paul himself wanted to go to Philippi, but had had to send Timothy in his place. But, what an honor! Timothy was not only Paul's "son," and Paul's servant, but he became Paul's substitute. His name is held in high regard by Christians today, something that young Timothy never dreamed of when he was busy serving Christ.

The submissive mind is not the product of an hour's sermon, or a week's seminar, or even a year's service. The submissive mind grows in us as, like Timothy, we yield to the Lord and seek to serve others.

Applying God's Truth:

1. Who is the person you know who best fits the description of Timothy given in this section?

2. Do you have anyone you can count on in the same way that Paul counted on Timothy? If not, how might you begin such a relationship with someone?

3. In the areas of your personal ministry, how are you training people to take your place when you move on to new places or other opportunities?

Scripture: Read Philippians 3:1-3

"It is we who are the circumcision, we who worship by the Spirit of God, who glory in Christ Jesus, and who put no confidence in the flesh" (Phil. 3:3).

NO CONFIDENCE IN THE FLESH

The popular religious philosophy of today is, "The Lord helps those who help themselves." It was also popular in Paul's day, and it is just as wrong today as it was then. By "the flesh," Paul means "the old nature" that we received at birth. The Bible has nothing good to say about "flesh," and yet most people today depend entirely on what they themselves can do to please God. Flesh only corrupts God's way on earth. It profits nothing as far as spiritual life is concerned. It has nothing good in it. No wonder we should put no confidence in the flesh!

A lady was arguing with her pastor about this matter of faith and works. "I think that getting to heaven is like rowing a boat," she said. "One oar is faith, and the other is works. If you use both, you get there. If you use only one, you go around in circles."

"There is only one thing wrong with your illustration," replied the pastor. "Nobody is going to heaven *in a rowboat!*"

There is only one "good work" that takes the sinner to heaven: the finished work of Christ on the cross.

Applying God's Truth:

1. What are some ways that you have observed people "put confidence in the flesh"?

2. Create your own model (pie chart, graph, etc.) to indicate how you think faith and works are related.

3. In contrast to putting confidence in the flesh, what does it mean to "worship by the Spirit of God"?

Scripture: Read Philippians 3:4-7

"If anyone else thinks he has reasons to put confidence in the flesh, I have more. . . . But whatever was to my profit I now consider loss for the sake of Christ" *(Phil. 3:4, 7).*

MEASURING STICKS

Every Jew could boast of his own blood heritage. Some Jews could boast of their faithfulness to the Jewish religion. But Paul could boast of those things *plus* his zeal in persecuting the church. We might ask, "How could a sincere man like Saul of Tarsus be so wrong?" The answer is: *he was using the wrong measuring stick*!

Like the rich young ruler (Mark 10:17-22) and the Pharisee in Christ's parable (Luke 18:10-14), Saul of Tarsus was looking at the *outside* and not the *inside*. He was comparing himself with standards set by men, not by God. As far as obeying *outwardly* the demands of the Law, Paul was a success, but he did not stop to consider the *inward* sins he was committing. In the Sermon on the Mount, Jesus makes it clear that there are sinful *attitudes* and *appetites* as well as sinful actions (Matt. 5:21-48).

When he looked at himself or looked at others, Saul of Tarsus considered himself to be righteous. But one day he saw himself as compared with Jesus Christ! It was then that he changed his evaluations and values, and abandoned "works righteousness" for the righteousness of Jesus Christ.

Applying God's Truth:

1. Can you recall a time when you devoted a lot of time and energy to a project that didn't ultimately accomplish much? If so, how can you more effectively channel your efforts in the future?

2. Paul had worked very hard on his religion. Why do you think he was so quick to "consider [it] loss for the sake of Christ"?

3. Can you think of anything you might be clinging to that would be better to "consider loss" in order to continue to grow spiritually?

Scripture: Read Philippians 3:8-11

"I consider everything a loss compared to the surpassing greatness of knowing Christ Jesus my Lord, for whose sake I have lost all things. I consider them rubbish, that I may gain Christ" (Phil. 3:8).

GAINING AND LOSING

Remember Jim Elliot's words: "He is no fool who gives what he cannot keep to gain what he cannot lose." This is what Paul experienced: he lost his religion and his reputation, but he gained far more than he lost. In fact, the gains were so thrilling that Paul considered all other things nothing but garbage in comparison!

No wonder he had joy—his life did not depend on the cheap things of the world but on the eternal values found in Christ. Paul had the "spiritual mind" and looked at the things of earth from heaven's point of view. People who live for things are never really happy because they must constantly protect their treasures and worry lest they lose their value. Not so the believer with the spiritual mind; his treasures in Christ can never be stolen and they never lose their value.

Maybe now is a good time for you to become an accountant and evaluate the things that matter most to you.

Applying God's Truth:

1. What is the single force that drives you more than any other?

2. What did you formerly value that you now consider "rubbish"? Why?

3. List the things you tend to value and contrast them with the eternal values made possible by Christ. Do your feelings toward your possessions tend to change? In what ways?

Scripture: Read Philippians 3:12-13a

"I press on to take hold of that for which Christ Jesus took hold of me. Brothers, I do not consider myself yet to have taken hold of it" (Phil. 3:12-13a).

BEYOND COMPARE

Harry came out of the manager's office with a look on his face dismal enough to wilt the roses on the secretary's desk.

"You didn't get fired?" she asked.

"No, it's not that bad. But he sure did lay into me about my sales record. I can't figure it out; for the past month I've been bringing in plenty of orders. I thought he'd compliment me, but instead he told me to get with it." Later in the day, the secretary talked to her boss about Harry. The boss chuckled. "Harry is one of our best salesmen and I'd hate to lose him. But he has a tendency to rest on his laurels and be satisfied with his performance. If I didn't get him mad at me once a month, he'd never produce!"

Many Christians are self-satisfied because they compare their "running" with that of other Christians, usually those who are not making much progress. Had Paul compared himself with others, he would have been tempted to be proud and perhaps to let up a bit. After all, there were not too many believers in Paul's day who had experienced all that he had! But Paul did not compare himself with others; he compared himself *with himself* and with *Jesus Christ*! The mature Christian honestly evaluates himself and strives to do better.

Applying God's Truth:

1. Do you think comparing yourself to others is always wrong? Why?

2. In a spiritual sense, can you identify any recent times when you may have tended to compare yourself to someone else rather than imitating the model Jesus has set?

3. When was the last time you tried to objectively evaluate your spiritual growth for the past month or year? How can you ensure that you don't "coast" too long without checking for progress?

Scripture: Read Philippians 3:13b-14

"But one thing I do: Forgetting what is behind and straining toward what is ahead, I press on toward the goal to win the prize for which God has called me heavenward in Christ Jesus" (Phil. 3:13b-14).

FINDING A SPECIALTY

Before the tragedy of the Chicago fire in 1871, D.L. Moody was involved in Sunday School promotion, YMCA work, evangelistic meetings, and many other activities; but after the fire, he determined to devote himself exclusively to evangelism. "One thing I do" became a reality to him. As a result, millions of people heard the Gospel.

The believer must devote himself to "running the Christian race." No athlete succeeds by doing everything; he succeeds by *specializing*. There are those few athletes who seem proficient in many sports, but they are the exception. The winners are those who concentrate, who keep their eyes on the goal and let nothing distract them. They are devoted entirely to their calling. Like Nehemiah the wall-building governor, they reply to the distracting invitations, "I am carrying on a great project and cannot go down" (Neh. 6:3).

Concentration is the secret of power. If a river is allowed to overflow its banks, the area around it becomes a swamp. But if that river is dammed and controlled, it becomes a source of power. It is wholly a matter of values and priorities, living for that which matters most.

Applying God's Truth:

1. In "running the Christian race," would you say you are better in the short sprints or the long distance runs?

2. What would you say is one area of ministry in which you could "specialize"?

3. Are you able to forget what is behind and press on toward the goal to win the prize? Or are certain events of your past weighing you down and impeding your progress?

Scripture: Read Philippians 3:15-16

"All of us who are mature should take such a view of things. And if on some point you think differently, that too God will make clear to you. Only let us live up to what we have already attained" (Phil. 3:15-16).

RULES OF THE RACE

It is not enough to run hard and win the race; the runner must also obey the rules. In the Greek games, the judges were very strict about this. One day each Christian will stand before the judgment seat of Christ (Rom. 14:10-12). The Greek word for "judgment seat" is *bema*, the very same word used to describe the place where the Olympic judges gave out the prizes! If we have disciplined ourselves to obey the rules, we shall receive a prize.

Biblical history is filled with people who began the race with great success but failed at the end because they disregarded God's rules. They did not lose their salvation, but they did lose their rewards. It happened to Lot, Samson, Saul, and Ananias and Sapphira. And it can happen to us!

It is an exciting experience to run the race daily, "fixing our eyes on Jesus" (Heb. 12:1-2). It will be even more exciting when we experience that "upward calling" and Jesus returns to take us to heaven! Then we will stand before the *bema* to receive our rewards! It was this future prospect that motivated Paul, and it can also motivate us.

Applying God's Truth:

1. What "rules" of Christian living do you find hardest to obey on a regular basis?

2. How do you feel as you think about standing at the judgment seat of Christ to receive your rewards? Why?

3. What are three things you can do to ensure that you don't lose your rewards?

Scripture: Read Philippians 3:17-19

"As I have often told you before and now say again even with tears, many live as enemies of the cross of Christ" (Phil. 3:18).

ENEMIES OF THE CROSS

The cross of Jesus Christ is the theme of the Bible, the heart of the Gospel, and the chief source of praise in heaven. The cross is the proof of God's love for sinners and God's hatred for sin. In what sense were the Judaizers the "enemies of the cross of Christ"? For one thing, the cross ended the Old Testament religion. By His death and resurrection, Jesus accomplished a "spiritual circumcision" that made ritual circumcision unnecessary (Col. 2:10-13). Everything the Judaizers advocated had been eliminated by the death of Christ on the cross.

Furthermore, everything that they lived for was condemned by the cross. Jesus had broken down the wall that stood between Jews and Gentiles, and the Judaizers were rebuilding that wall!

The true believer crucifies the flesh. He also crucifies the world. Yet, the Judaizers were minding "earthly things." It is the cross that is central in the life of the believer. He does not glory in men, in religion, or in his own achievements; he glories in the cross.

Applying God's Truth:

1. Do you know people you would consider "enemies of the cross of Christ"? How would you describe them?

2. What are your feelings toward people who are openly hostile to Christian teaching? Why?

3. How much thought have you put into the significance of the cross? Would you say you "glory" in the cross, or do you need to think some more about this subject?

Scripture: Read Philippians 3:20-21

"Our citizenship is in heaven. And we eagerly await a Savior from there, the Lord Jesus Christ" (Phil. 3:20).

DUAL CITIZENSHIP

The citizens of Philippi were privileged to be Roman citizens away from Rome. When a baby was born in Philippi, it was important that its name be registered on the legal records. When the lost sinner trusts Christ and becomes a citizen of heaven, his name is written in "the book of life" (Phil. 4:3).

Citizenship is important. When you travel to another country, it is essential that you have a passport that proves your citizenship. None of us wants to suffer the fate of Philip Nolan in the classic tale *The Man Without a Country*. Because he cursed the name of his country, Nolan was sentenced to live aboard ship and never again see his native land or even hear its name or news about its progress. For fifty-six years he was on an endless journey from ship to ship and sea to sea, and finally was buried at sea. He was a "man without a country."

The Christian's name is written in "the book of life," and this is what determines his final entrance into the heavenly country. When you confess Christ on earth, He confesses your name in heaven. Your name is written down in heaven and it stands written forever.

Applying God's Truth:

1. Think of some groups and organizations to which you belong. What privileges do you have as a member of each group?

2. What privileges are you entitled to as a "citizen of heaven"?

3. What are your responsibilities as a citizen of heaven?

Scripture: Read Philippians 4:1-5

"Rejoice in the Lord always. I will say it again: Rejoice! Let your gentleness be evident to all. The Lord is near" (Phil. 4:4-5).

THE ANTIDOTE TO WORRY

If anybody had an excuse for worrying, it was the Apostle Paul. His beloved Christian friends at Philippi were disagreeing with one another, and he was not there to help them. We have no idea what Euodia and Syntyche were disputing about, but whatever it was, it was bringing division into the church. Along with the potential division at Philippi, Paul had to face division among the believers at Rome (Phil. 1:14-17). Added to these burdens was the possibility of his own death! Yes, Paul had a good excuse to worry—but he did not! Instead, he takes time to explain to us the secret of victory over worry.

The Old English root from which we get our word "worry" means "to strangle." If you have ever really worried, you know how it does strangle a person! In fact, worry has definite physical consequences: headaches, neck pains, ulcers, even back pains. Worry affects our thinking, our digestion, and even our coordination.

The antidote to worry is the secure mind: "The peace of God . . . will guard your hearts and your minds in Christ Jesus" (Phil. 4:7). When you have the secure mind, the peace of God guards you and the God of peace guides you! With that kind of protection—why worry?

Applying God's Truth:

1. What are three things you are worried about right now? If you begin to rejoice about other, more positive things, how do you think your worries would be affected?

2. Do you think it's really possible to rejoice always? Explain.

3. How might you reduce your amount of worrying in the future?

Scripture: Read Philippians 4:6-7

"Do not be anxious about anything, but in everything, by prayer and petition, with thanksgiving, present your requests to God" (Phil. 4:6).

MIND GUARDING

Paul counsels us to take everything to God in prayer. "Don't worry about *anything*, but pray about *everything*!" is his admonition. We are prone to pray about the "big things" in life and forget to pray about the so-called "little things"—until they grow and become big things! Talking to God about *everything* that concerns us and Him is the first step toward victory over worry.

The result is that the "peace of God" guards the heart and the mind. You will remember that Paul is chained to a Roman soldier, guarded day and night. In like manner, "the peace of God" stands guard over the two areas that create worry—the heart (wrong feeling) and the mind (wrong thinking). When we give our hearts to Christ in salvation, we experience "peace with God" (Rom. 5:1); but the "peace of God" takes us a step further into His blessings. This does not mean the absence of trials on the outside, but it does mean a quiet confidence within, regardless of circumstances, people, or things.

Applying God's Truth:

1. What are some "little things" in your life that concern you, yet that you may feel are too insignificant to pray about? (Whatever you think of, commit it to prayer and trust God to deal with the little things as well as the big ones.)

2. We tend to think of peace as an *inner* emotion. How do you feel when you envision God's peace as something that can protect you from outside influences?

3. What requests do you need to present to God today? What reasons do you have to offer thanksgiving today?

Scripture: Read Philippians 4:8-9

"Whatever is true, whatever is noble, whatever is right, whatever is pure, whatever is lovely, whatever is admirable—if anything is excellent or praiseworthy—think about such things. Whatever you have learned or received or heard from me, or seen in me—put it into practice" (Phil. 4:8-9).

THE RIGHT BALANCE

Paul balances four activities: "learned and received" and "heard and seen." It is one thing to *learn* a truth, but quite another to *receive* it inwardly and make it a part of our inner self. Facts in the head are not enough; we must also have truths in the heart. In Paul's ministry, he not only taught the Word but also lived it so that his listeners could see the truth in his life. Paul's experience ought to be our experience. We must learn the Word, receive it, hear it, and do it.

The peace of God is one test of whether or not we are in the will of God. If we are walking with the Lord, then the peace of God and the God of peace exercise their influence over our hearts. Whenever we disobey, we lose that peace and we know we have done something wrong.

Right praying, right thinking, and right living: these are the conditions for having the secure mind and victory over worry.

Applying God's Truth:

1. Of learning, receiving, hearing, and seeing God's Word, which do you feel you do best? In which area do you need the most work?

2. What can you do to keep your thoughts true, pure, lovely, and so forth? How do you prevent less noble thoughts from sneaking in?

3. What are some things you can "think about" right now that will help purify your thought patterns?

Scripture: Read Philippians 4:10-12

"I have learned to be content whatever the circumstances. I know what it is to be in need, and I know what it is to have plenty" *(Phil. 4:11-12).*

LEARNING CONTENTMENT

Contentment is not complacency, nor is it a false peace based on ignorance. The complacent believer is unconcerned about others, while the contented Christian wants to share his blessings. Contentment is not escape from the battle, but rather an abiding peace and confidence in the midst of the battle. Two words in verse 11 are vitally important—"learned" and "content."

The verb *learned* means "learned by experience." Paul's spiritual contentment was not something he had immediately after he was saved. He had to go through many difficult experiences of life in order to learn how to be content.

The word *content* actually means "contained." It is a description of the man whose resources are within him so that he does not have to depend on substitutes without. The Greek word means "self-sufficient" and was a favorite word of the Stoic philosophers. But the Christian is not sufficient in himself; he is sufficient in Christ. Because Christ lives within us, we are adequate for the demands of life.

Applying God's Truth:

1. What are your major sources of discontentment? What causes you to be content?

2. Do you think you can learn to be content most of the time without undergoing suffering first? Why?

3. What would need to happen before you feel that you could be content—no matter *what* happens?

Scripture: Read Philippians 4:13-23

"I can do everything through him who gives me strength" (Phil. 4:13).

NEEDS AND GREEDS

God has not promised to supply all our "greeds." When the child of God is in the will of God, serving for the glory of God, then he will have every need met. Hudson Taylor often said, "When God's work is done in God's way for God's glory, it will not lack for God's supply."

A young pastor came to a church that had been accustomed to raising its annual budget by means of suppers, bazaars, and the like. He told his officers he could not agree with their program. "Let's pray and ask God to meet every need," he suggested. "At the end of the month, pay all the bills and leave my salary till the last. If there isn't enough money for my salary, then I'm the one who suffers, and not the church. But I don't think anybody is going to suffer!" The officers were sure that both the pastor and the church would die, but such was not the case. Each month every bill was paid, and at the end of the year there was a surplus in the treasury for the first time in many years.

Contentment comes from adequate resources. Our resources are the providence of God, the power of God, and the promises of God. These resources made Paul sufficient for every demand of life, and they can make us sufficient too.

Applying God's Truth:

1. Are you careful to separate your needs from your "greeds"? Can you think of anything you've been praying for that may not be a legitimate need?

2. Can you think of anything you've been wanting to ask God for, yet are hesitant because it seems like too great a request? Based on today's verse, are you ready now to ask for it?

3. Can you think of ways that God might use *you* to supply someone else's need?

INTEGRITY

30 Daily Readings from the Book of 1 John

WE MUST BE CAREFUL TO PROTECT OUR OWN PERSONAL INTEGRITY. When integrity goes, then character starts to decay; when character goes, we've lost everything important. No matter what you may possess—money, popularity, talent, friends—if you don't have character, you don't have anything.

But character depends on integrity. People with integrity are people who are honest with themselves, with others, and with God. They don't wear masks and they don't waste energy pretending to be what they aren't. They're not afraid of what others may find out about them because they have nothing to hide.

The alternative to integrity is hypocrisy, and that eventually leads to duplicity—becoming two persons inside, neither of whom knows the other. Without inner wholeness, we can't function successfully in life or enjoy all that God wants us to enjoy.

We must cultivate integrity. That means knowing God, God's forgiveness, God's truth, God's church, and God's love. John's First Epistle is a guidebook for the kind of personal integrity that comes from a faithful walk with Jesus Christ, what John calls "walking in the light." No shadows—nothing to hide.

As you ponder this letter these next thirty days, you can discover the joyful inner healing that comes from being exposed to the loving light of God's truth and being honest with God. I pray that this will indeed be your experience.

Scripture: Read 1 John 1:1

"That which was from the beginning, which we have heard, which we have seen with our eyes, which we have looked at and our hands have touched—this we proclaim concerning the Word of life" (1 John 1:1).

REVEALING WORDS

If you were God, how would you go about revealing yourself to men? How could you tell them about, and give them, the kind of life you wanted them to enjoy?

God has revealed Himself in creation (Rom. 1:20), but creation alone could never tell us the story of God's love. God has also revealed Himself much more fully in His Word, the Bible. But God's final and most complete revelation is in His Son, Jesus Christ. Jesus said, "Anyone who has seen me has seen the Father" (John 14:9).

Because Jesus is God's revelation of Himself, He has a very special name: "The Word of Life" (1 John 1:1). This same title opens John's Gospel: "In the beginning was the Word, and the Word was with God, and the Word was God" (John 1:1).

Why does Jesus Christ have this name? Because Christ is to us what our words are to others. Our words reveal to others just what we think and how we feel. Christ reveals to us the mind and heart of God. He is the living means of communication between God and men. To know Jesus Christ is to know God!

Applying God's Truth:

1. What are some things you know about God based on His creation? What do you know about Him from reading the Bible?

2. What other things have you determined to be true about God primarily from examining the life of Jesus?

3. Based on your words during the past twenty-four hours, what have you revealed to other people about yourself?

Scripture: Read 1 John 1:2

"The life appeared; we have seen it and testify to it, and we proclaim to you the eternal life, which was with the Father and has appeared to us" (1 John 1:2).

DON'T BE FOOLED BY IMITATIONS

There are two kinds of children in this world: the children of God and the children of the devil (3:10). You would think that a "child of the devil" would be a person who lives in gross sin, but such is not always the case. An unbeliever is a "child of the devil." He may be moral and even religious; he may be a counterfeit Christian. But because he has never been "born of God" and experienced spiritual life personally, he is still Satan's "child."

A counterfeit Christian—and they are common—is something like a counterfeit ten-dollar bill. Suppose you have a counterfeit bill and actually think it is genuine. You use it to pay for a tank of gas. The gas station manager uses the bill to buy supplies. The supplier uses the bill to pay the grocer. The grocer bundles the bill up with forty-nine other ten-dollar bills and takes it to the bank. And the teller says, "I'm sorry, but *this* bill is a counterfeit."

That ten-dollar bill may have done a lot of good while it was in circulation, but when it arrived at the bank it was exposed for what it *really* was, and put out of circulation.

So with a counterfeit Christian. He may do many good things in this life, but when he faces the final judgment he will be rejected. Each of us must ask himself honestly, "Am I a true child of God or am I a counterfeit Christian? Have I truly been born of God?"

Applying God's Truth:

1. Was there a time in your life when you were moral, or even religious, yet not a "child of God"? If so, what happened to help you see your situation more clearly?

2. By what characteristics do you identify "counterfeit Christians" with whom you might come into contact?

3. Even when one's Christian commitment is genuine, what are some "counterfeit" behaviors that can affect spiritual growth?

Scripture: Read 1 John 1:3

"We proclaim to you what we have seen and heard, so that you also may have fellowship with us. And our fellowship is with the Father and with his Son, Jesus Christ" (1 John 1:3).

REAL LIFE

When God made us, He made us in His own image (Gen. 1:26-27). This means that we have a personality patterned after God's. We have a *mind* to think with, a *heart* to feel with, and a *will* with which to make decisions. We sometimes refer to these aspects of our personality as *intellect, emotion,* and *will.*

The life that is real *must involve all the elements of the personality.*

Most people are dissatisfied today because their total personality has never been controlled by something real and meaningful. When a person is born of God through faith in Christ, God's Spirit comes into his life to live there forever. As he has fellowship with God in reading and studying the Bible and in prayer, the Holy Spirit is able to control his mind, heart, and will. And what happens then?

A Spirit-controlled *mind* knows and understands *truth.*

A Spirit-controlled *heart* feels *love.*

A Spirit-controlled *will* inclines us to *obedience.*

John wants to impress this fact on us, and that is why he uses a series of contrasts in his letter: truth vs. lies, love vs. hatred, and obedience vs. disobedience. There is no middle ground in the life that is real. We must be on one side or on the other.

This, then, is the life that is real. It was revealed in Christ; it was experienced by those who trusted in Christ; and it can be shared today.

Applying God's Truth:

1. Of your own intellect, emotion, and will, which would you say is most in need of further development?

2. Which of the three aspects of personality do you think most people find hardest to submit to God? Why?

3. For each of the three areas, what is one thing you can do this week to give the Holy Spirit more control?

Scripture: Read 1 John 1:5-7

"If we walk in the light, as He is in the light, we have fellowship with one another, and the blood of Jesus, his Son, purifies us from all sin" (1 John 1:7).

WALK ON

E very form of life has its enemies. Insects have to watch out for hungry birds, and birds must keep an eye on hungry cats and dogs. Even human beings have to dodge automobiles and fight off germs.

The life that is real also has an enemy, and we read about it in this section. This enemy is *sin*. John illustrates his theme by using the contrast between light and darkness: God is light; sin is darkness.

The New Testament calls the Christian life a "walk." This *walk* begins with a step of faith when we trust Christ as our Savior. But salvation is not the end—it's only the beginning—of spiritual life. "Walking" involves progress, and Christians are supposed to advance in the spiritual life. Just as a child must learn to walk and must overcome many difficulties in doing so, a Christian must learn to "walk in the light." And the fundamental difficulty involved here is this matter of *sin*.

Applying God's Truth:

1. What sins have proven to be most threatening and powerful to you in the past?

2. When you identify a recurring sin in your life, how do you deal with it? Can you think of any potential sin in your life right now that needs attention?

3. Do you agree that "walk" is a good description of your spiritual progress? If not, what other word would you choose? (Crawl? Sprint? Jog? Standstill? Etc.)

Scripture: Read 1 John 1:8-9

"If we claim to be without sin, we deceive ourselves and the truth is not in us" (1 John 1:8).

SELF-DECEIT

A dishonest person loses his fellowship with God and with God's people. As a result, prayer becomes an empty form to him. Worship is a dull routine. He becomes critical of other Christians and starts staying away from church.

A group of church members were discussing their new pastor.

"For some reason," said one man, "I really don't feel at ease with him. I believe he's a good man, all right—but something seems to stand between us."

Another member replied, "Yes, I think I know what you mean. I used to have that same problem with him, but now I don't have it anymore. The pastor and I have great fellowship."

"What did he do to make things better?"

"*He* didn't do anything," said the friend. "*I* did the changing."

"*You* did the changing?"

"Yes, I decided to be open and honest about things, the way our pastor is. You see, there isn't one stain of hypocrisy in his life, and there was so much pretending in *my* life that we just didn't make it together. He and I both knew I was a phony. Since I've started to live an honest Christian life, *everything* is better."

Applying God's Truth:

1. Most people never *verbally* claim to be "without sin," so how can you tell when someone is being dishonest with himself or herself?

2. When your own praying becomes empty and worship becomes dull, what do you do to get back "on track"?

3. When fellow Christians criticize you, do you consider they may be going through a personal spiritual problem and "cut them some slack"? What are some recent examples of conflict where this might have been the case?

Scripture: Read 1 John 2:1-6

"If anyone obeys his word, God's love is truly made complete in him" (1 John 2:5).

MOTIVES FOR OBEDIENCE

Obedience to God's Word is proof of our love for Him. There are three motives for obedience. We can obey because we *have to*, because we *need to*, or because we *want to*.

A slave obeys because he *has* to. If he doesn't obey he will be punished. An employee obeys because he *needs* to. He may not enjoy his work, but he *does* enjoy getting his paycheck! He needs to obey because he has a family to feed and clothe. But a Christian is to obey his Heavenly Father because he *wants* to—for the relationship between him and God is one of love. "If you love me, you will obey what I command" (John 14:15).

This is the way we learned obedience when we were children. First, we obeyed because we *had* to. If we didn't obey, we were spanked! But as we grew up, we discovered that obedience meant enjoyment and reward; so we started obeying because it met certain *needs* in our lives. And it was a mark of real maturity when we started obeying because of love.

"Baby Christians" must constantly be warned or rewarded. Mature Christians listen to God's Word and obey it simply because they love Him.

Applying God's Truth:

1. What are some laws you obey primarily because you have to? What are some you obey because you need to?

2. What are some of God's commands you obey primarily out of obligation? Which do you obey because of the benefits you receive?

3. Of the things that came to mind in both of the previous questions, how do you think you might eventually learn to obey the laws/commands out of genuine personal desire?

Scripture: Read 1 John 2:7-8a

"I am not writing you a new command but an old one. . . . Yet I am writing you a new command" (1 John 2:7-8).

SOMETHING OLD, SOMETHING NEW

The Christian life—the life that is real—is a beautiful blending of "something old, something new." The Holy Spirit takes the "old things" and makes them "new things" in our experience. When you stop to think about it, the Holy Spirit never grows old! He is always young! And He is the only Person on earth *today* who was here centuries ago when Jesus lived, taught, died, and rose again. He is the only One who can take "old truth" and make it fresh and new in our daily experience at this present time.

There are other exciting truths in the rest of John's letter, but if we fail to obey in the matter of love, the rest of the letter may well be "darkness" to us. Perhaps the best thing we can do, right *now*, is to search our hearts to see if we hold anything against a brother, or if someone has anything against us. The life that is real is an honest life—and it is a life of *doing*, not merely *saying*. It is a life of active love in Christ. This means forgiveness, kindness, long-suffering. But it also means joy and peace and victory.

The love life is the only life, because it is the life that is real!

Applying God's Truth:

1. What are some elements of your "old" life that God made new after you became a Christian?

2. Are you currently involved in an resolved conflict? If so, what steps can you take to try to deal with the matter?

3. Can you think of anything you might be *saying* that you aren't actually *doing*? Can you foresee any potential problems if your actions don't soon begin to support your words?

Scripture: Read 1 John 2:8

"I am writing you a new command; its truth is seen in him and you, because the darkness is passing and the true light is already shining" (1 John 2:8).

TWO "NEW"S? (WHO KNEW?)

The Greeks had two different words for *new*—one means "new in time," and the other means "new in quality." For example, you would use the first word to describe the latest car, a recent model. But if you purchased a car that was so revolutionary that it was *radically* different, you would use the second word—new in quality.

The commandment to love one another is not new in time, but it is new in character. Because of Jesus Christ, the old commandment to "love one another" has taken on new meaning.

It is important that we understand the meaning of Christian love. It is not a shallow sentimental emotion that Christians try to "work up" so they can get along with each other. It is a matter of the *will* rather than an *emotion*—an affection for and attraction to certain persons. It is a matter of determining—of making up your mind—that you will allow God's love to reach others through you, and then of acting toward them in loving ways. You are not to act "as if you loved them," but *because* you love them. This is not hypocrisy—it is obedience to God.

Perhaps the best explanation of Christian love is 1 Corinthians 13. You should read a modern translation of this chapter to get the full force of its message: the Christian live without love is NOTHING!

Applying God's Truth:

1. How do you think Jesus' coming to earth affected the way people defined "love"?

2. Have you recently experienced love that you would consider "new in quality" or "fresh"? How would you describe it to a friend?

3. In what ways is love a matter of the will for you? Give some specific examples.

Scripture: Read 1 John 2:9-11

"Whoever loves his brother lives in the light, and there is nothing in him to make him stumble" (1 John 2:10).

LIGHTEN UP

It is bad enough when an unloving believer hurts himself (v. 9), but when he starts to hurt *others* the situation is far more serious. It is *serious* to walk in the darkness. It is *dangerous* to walk in the darkness when stumbling blocks are in the way! An unloving brother stumbles himself, and in addition he causes others to stumble.

A man who was walking down a dark street one night saw a pinpoint of light coming toward him in a faltering way. He thought perhaps the person carrying the light was ill or drunk; but as he drew nearer he could see a man with a flashlight carrying a *white cane.*

"Why would a blind man be carrying a light?" the man wondered, and then he decided to ask.

The blind man smiled. "I carry my light, not so *I* can see, but so that *others* can see me. I cannot help being blind," he said, "but I can help being a stumbling block."

The best way to help other Christians not to stumble is to love them. Love makes us stepping-stones; hatred (or any of its "cousins," such as envy or malice) makes us stumbling blocks. It is important that Christians exercise love in a local church, or else there will always be problems and disunity. When we are falling over each other, instead of lifting each other higher, we will never become a truly happy spiritual family.

Applying God's Truth:

1. In what ways do believers harm themselves when they "walk in darkness"?

2. How can believers who become stumbling blocks hurt *others*?

3. For each of the answers that came to mind in the previous questions, how can love act as an antidote to those harmful things?

Scripture: Read 1 John 2:12-15

"Do not love the world or anything in the world. If anyone loves the world, the love of the Father is not in him" (1 John 2:15).

THE LOVE GOD HATES

John's epistle has reminded us to exercise love (1 John 2:7-11)—the right kind of love. Now it warns us that there is a *wrong* kind of love, a love that God hates. This is love for what the Bible calls "the world."

The New Testament word *world* has at least three different meanings. It sometimes means the *physical* world, *the earth*. It also means the *human* world, *mankind*. But the warning, "Do not love the world," is not about the world of nature or the world of men. Christians ought to appreciate the beauty and usefulness of the earth God has made, since He "richly provides us with everything for our enjoyment" (1 Tim. 6:17). And they certainly ought to love people—not only their friends, but even their enemies.

This "world" named here as our enemy is an invisible spiritual system opposed to God and Christ. "The world," in the Bible, is Satan's system for opposing the work of Christ on earth. It is the very opposite of what is godly (1 John 2:16) and holy and spiritual.

The believer is somewhat like a scuba diver. The water is not man's natural habitat, for he is not equipped for life in (or under) it. When a scuba diver goes under, he has to take special equipment with him so that he can breathe.

Were it not for the Holy Spirit's living within us, and the spiritual resources we have in prayer, Christian fellowship, and the Word, we could never "make it" here on earth.

Applying God's Truth:

1. Based on the author's definition of the "world," what are some "worldly" things we need to watch out for?

2. Do you think the best solution to the threat of worldliness is to remove yourself completely from anything that is worldly? Explain.

3. What are some things you've done during the past week to combat the influence of worldliness in your life?

Scripture: Read 1 John 2:16

"Everything in the world—the cravings of sinful man, the lust of his eyes and the boasting of what he has and does—comes not from the Father but from the world" *(1 John 2:16).*

SLOW AND STEADY LOSES THE RACE

The world appeals to a Christian through the lust of the flesh, the lust of the eyes, and the pride of life. And once the world takes over in one of these areas, a Christian will soon realize it. He will lose his enjoyment of the Father's love and his desire to do the Father's will. The Bible will become boring and prayer a difficult chore. Even Christian fellowship may seem empty and disappointing. It is not that there is something wrong with others, however—what's wrong is the Christian's worldly heart.

It is important to note that no Christian becomes worldly all of a sudden. Worldliness creeps up on a believer; it is a gradual process. Among Christians, worldliness rears its ugly head in many subtle and unrecognized forms. Sometimes we tend to idolize great athletes, TV stars, or political leaders who profess to be Christians—as if these individuals were able to be of special help to Almighty God. Or we cater to wealthy and "influential" persons in our local church, as if God's work would fold up without their good will or financial backing. Many forms of worldliness do not involve reading the wrong books and indulging in "carnal" amusements.

Applying God's Truth:

1. What are some worldly appeals you've recently faced in each of these categories: (1) Sinful cravings; (2) The lust of the eyes; and (3) Pride/boasting?

2. If worldliness is a gradual process, what do you think is the *first* symptom?

3. Are there any people you hold in such high esteem that it may approach worldly idolization? How can you prevent from going too far in your devotion and admiration?

Scripture: Read 1 John 2:17

"The world and its desires pass away, but the man who does the will of God lives forever" (1 John 2:17).

AVOIDING OBLIVION

E very great nation in history has become decadent and has finally been conquered by another nation. There is no reason why we should suppose that *our* nation will be an exception. Some nineteen world civilizations, in the past, have slipped into oblivion. There is no reason why we should think that our present civilization will endure forever. "Change and decay in all around I see," wrote Henry F. Lyte (1793–1847), and if our civilization is not eroded by change and decay it will certainly be swept away and replaced by a new order of things at the coming of Christ, which could happen at any time.

Slowly but inevitably, and perhaps sooner than even Christians think, the world is passing away; but the man who does God's will abides forever. Long after this world system, with its vaunted culture, its proud philosophies, its egocentric intellectualism, and its godless materialism, has been forgotten, and long after this planet has been replaced by the new heavens and the new earth, God's faithful servants will remain—sharing the glory of God for all eternity.

And this prospect is not limited to Moody, Spurgeon, Luther, or Wesley and their likes—it is open to each and every humble believer. If you are trusting Christ, it is for *you*.

Applying God's Truth:

1. How do you think your nation will be different fifty years from now? (Consider potential geographic changes, economic considerations, spiritual condition, and so forth.)

2. Considering that the world system is eventually going to slip into oblivion, what things are you regularly involved in that may prove to be counterproductive or a waste of time?

3. If you're expecting to "share the glory of God for all eternity," what things are you doing now to prepare for such an encounter?

Scripture: Read 1 John 2:18-20

"You have an anointing from the Holy One, and all of you know the truth" *(1 John 2:20).*

SINCERELY WRONG

I t makes no difference what you believe, just as long as you are sincere!" That statement expresses the personal philosophy of many people today, but it is doubtful whether most of those who make it have really thought it through. Is "sincerity" the magic ingredient that makes something *true*? If so, then you ought to be able to apply it to any area of life, and not only to religion.

A nurse in a city hospital gives some medicine to a patient, and the patient becomes violently ill. The nurse is sincere but the medicine is wrong, and the patient almost dies.

A man hears noises in the house one night and decides a burglar is at work. He gets his gun and shoots the "burglar," who turns out to be his daughter! Unable to sleep, she has gotten up for a bite to eat. She ends up the victim of her father's "sincerity."

It takes more than "sincerity" to make something true. Faith in a lie will always cause serious consequences; faith in the truth is never misplaced. *It does make a difference what a man believes!* If a man wants to drive from Chicago to New York, no amount of sincerity will get him there if the highway is taking him to Los Angeles. A person who is real builds his life on truth, not superstition or lies. It is impossible to live a real life by believing lies.

Applying God's Truth:

1. When is the last time you can remember feeling strongly about something you were very sincere about, only to eventually discover you were wrong?

2. On a scale of 1 (least) to 10 (most), how strongly would you say you value the truth? (For example, if a "white lie" would spare someone some pain, would you still be completely honest?)

3. What connections have you discovered between faith and truth in your own life?

Scripture: Read 1 John 2:21-25

"Who is the liar? It is the man who denies that Jesus is the Christ. . . . No one who denies the Son has the Father; whoever acknowledges the Son has the Father also" (1 John 2:22-23).

DISCERN AS YOU LEARN

We are warned against letting any man be our teacher, for God has given us the Spirit to teach us His truth. This does not deny the office of human teachers in the church (Eph. 4:11-12); but it means that under the guidance of the Spirit you must test the teaching of men as you search the Bible for yourself.

A missionary to the American Indians was in Los Angeles with an Indian friend who was a new Christian. As they walked down the street, they passed a man on the corner who was preaching with a Bible in his hand. The missionary knew the man represented a cult, but the Indian saw only the Bible. He stopped to listen to the sermon.

"I hope my friend doesn't get confused," the missionary thought to himself, and he began to pray. In a few minutes the Indian turned away from the meeting and joined his missionary friend.

"What did you think of that preacher?" the missionary asked.

"All the time he was talking," exclaimed the Indian, "something in my heart kept saying, 'Liar! Liar!'"

That "something" in his heart was "Someone"—the Holy Spirit of God! The Spirit guides us into the truth and helps us to recognize error. This anointing of God is "no lie," because "the Spirit is truth" (1 John 5:6).

Applying God's Truth:

1. How do you respond to attempts by cult members or other false teachers who approach you with a distorted version of the truth of the Gospel?

2. Can you think of a specific time when the Holy Spirit alerted you to a cleverly disguised falsehood being promoted by someone?

3. How hard do you work to keep from being taken in by someone? Are you quick to let someone speak for you, or do you do a lot of careful examination of Scripture on your own?

Scripture: Read 1 John 2:26-29

"Now, dear children, continue in him, so that when he appears we may be confident and unashamed before him at his coming" *(1 John 2:28)*.

TRUTH OR YOU-KNOW-WHAT

A person who *professes* to be a Christian, but who does not live in obedience, love, and truth, is either deceived or a deceiver. A child bears the nature of his father, and a person who has been "born of God" will reveal the characteristics of the Heavenly Father.

A Sunday School class seemed to be having constant problems. The pastor and the superintendent met with the teacher and officers, but made no apparent progress. Then, one Sunday morning, the teacher of the class came down the aisle during the closing hymn of the service. "I suppose she wants to dedicate her life to the Lord," the pastor thought.

"Pastor," she said, "I want to confess Christ as my Savior. All these years I thought I was saved, but I wasn't. There was always something lacking in my life. The class problems were *my* problems, but now they've been solved. Now I *know* I'm saved."

"Examine yourselves to see whether you are in the faith; test yourselves" (2 Cor. 13:5). Does your life bear the marks of obedience, love, and truth? Is your Christian life something *real—genuine—authentic*? Or is it counterfeit?

It is a question of truth—or consequences! And if you do not face the truth, you must pay the consequences!

Applying God's Truth:

1. Can you think of any professed Christians you suspect to be deceived? Do you know any deceivers? How do you tend to identify such people?

2. What are some of your characteristics that reflect the characteristics of God?

3. What would it take to make your Christian life more real, genuine, and authentic?

Scripture: Read 1 John 3:1-3

"We know that when he appears, we shall be like him, for we shall see him as he is" (1 John 3:2).

AIN'T NOTHING LIKE THE REAL THING

The United States Treasury Department has a special group of men whose job it is to track down counterfeiters. Naturally, these men need to know a counterfeit bill when they see it.

How do they learn to identify fake bills?

Oddly enough, they are not trained by spending hours examining counterfeit money. Rather, they study *the real thing*. They become so familiar with authentic bills that they can spot a counterfeit by looking at it or, often, simply by feeling it.

This is the approach in 1 John 3, which warns us that in today's world there are counterfeit Christians—"children of the devil" (v. 10). But instead of listing the evil characteristics of Satan's children, the Scripture gives us a clear description of God's children. The contrast between the two is obvious.

An unsaved person (even if he professes to be a Christian but is a counterfeit) lives a life of *habitual sin*. Sin—especially the sin of unbelief—is the normal thing in his life (Eph. 2:1-3). He has no divine resources to draw upon. His profession of faith, if any, is not real. A true believer does not live in habitual sin. He may *commit* sin—an occasional wrong act—but he will not *practice* sin—make a settled habit of it.

Applying God's Truth:

1. By what means do you identify "counterfeit" Christians?

2. What are some of the habitual sins you've found hardest to eliminate from your life? Why do you think these are such problem areas for you?

3. Since our goal is to "be like [Jesus]," in what areas do you think you're doing fairly well? What areas still need a lot of work?

Scripture: Read 1 John 3:4-6

"No one who lives in him keeps on sinning. No one who continues to sin has either seen him or known him" (1 John 3:6).

THE WAR IS OVER

For many months after the close of World War II, Japanese troops were discovered hidden in the caves and jungles of the Pacific islands. Some of these stragglers were living like frightened savages; they didn't know the war was over. Once they understood that it was no longer necessary for them to fight, they surrendered.

Christians may rest in the truth that Satan is a defeated enemy. He may still win a few battles here and there, but *he has already lost the war!* Sentence has been pronounced on him, but it will be a while before the punishment is meted out. A person who knows Christ, and who has been delivered from the bondage of sin through Christ's death on the cross, has no desire to obey Satan and live like a rebel.

Counterfeit Christians were trying to convince true believers that a person could be "saved" and still practice sin. John does not deny that Christians sin, but he *does* deny that Christians can *live in sin.* A person who can *enjoy* deliberate sin and who does not feel convicted or experience God's chastening had better examine himself to see whether or not he is really born of God.

Applying God's Truth:

1. In what ways do you live in celebration of the fact that the war with Satan is over and that he has lost?

2. Would any of your actions or attitudes indicate that your victory is in doubt?

3. What would you tell a friend who professed to be a Christian, yet claimed to enjoy indulging in a particular sin on a regular basis?

Scripture: Read 1 John 3:7-10

"Do not let anyone lead you astray. He who does what is right is righteous, just as he is righteous. He who does what is sinful is of the devil" (1 John 3:7-8).

BACKSLIDING IS NOT GOOD EXERCISE

Unconfessed sin is the first step in what the Bible calls "backsliding"— gradually moving away from a close walk with Christ into a life filled with the alien world in which we live.

God's promise, "I will cure you of backsliding" (Jer. 3:22), implies that backsliding resembles physical sickness. First is the secret invasion of the body by a disease germ. Then infection follows and there is a gradual decline: no pep, no appetite, no interest in normal activities. Then comes the collapse!

Spiritual decline works in a similar way. First sin invades us. Instead of fighting it, we yield to it (cf. James 1:14) and infection sets in. A gradual decline follows. We lose our appetite for spiritual things, we become listless and even irritable, and finally we collapse. The only remedy is to confess and forsake our sin and turn to Christ for cleansing and healing.

The inner man not only needs food and cleansing, but he also needs exercise. "Train yourself to be godly" (1 Tim. 4:7). A person who eats but does not exercise will become overweight; a person who exercises without eating will kill himself. There must be proper balance. "Spiritual exercise" for a believer includes sharing Christ with others, doing good works in Christ's name, and helping to build up other believers.

Applying God's Truth:

1. What would you say was your most recent incident of "backsliding"? Can you identify what caused the initial lack of spiritual momentum?

2. With what have you fed your appetite for spiritual things during this past week?

3. What kinds of spiritual "exercise" have you had this week? Do you think you may need to increase your exercise? If so, what other activities might you add?

Scripture: Read 1 John 3:11-15

"We know that we have passed from death to life, because we love our brothers. . . . Anyone who hates his brother is a murderer" *(1 John 3:14-15).*

KILLER INSTINCT

A visitor at the zoo was chatting with the keeper of the lion house. "I have a cat at home," said the visitor, "and your lions act just like my cat. Look at them sleeping so peacefully! It seems a shame that you have to put those beautiful creatures behind bars."

"My friend," the keeper laughed, "these may look like your cat, but their disposition is radically different. There's murder in their hearts. You'd better be glad the bars are there."

The only reason some people have never actually murdered anyone is because of the "bars" that have been put up: the fear of arrest and shame, the penalties of the law, and the possibility of death. But we are going to be judged by "the law of liberty" (James 2:12). The question is not so much, "What did you *do?*" but "What did you *want* to do? What would you have done if you had been at liberty to do as you pleased?" This is why Jesus equates hatred with murder (Matt. 5:21-26) and lust with adultery (vv. 27-30).

This does not mean, of course, that hatred in the heart does the same amount of damage, or involves the same degree of guilt, as actual murder. Your neighbor would rather you hate him than kill him! But in God's sight, hatred is the moral equivalent of murder, and if left unbridled it leads to murder.

Applying God's Truth:

1. What are some of the emotions you've recently felt or expressed that you realized were stronger than you thought? Might such emotions "mask" deeper feelings?

2. What are some "bars" that keep you from acting on all of your feelings?

3. If you were judged today for all the things you *wanted* to do during the past week, how would you do? After you eliminate most of the sinful *actions* from your life, how can you get rid of the sinful *attitudes* as well?

Scripture: Read 1 John 3:16-17

"This is how we know what love is: Jesus Christ laid down his life for us. And we ought to lay down our lives for our brothers" (1 John 3:16).

GOOD AND CHEAP

In these days of multiplied social agencies, it is easy for Christians to forget their obligations. "Let us do good to all people, especially to those who belong to the family of believers" (Gal. 6:10).

This "doing good" need not be in terms of money or material supplies. It may include personal service and the giving of oneself to others. There are many individuals in our churches who lack love and would welcome friendship.

A young mother admitted, in a testimony meeting, that she never seemed to find time for her own personal devotions. She had several little children to care for, and the hours melted away.

Imagine her surprise when two of the ladies from the church appeared at her front door.

"We've come to take over," they explained. "You go into the bedroom and get started on your devotions." After several days of this kind of help, the young mother was able to develop her devotional life so that the daily demands on her time no longer upset her.

If we want to experience and enjoy the love of God in our own hearts, we must love others, even to the point of sacrifice.

Applying God's Truth:

1. What would you consider the most sacrificial act you've done for someone else?

2. What are some "little" ways you could help others in your church, family, or neighborhood this week?

3. What are some things you wish people would do for you occasionally? Have you ever made your needs known to others?

Scripture: Read 1 John 3:18-24

"This then is how we know that we belong to the truth, and how we set our hearts at rest in his presence whenever our hearts condemn us. For God is greater than our hearts, and he knows everything" (1 John 3:19-20).

AT EASE

A "condemning heart" is one that robs a believer of peace. An "accusing conscience" is another way to describe it. Sometimes the heart accuses us wrongly, because it "is deceitful above all things and beyond cure. Who can understand it?" (Jer. 17:9) The answer to that question is, "God understands the heart!"

Be careful lest the devil accuse you and rob you of your confidence (Rev. 12:10). Once you confess your sin and it is forgiven, you need not allow it to accuse you anymore.

No Christian should treat sin lightly, but no Christian should be harder on himself than God is. There is a morbid kind of self-examination and self-condemnation that is not spiritual. If you are practicing genuine love for the brethren, your heart must be right before God, for the Holy Spirit would not "shed abroad" His love in you if there were habitual sin in your heart. When you grieve the Spirit, you "turn off" the supply of God's love (Eph. 4:30–5:2).

Applying God's Truth:

1. Have you done something that God has forgiven, but that you're still condemning yourself for? What do you need to do to more fully experience His forgiveness?

2. In what ways does the devil "accuse you and rob you of your confidence"?

3. You don't want to be harder on yourself than God is. Is it possible that you might be harder on *someone else* than God is? If so, what do you need to do for the person(s) involved?

Scripture: Read 1 John 4:1-8

"Dear friends, let us love one another, for love comes from God. Everyone who loves has been born of God and knows God. Whoever does not love does not know God, because God is love" (1 John 4:7-8).

BACK TO (GOD'S) NATURE

Love is a valid test of our fellowship and our sonship because "God is love." Love is a part of the very being and nature of God. If we are united to God through faith in Christ, we share His nature. And since His nature is love, love is the test of the reality of our spiritual life.

A navigator depends on a compass to help him determine his course. But why a compass? Because it shows him his directions. And why does the compass point north? Because it is so constituted that it responds to the magnetic field that is part of the earth's makeup. The compass is responsive to the nature of the earth.

So with Christian love. The nature of God is love. And a person who knows God and has been born of God will respond to God's nature. As a compass naturally points north, a believer will naturally practice love because love is the nature of God. This love will not be a forced response; it will be a natural response. A believer's love for the brethren will be proof of his sonship and fellowship.

Applying God's Truth:

1. If God *is* love—if that is His nature—how does that affect His other attributes (justice, power, knowledge, etc.)?

2. Where do you think most Christians fall short of reflecting the complete love of God?

3. If God's complete love were indicated by due north on a compass, what direction would your own personal compass read? (How far off would you be?)

Scripture: Read 1 John 4:9-11

"This is love: not that we loved God, but that he loved us and sent his Son as an atoning sacrifice for our sins. Dear friends, since God so loved us, we also ought to love one another" (1 John 4:10-11).

TELL AND SHOW

A Salvation Army worker found a derelict woman alone on the street and invited her to come into the chapel for help, but the woman refused to move. The female worker assured her: "We love you and want to help you. God loves you. Jesus died for you." But the woman did not budge.

As if on divine impulse, the Army worker leaned over and kissed the woman on the cheek, taking her into her arms. The woman began to sob, and like a child was led into the chapel, where she ultimately trusted Christ.

"You *told* me that God loved me," she said later, "but it wasn't until you *showed* me that God loved me that I wanted to be saved."

Jesus did not simply preach the love of God; He proved it by giving His life on the cross. He expects His followers to do likewise. If we abide in Christ, we will abide in His love. If we abide in His love, we must share this love with others. Whenever we share this love, it is proof in our own hearts that we are abiding in Christ. In other words, there is no separation between a Christian's inner life and his outer life.

Applying God's Truth:

1. Jesus was an excellent teacher, but what do you think He would have accomplished if He had only taught and had not ministered to people and died on the cross?

2. Did you become a Christian because of something you heard, something you saw in the life of another person, or a combination of the two? How do you think most people are attracted to the Gospel of Christ?

3. Whom have you told about the love of God recently? Whom have you *shown*?

Scripture: Read 1 John 4:12-16

"If anyone acknowledges that Jesus is the Son of God, God lives in him and he in God" (1 John 4:15).

AHA!

In order to save money, a college drama class purchased only a few scripts of a play and cut them up into the separate parts. The director gave each player his individual part in order and then started to rehearse the play. But nothing went right. After an hour of missed cues and mangled sequences, the cast gave up.

At that point, the director sat the actors all on the stage and said: "Look, I'm going to read the entire play to you, so don't any of you say a word." He read the entire script aloud, and when he was finished, one of the actors said:

"So that's what it was all about!"

And when they understood the entire story, they were able to fit their parts together and have a successful rehearsal.

When you read 1 John 4:12-16, you feel like saying, "So that's what it's all about!" Here we discover what God had in mind when He devised His great plan of salvation.

Applying God's Truth:

1. Are there any "pieces" of your faith that you don't fully understand? If so, whom can you talk to this week to help see how they fit into the "entire story"?

2. Besides Jesus' sacrificial death on the cross, what are some other things He does (or did) to prove that God loves us?

3. If a stranger watched you for a week, could he tell that "God lives in you"? Why or why not?

Scripture: Read 1 John 4:17-19

"There is no fear in love. But perfect love drives out fear, because fear has to do with punishment. The man who fears is not made perfect in love" (1 John 4:18).

OVERCOMING FEAR

Two brand-new words come into John's vocabulary here: *fear* and *punishment*. And this is written to *believers!* Is it possible that Christians can actually live in fear? Yes, unfortunately, many professed believers experience both fear and torment day after day. And the reason is that they are not growing in the love of God.

If people are afraid, it is because of something in the past that haunts them, or something in the present that upsets them, or something in the future that they feel threatens them. Or it may be a combination of all three. A believer in Jesus Christ does not have to fear the past, present, or future, for he has experienced the love of God and this love is being perfected in him day by day.

God wants His children to live in an atmosphere of love and confidence, not fear and potential punishment. An immature Christian is tossed between fear and love; a mature Christian rests in God's love.

A growing confidence in the presence of God is one of the first evidences that our love for God is maturing.

Applying God's Truth:

1. Isn't "fear of the Lord" something we're supposed to have? Is there a difference between "fear of the Lord" and being afraid of God and what He might to do you?

2. Do you know Christians who seem to live in constant fear and/or dread of potential punishment? How might you be able to help?

3. What can *you* do this week to rest more securely in God's love?

Scripture: Read 1 John 4:20-21

"Anyone who does not love his brother, whom he has seen, cannot love God, whom he has not seen" (1 John 4:20).

PLEASING PRIORITIES

When our hearts are confident toward God, there is no need for us to pretend, either to God or to other people. A Christian who lacks confidence with God will also lack confidence with God's people. Part of the torment that fear generates is the constant worry, "How much do others really know about me?" But when we have confidence with God, this fear is gone and we can face both God and men without worry.

"How many members do you have in your church?" a visitor asked the pastor.

"Somewhere near a thousand," the pastor replied.

"That certainly is a lot of people to try to please!" the visitor exclaimed.

"Let me assure you, my friend, that I have never tried to please all my members, or even some of them," the pastor said with a smile. "I aim to please *one* person—the Lord Jesus Christ. If I am right with Him, then everything should be right between me and my people."

An immature Christian who is not growing in his love for God may think he has to impress others with his "spirituality." This mistake turns him into a liar! He is professing something that he is not really practicing: he is playing a role instead of living a life.

Applying God's Truth:

1. Who are the people you are reluctant to "be yourself" in front of? What's the worst that could happen if they "really knew about you"?

2. What do you do to encourage others to be more comfortable around you?

3. Do you think it's wrong to want to please or impress people from time to time? If not, what potential problems *might* arise out of such a desire to please others?

Scripture: Read 1 John 5:1-3

"This is love for God: to obey his commands. And his commands are not burden-some" (1 John 5:3).

THE SECRET OF JOYFUL OBEDIENCE

E verything in creation—except man—obeys the will of God. "Lightning and hail, snow and clouds, stormy winds . . . do his bidding" (Ps. 148:8). In the Book of Jonah, you see the winds and waves, and even the fish, obeying God's commands; but the prophet stubbornly wanted his own way.

Disobedience to God's will is a tragedy—but so is reluctant, grudging obedience. God does not want us to disobey Him, but neither does He want us to obey out of fear or necessity. What Paul wrote about *giving* also applies to *living*: "not reluctantly or under compulsion, for God loves a cheerful giver" (2 Cor. 9:7).

What is the secret of *joyful* obedience? It is to recognize that obedience is a family matter. We are serving a loving Father and helping our brothers and sisters in Christ. We have been born of God; we love God, and we love God's children. And we demonstrate this love by keeping God's commandments.

Applying God's Truth:

1. Can you think of anything you've done this week that was clearly disobedient to one of God's commands?

2. Can you think of anything you've done this week to obey God's commands, but that you did grudgingly or reluctantly? If so, why were you so resistant?

3. What are three specific things you would be willing to try this week to attempt to make your obedience more joyful?

Scripture: Read 1 John 5:4-5

"Who is it that overcomes the world? Only he who believes that Jesus is the Son of God" (1 John 5:5).

FRIENDS IN HIGH PLACES

A Civil War veteran used to wander from place to place, begging a bed and bite to eat and always talking about his friend, "Mr. Lincoln." Because of his injuries, he was unable to hold a steady job. But as long as he could keep going, he would chat about his beloved President.

"You say you knew Mr. Lincoln," a skeptical bystander retorted one day. "I'm not so sure you did. Prove it!"

The old man replied, "Why, sure, I can prove it. In fact, I have a piece of paper here that Mr. Lincoln himself signed and gave to me."

From his old wallet, the man took out a much-folded piece of paper and showed it to the man.

"I'm not much for reading," he apologized, "but I know that's Mr. Lincoln's signature."

"Man, do you know what you have here?" one of the spectators asked. "You have a generous federal pension authorized by President Lincoln. You don't have to walk around like a poor beggar! Mr. Lincoln has made you rich!"

To paraphrase what John wrote: "You Christians do not have to walk around defeated, because Jesus Christ has made you victors! He has defeated every enemy and you share His victory. Now, *by faith*, claim His victory."

Applying God's Truth:

1. What does it mean to you that you "have overcome the world"?

2. In what ways do you occasionally feel defeated by the events you face in life?

3. You can "claim victory" by faith, but what will it take for you to truly *feel* victorious?

Scripture: Read 1 John 5:6-15

"This is the assurance we have in approaching God: that if we ask anything according to his will, he hears us" (1 John 5:14).

CONFIDENT OF ANSWERS

What breathing is to a physical man, prayer is to a spiritual man. Prayer is not only the utterance of the lips; it is also the desire of the heart. "Pray continually" (1 Thes. 5:17) does not mean that a Christian is always saying an audible prayer. We are not heard for our much speaking (Matt. 6:7). No, "Pray continually" suggests the attitude of the heart as well as the words of the lips. A Christian who has his heart fixed on Christ and is trying to glorify Him is praying even when he is not conscious of it.

Charles Spurgeon, the famous preacher, was working hard on a message but was unable to complete it. It grew late and his wife said, "Why don't you go to bed. I'll wake you up early and you can finish your sermon in the morning."

Spurgeon dozed off and in his sleep began to preach the sermon that was giving him so much trouble! His wife wrote down what he said and the next morning gave her preacher-husband the notes.

"Why, that's exactly what I wanted to say!" exclaimed the surprised preacher. The message had been in his heart; it had simply needed expression. So with prayer: if we are abiding in Christ, the very desires of our heart are heard by God whether we voice them or not.

Applying God's Truth:

1. How do you determine whether or not you are praying "according to [God's] will"?

2. During the times when it seems that God isn't hearing you, do you continue to pray faithfully? Or do you get discouraged during those times? How can you maintain a positive outlook even when your immediate feelings don't support it?

3. What are some of the "desires of your heart" that you haven't expressed to God in a while? Are you confident enough to ask Him again for those things?

Scripture: Read 1 John 5:16-21

"We are in him who is true—even in his Son Jesus Christ. He is the true God and eternal life" (1 John 5:20).

FOR REAL

The world boasts of enlightenment, but a Christian walks in the *real* light, because God is light. The world talks about love, but it knows nothing of the *real* love which a Christian experiences because "God is love." The world displays its wisdom and learning, but a Christian lives in truth because "the Spirit is truth." God is light, love, and truth; and these together make a life that is *real*.

"But it makes no difference what a man believes so long as he is sincere!"

This popular excuse hardly needs refutation. Does it make any difference what the pharmacist believes, or the surgeon, or the chemist? It makes all the difference in the world.

Shed a tear for Jimmy Brown;
Poor Jimmy is no more.
For what he thought was H_2O
Was H_2SO_4.

(H_2O is water. H_2SO_4 is sulfuric acid.)

A Christian has "turned to God from idols to serve the living and true God" (1 Thes. 1:9). Idols are dead, but Christ is the living God. Idols are false, but Christ is the true God. This is the secret of the life that is real!

So John's admonition, "Keep yourselves from idols," can be paraphrased, "Watch out for the imitation and the artificial and be real!"

Applying God's Truth:

1. What is the most significant thing you've learned (or reviewed) by going through the Book of 1 John?

2. What is an evidence from your own life that God is light? Love? Truth?

3. What are three specific things you can do to begin to live a more real life from this moment forward?

CONFIDENCE

30 Daily Readings from the Book of Hebrews

HAVE YOU NOTICED HOW OFTEN THE WORDS CONFIDENT AND CONFIDENCE show up in contemporary advertising?

An automobile manufacturer tells us we can drive his product with confidence because the designers have built into the vehicle the latest safety features. (Wouldn't it be nice to have safety features in our daily lives?)

A pharmaceutical firm announces that we can use their latest cold medication with confidence because it will take away the cold symptoms but won't make us drowsy. (It can't cure the cold, but that's another story.)

Publishers assure us we can read their newspapers and magazines with confidence because they print only the truth—the facts—and nobody has ever caught them in a lie.

Confidence is a matter of *trust*. In fact, that's what the word means: *to trust*. Everybody lives by faith in something, *and your faith is only as good as whatever or whomever you're trusting*. Do you have confidence in the object of your faith?

The Epistle to the Hebrews is about faith in Jesus Christ, the Son of God. It is one of three books in the New Testament written to explain one Old Testament verse of Scripture: "The righteous will live by his faith" (Hab. 2:4). The Epistle to the Romans explains who "the righteous" are; the Epistle to the Galatians describes how they "live"; and the Epistle to the Hebrews tells us what it means to live "by faith."

When you learn to live "by faith," you have confidence and you aren't blown over by every wind that comes along. Every Christian knows what Jesus Christ did on earth, but the Epistle to the Hebrews tells you what Jesus Christ is doing for His people *right now in heaven*. What a difference it makes when you trust Him *for everything* and have confidence in His promises and His power.

The Epistle to the Hebrews relates how God takes ordinary people and helps them face tremendous challenges and do incredible things *because they have confidence in God*. Once you understand what Jesus Christ is doing for you in heaven today, your own confidence will grow, your life will be transformed, and you will know the joy and excitement of living by faith.

Scripture: Read Hebrews 1

"In the past God spoke to our forefathers through the prophets at many times and in various ways, but in these last days he has spoken to us by his Son" (Heb. 1:1-2).

HEAR AND NOW

A man from Leeds, England, visited his doctor to have his hearing checked. The doctor removed the man's hearing aid, and the patient's hearing immediately improved! He had been wearing the device *in the wrong ear* for over twenty years!

I once asked a pastor friend, "Do you have a deaf ministry in your church?" He replied, "There are times when I think the whole church needs a deaf ministry—they just don't seem to hear me."

There is a difference between *listening* and really *hearing.* Jesus often cried, "He who has ears to hear, let him hear!" This statement suggests that it takes more than physical ears to hear the voice of God. It also requires a receptive heart.

Many people have avoided the Epistle to the Hebrews and, consequently, have robbed themselves of practical spiritual help. Some have avoided this book because they are "afraid of it." The "warnings" in Hebrews have made them uneasy. Others have avoided this book because they think it is "too difficult" for the average Bible student. To be sure, there are some profound truths in Hebrews, and no preacher or teacher would dare to claim that he knows them all! But the general message of the book is clear and there is no reason why you and I should not understand and profit from it.

Applying God's Truth:

1. When you go to church, what percent of the time would you say you are truly *hearing* as opposed to merely *listening?*

2. How can you hear more clearly, given that God "has spoken to us by His Son"?

3. What do you hope to accomplish through your readings from the Book of Hebrews?

Scripture: Read Hebrews 2:1

"We must pay more careful attention, therefore, to what we have heard, so that we do not drift away" *(Heb. 2:1)*.

A DOWNWARD CYCLE

If we do not listen to God's Word and really *hear* it, we will start to *drift*. Neglect always leads to drifting, in things material and physical as well as spiritual. As we drift from the Word, we start to *doubt* the Word; because *faith* comes by hearing the Word of God (Rom. 10:17). We start to get hard hearts, and this leads to spiritual sluggishness which produces *dullness* toward the Word. We become "dull of hearing"—lazy listeners! This leads to a *despiteful* attitude toward the Word to the extent that we willfully *disobey* God; and this gradually develops into a *defiant* attitude—we almost "dare" God to do anything!

Now what does God do while this spiritual regression is going on? He keeps speaking to us, encouraging us to get back to the Word. If we fail to listen and obey, then He begins to chasten us. This chastening process is the theme of Hebrews 12, the climactic chapter in the epistle. "The Lord will judge *His people*" (Heb. 10:30, italics mine). God does not allow His children to become "spoiled brats" by permitting them willfully to defy His word. He always chastens in love.

Applying God's Truth:

1. Can you recall a time when you were caught in the drifting/doubting/dullness/despising/disobeying/defying cycle? What was the lowest level you reached? How did you break out of the downward spiral?

2. How can you keep from beginning to drift in the first place?

3. Have you ever experienced God's loving chastening? In what ways?

Scripture: Read Hebrews 2:2-3a

"For if the message spoken by angels was binding . . . how shall we escape if we ignore such a great salvation?" (Heb. 2:2-3a)

STREAMS OF MERCY

The next time you sing "Come Thou Fount of Every Blessing," recall that the composer, Robert Robinson, was converted under the mighty preaching of George Whitefield, but that later he drifted from the Lord. He had been greatly used as a pastor, but neglect of spiritual things led him astray. In an attempt to find peace, he began to travel. During one of his journeys, he met a young woman who was evidently very spiritually minded.

"What do you think of this hymn I have been reading?" she asked Robinson, handing him the book. *It was his own hymn!* He tried to avoid her question but it was hopeless, for the Lord was speaking to him. Finally, he broke down and confessed who he was and how he had been living away from the Lord.

"But these 'streams of mercy' are still flowing," the woman assured him; and through her encouragement, Robinson was restored to fellowship with the Lord.

It is easy to drift with the current, but it is difficult to return against the stream. Our salvation is a "great salvation," purchased at a great price. It brings with it great promises and blessings, and it leads to a great inheritance in glory. How can we neglect it?

Applying God's Truth:

1. In what ways are God's "streams of mercy" flowing through your life?

2. When was a recent time you experienced great difficulty "going against the current" in order to follow God when no one else seemed to want to?

3. In what way is yours a "great salvation"?

Scripture: Read Hebrews 2:3b-9

"This salvation, which was first announced by the Lord, was confirmed to us by those who heard him" (Heb. 2:3b).

SINS OF THE SAINTS

We have the idea that believers today "under grace" can escape the chastening hand of God that was so evident "under Law." But to whom much is given, much shall be required. Not only have we received the Word from the Son of God, but that Word has been confirmed by apostolic miracle (v. 4). The phrase "signs and wonders" is found eleven times in the New Testament. Here it refers to the miracles that witnessed to the Word and gave confirmation that it was true. These miracles were performed by the apostles. Today we have the completed Word of God; so there is no need for these apostolic miracles. God now bears witness through His Spirit using the Word. The Spirit also gives spiritual gifts to God's people so that they may minister in the church.

I have often told the story about the pastor who preached a series of sermons on "the sins of the saints." He was severely reprimanded by one of the members of the church. "After all," said the member, "sin in the life of a Christian is different from sin in the lives of other people."

"Yes," replied the pastor, "it's worse!"

Applying God's Truth:

1. If a stranger were to ask you today, "Why do you believe in God?" what reasons would you give?

2. What are some of the gifts of the Holy Spirit that you feel have been "distributed" to you? Be specific.

3. Do you agree that sin in the life of a Christian is worse than sin in the lives of other people? Why?

Scripture: Read Hebrews 2:10-18

"For this reason [Jesus] had to be made like his brothers in every way, in order that he might become a merciful and faithful high priest in service to God, and that he might make atonement for the sins of the people" (Heb. 2:17).

MERCY AND FAITHFULNESS

If you want an example of a man who was *not* a merciful and faithful high priest, then read the account about Eli (1 Sam. 2:27-36). Here was a high priest who did not even lead his own sons into a faithful walk with God. Eli even accused brokenhearted Hannah of being drunk! (1 Sam. 1:9-18)

Jesus Christ is both merciful and faithful; He is merciful toward people and faithful toward God. He can never fail in His priestly ministries. He made the necessary sacrifice for our sins so that we might be reconciled to God. He did not need to make a sacrifice for Himself because He is sinless.

But what happens when we who have been saved are tempted to sin? He stands ready to help us! He was tempted when He was on earth, but no temptation ever conquered Him. Because He has defeated every enemy, He is able to give us the grace that we need to overcome temptation. The word translated "succour" in the *King James Version* (or "help" in the *New International Version*) in Hebrews 2:18 literally means "to run to the cry of a child." It means "to bring help when it is needed." Angels are able to *serve* us (1:14), but they are not able to *succour* us in our times of temptation. Only Jesus Christ can do that, and He can do it because He became a man and suffered and died.

Applying God's Truth:

1. What are some specific ways that Jesus has been merciful to you lately? In so doing, how has He been faithful toward God?

2. List all the temptations you have faced during the past week.

3. For each of the temptations you listed, how would you like Jesus to help you stand firmly against it?

Scripture: Read Hebrews 3:1-11

"Fix your thoughts on Jesus, the apostle and high priest whom we confess. He was faithful to the one who appointed him, just as Moses was faithful in all God's house" (Heb. 3:1-2).

TWO GOOD EXAMPLES

Jesus Christ is not only the Apostle, but He is also the High Priest. Moses was a prophet who on occasion served as a high priest. That title belonged to his brother Aaron. In fact, Jesus Christ has the title "Great High Priest" (4:14).

As the Apostle, Jesus Christ represented God to men, and as the High Priest, He now represents men to God in heaven. Moses, of course, fulfilled similar ministries; for he taught Israel God's truth, and he prayed for Israel when he met God on the mount. (See Ex. 32:30-32.) Moses was primarily the prophet of Law, while Jesus Christ is the messenger of God's grace. Moses helped prepare the way for the coming of the Savior to the earth.

However, the writer of Hebrews notes that Moses and Jesus Christ were both faithful in the work God gave them to do. Moses was not sinless, as was Jesus Christ, but he was faithful and obeyed God's will (Num. 12:7). This would be an encouragement to those first-century Jewish believers to remain faithful to Christ, even in the midst of the tough trials they were experiencing. Instead of going back to Moses, they should *imitate* Moses and be faithful in their calling.

Applying God's Truth:

1. How does Jesus serve as an *apostle* ("one sent with a commission")? How does He serve as your *high priest*?

2. How might your spiritual life improve if you were to imitate the faithfulness of Moses? How might you better imitate Christ?

3. Specifically, what are some things you can do to "fix your thoughts on Jesus"?

Scripture: Read Hebrews 3:12-19

"See to it, brothers, that none of you has a sinful, unbelieving heart that turns away from the living God. But encourage one another daily . . . so that none of you may be hardened by sin's deceitfulness" (Heb. 3:12-13).

HEART PROBLEMS

The heart of every problem is a problem in the heart. The people of Israel (except Moses, Joshua, and Caleb) erred in their hearts, which means that their hearts wandered from God and His Word. They also had evil hearts of unbelief; they did not believe that God would give them victory in Canaan. They had seen God perform great signs in Egypt, yet they doubted He was adequate for the challenge of Canaan.

When a person has an *erring* heart and a *disbelieving* heart, the result will also be a *hard* heart. This is a heart that is insensitive to the Word and work of God. So hard was the heart of Israel that the people even wanted to return to Egypt! Imagine wanting to exchange their freedom under God for slavery in Egypt! Of course, all this history spoke to the hearts of the readers of this letter, because they were in danger of "going back" themselves.

Believers who doubt God's Word and rebel against Him do not miss heaven, but they do miss out on the blessing of their inheritance today, and they must suffer the chastening of God.

Applying God's Truth:

1. When was the last time your heart was "hardened by sin's deceitfulness"?

2. What are some blessings we stand to lose if we don't deal with hard-heartedness?

3. We are commanded to "encourage one another daily." How do you think this helps alleviate forming a "hard heart" toward God? Whom have you encouraged today?

Scripture: Read Hebrews 4

"Since the promise of entering his rest still stands, let us be careful that none of you be found to have fallen short of it" (Heb. 4:1).

A Lesson in Geography

We must understand that there are spiritual lessons in the geography of Israel's experiences. The nation's bondage in Egypt is an illustration of a sinner's bondage in this world. Much as Israel was delivered from Egypt by the blood of lambs and the power of God, so a sinner who believes on Christ is delivered from the bondage of sin.

It was not God's will that Israel remain either in Egypt or in the wilderness. His desire was that the people enter their glorious inheritance in the land of Canaan. But when Israel got to the border of their inheritance, they delayed because they doubted the promise of God (Num. 13–14). "We are not able," wept the ten spies and the people. "We are able with God's help!" said Moses, Joshua, and Caleb. Because the people went backward in unbelief instead of forward by faith, they missed their inheritance and died in the wilderness.

What does Canaan represent to us as Christians today? It represents our spiritual inheritance in Christ. Israel had to cross the Jordan River by faith (a picture of the believer as he dies to self and the world). They had to step out by faith (Josh. 1:3) and claim the land for themselves, just as believers today must do.

Applying God's Truth:

1. Do you feel that you are "in bondage" in any way? How might faith help you experience real freedom?

2. Do you ever want, even briefly, to return to the lifestyle you had before becoming a Christian? If so, why? How do you deal with such feelings?

3. What do you think it means to "enter [God's] rest"?

Scripture: Read Hebrews 5:1-6

"Every high priest is selected from among men and is appointed to represent them in matters related to God, to offer gifts and sacrifices for sins. . . . No one takes this honor upon himself; he must be called by God" (Heb. 5:1, 4).

THE RIGHT TO SERVE

When I became pastor of the Calvary Baptist Church in Covington, Kentucky, it was necessary for me to go to the city hall and be bonded. Otherwise, I would not have the authority to perform marriages. I had to show my ordination certificate and prove that I was indeed ministering at the church.

One day I received a frantic phone call from one of our members. Some Christian friends were being married the next day by a relative from Michigan, and they discovered that he was not authorized to perform the ceremony! Could I help them? The visiting pastor could read the ceremony as well as I could, and he knew the couple better than I did; but he lacked the authority to minister.

No man could appoint himself as a priest, let alone *high* priest. The very existence of a priesthood and a system of sacrifices gave evidence that man is estranged from God. It was an act of grace on God's part that He instituted the whole levitical system. Today, that system is fulfilled in the ministry of Jesus Christ. He is both the sacrifice and the High Priest who ministers to God's people on the basis of His once-for-all offering on the cross.

Applying God's Truth:

1. How was Jesus given "authority to minister" in His role as high priest?

2. What requests do you need to make of Jesus today specifically in regard to His high-priestly duties?

3. What makes Jesus the ideal high priest to represent us before God?

Scripture: Read Hebrews 5:7-8

"During the days of Jesus' life on earth, he offered up prayers and petitions with loud cries and tears to the one who could save him from death, and he was heard because of his reverent submission. Although he was a son, he learned obedience from what he suffered" (Heb. 5:7-8).

SUPERIOR SYMPATHY

Every Old Testament high priest had to minister to people who were "ignorant and . . . going astray" (v. 2). God made no provision but judgment for the high-handed sins of rebellion. But he did make provision when people sinned through ignorance or weakness. An Old Testament priest could identify with the sinners since he himself was a sinner. In fact, on the Day of Atonement, the high priest had to offer a sacrifice for himself before he could offer one for the nation! (Lev. 16; Heb. 9:7)

You would think that one sinner would have compassion for another sinner, but this is not always the case. Sin makes a person selfish. Sin can blind us to the hurts of others. Sin can harden our hearts and make us judgmental instead of sympathetic. Remember how heartbroken Hannah, who was praying for a son, was accused by high priest Eli of being drunk? (1 Sam. 1:9-18) And when King David was confronted with a story of a rich man's sin, he had no sympathy for him, even though David himself was a worse sinner (2 Sam. 12).

No, it is the spiritually minded person with a clean heart who sympathizes with a sinner and seeks to help him. Because we are so sinful, we have a hard time helping other sinners; but because Jesus is perfect, He is able to meet our needs after we sin.

Applying God's Truth:

1. On a scale of 1 (least) to 10 (most), what would you say is your average level of compassion shown toward the sinful people you come into contact with?

2. What can you learn from Jesus' example of "reverent submission"? Be specific.

3. Is your status as "child of God" something you've begun to take for granted or, like Jesus, do you strive to continue to learn obedience from your sufferings?

Scripture: Read Hebrews 5:9-10

"Once made perfect, [Jesus] became the source of eternal salvation for all who obey him" (Heb. 5:9).

NO REPUTATION

No matter what trials we meet, Jesus Christ is able to understand our needs and help us. We need never doubt His ability to sympathize and strengthen. It is also worth noting that sometimes God puts *us* through difficulties that we might better understand the needs of others and become able to encourage them.

When Charles Haddon Spurgeon was a young preacher in London, his successful ministry aroused the envy of some of the clergy, and they attacked him with various kinds of slander and gossip. His sermons were called "trashy," and he was called "an actor" and "a pulpit buffoon." Even after his ministry was established, Spurgeon was lied about in the press (including the *religious* press), and this was bound to discourage him.

After one particularly scurrilous report in the press, Spurgeon fell before the Lord and prayed, "O Lord Jesus, Thou didst make Thyself of no reputation for me. I willingly lay my reputation down for Thy sake." From that time on, Spurgeon had peace in his heart. He knew that his Great High Priest understood his need and would give him the grace that he needed for each hour.

Applying God's Truth:

1. What trials are you facing today in which Jesus is the only person who can help you?

2. Have you ever been so devoted to Jesus (and your own spiritual growth) that your motives or reputation were called into question by others? If so, how did you respond?

3. Try to recall a difficulty you once faced, after which you were able to minister effectively to someone else facing the same or a similar problem. How did you feel to be able to help someone based on your previous personal experience?

Scripture: Read Hebrews 5:11-14

"Anyone who lives on milk, being still an infant, is not acquainted with the teaching about righteousness. But solid food is for the mature" (Heb. 5:13-14).

SPIRITUAL SENSES

Just as our physical bodies have senses, without which we could not function, so our inner "spiritual man" has "spiritual senses." As we feed on the Word of God, and apply it in daily life, our inner "spiritual senses" get their exercise and become strong and keen. Paul called this process training ourselves to be godly (1 Tim. 4:7-8).

The ability to discern good and evil is a vital part of Christian maturity. The nation of Israel in Moses' day lacked this discernment and failed to claim their promised inheritance. The readers of this letter were in danger of making the same mistake. It is impossible to stand still in the Christian life: we either go forward and claim God's blessing, or we go backward and wander about aimlessly.

I once heard a preacher say, "Most Christians are 'betweeners.' "

"What do you mean by that?" I asked.

"They are between Egypt and Canaan—out of the place of danger, but not yet into the place of rest and rich inheritance," he replied. "They are between Good Friday and Easter Sunday—saved by the blood but not yet enjoying newness of resurrection life."

Are *you* a "betweener"?

Applying God's Truth:

1. At what level of spiritual understanding would you say you are: (A) Milk/Liquid diet; (B) Baby food; (C) Junk food; (D) Soft foods; or (E) Steak and potatoes? Explain.

2. On a scale where 1 is "Egypt" and 10 is "Canaan," where would you place your spiritual progress? Are you moving forward at this point in your spiritual journey?

3. What are some ways that you train yourself to distinguish between good and evil?

Scripture: Read Hebrews 6

"We have this hope as an anchor for the soul, firm and secure. It enters the inner sanctuary behind the curtain, where Jesus, who went before us, has entered on our behalf" (Heb. 6:19-20).

DROP ANCHOR

Our hope in Christ is like an anchor for the soul. The anchor was a popular symbol in the early church. At least sixty-six pictures of anchors have been found in the catacombs. The Greek Stoic philosopher Epictetus wrote: "One must not tie a ship to a single anchor, nor life to a single hope." Christians have but one anchor—Jesus Christ our hope (Col. 1:5; 1 Tim. 1:1).

However, this spiritual anchor is different from material anchors on ships. For one thing, we are anchored *upward*—to heaven—not downward. We are anchored, not to stand still, but to *move ahead!* Our anchor is "firm"—it cannot break—and "secure"—it cannot slip. No earthly anchor can give that kind of security!

The writer then clinches the argument: this Savior is our "forerunner." The Old Testament high priest was *not* a "forerunner" because nobody could follow him into the holy of holies. But Jesus Christ has gone ahead to heaven so that one day we may follow!

Applying God's Truth:

1. In what ways would you say Jesus is your "anchor"?

2. What are some areas of your life that aren't anchored as securely as you wish they were?

3. What are some ways that being anchored to Jesus has helped you move *ahead?*

Scripture: Read Hebrews 7:1-2

"Melchizedek was king of Salem and priest of God Most High. . . . First, his name means 'king of righteousness'; then also, 'king of Salem' means 'king of peace'" (Heb. 7:1-2).

WHAT'S IN A NAME?

In the Bible, names and their meanings are often important. We name our children today without much consideration for what their names mean, but this was not the case in Bible days. Sometimes, a great spiritual crisis was the occasion for changing a person's name (see Gen. 32:24-32; John 1:35-42).

The name *Melchizedek* means "king of righteousness" in the Hebrew language. The word *Salem* means "peace" (the Hebrew word *shalom*), so that Melchizedek is "king of peace" as well as "king of righteousness."

"Righteousness" and "peace" are often found together in Scripture. In Psalm 85:10, for example, we are told: "Righteousness and peace kiss each other." And God's purpose for His people is that they bear "a harvest of righteousness and peace" (Heb. 12:10-11).

True peace can be experienced only on the basis of righteousness. If we want to enjoy "peace with God," we must be "justified by faith." Man cannot produce righteousness by keeping the Old Testament Law (Gal 2:21). It is only through the work of Jesus Christ on the cross that righteousness and peace can "kiss each other."

Applying God's Truth:

1. What do you think would be an appropriate "biblical" name for you (such as "king of peace," or "king of righteousness")?

2. In what ways is Jesus your King of peace?

3. In what ways is Jesus your King of righteousness?

Scripture: Read Hebrews 7:3-28

"Without father or mother, without genealogy, without beginning of days or end of life, like the Son of God [Melchizedek] remains a priest forever" (Heb. 7:3).

WITHOUT GENEALOGY

Melchizedek was a man, so he had to have had a mother and a father. But there is no *record* of his genealogy (descent) in the Old Testament; and this is significant because most great persons in the Old Testament have their ancestry identified. It was especially important that the priests be able to prove their ancestry. Here the writer of Hebrews uses an argument from silence, but it is a valid one.

Melchizedek was not an angel or some superhuman creature; nor was he an Old Testament appearance of Jesus Christ. He was a real man, a real king, and a real priest in a real city. But as far as the record is concerned, he was not born, nor did he die. In this way, he is a picture of the Lord Jesus Christ, the eternal Son of God. Though Jesus Christ did die, Calvary was not the end; for He arose from the dead and today he lives in "the power of an indestructible life" (v. 16). Since there is no account of Melchizedek's death, as far as the record is concerned, it seems that Melchizedek is still serving as a priest and king. This is another way in which he is like the eternal Son of God.

The application is clear: neither Aaron nor any of his descendants could claim to be "without genealogy." They could not claim to have an eternal ministry. Nor could they claim to be both kings and priests, like Jesus Christ.

Applying God's Truth:

1. How might your life be different if you had no knowledge of your father or mother? What things might you do differently?

2. How important is your genealogy to you? Why?

3. Why is it significant that Jesus "remains a priest forever"?

Scripture: Read Hebrews 8:1-6

"We do have such a high priest, who sat down at the right hand of the throne of the Majesty in heaven, and who serves in the sanctuary, the true tabernacle set up by the Lord, not by man" (Heb. 8:1-2).

A SEAT OF HONOR

Today our Lord is *seated* because His work is completed. There were no chairs in the Old Testament tabernacle because the work of the priests was never finished. Each repeated sacrifice was only a reminder that none of the sacrifices ever provided a finished salvation. The blood of animals did not wash away sin or cleanse the guilty conscience; it only covered sin until that day when Jesus Christ died to take away the sin of the world (John 1:29).

Jesus Christ is not just "seated." It is *where* He is seated that adds glory to His person and His work. He is seated on the throne in heaven, at the right hand of the Father. This great truth was introduced early in this epistle (1:3), and it will be mentioned again (10:12; 12:2). This enthronement was the fulfillment of the Father's promise to the Son, "Sit at my right hand until I make your enemies a footstool for your feet" (Ps. 110:1). Not only did the high priest of Israel never sit down, but he never sat down on a throne. Only a priest "after the order of Melchizedek" could be enthroned, for Melchizedek was both king and priest.

Applying God's Truth:

1. With all the turbulence in this world, what shows you that Jesus' work is actually completed?

2. As you think of Jesus seated in heaven, what are some assurances you feel related to the work He has finished?

3. What do you find significant about the fact that Jesus is seated on a throne?

Scripture: Read Hebrews 8:7-12

"I will forgive their wickedness and will remember their sins no more" (Heb. 8:12).

SHORT-TERM MEMORY

What does it mean that God remembers our sins no more? This important statement is quoted again in 10:16-17. Does it mean that our all-knowing God can actually *forget* what we have done? If God forgot anything, He would cease to be God! The phrase "remember no more" means "hold against us no more." God recalls what we have done, but He does not hold it against us. He deals with us on the basis of grace and mercy, not law and merit. Once sin has been forgiven, it is never brought before us again. The matter is settled eternally.

As a pastor in counseling ministry, I have often heard people say, "Well, I can forgive—but I cannot forget!"

"Of course you can't forget," I usually reply. "The more you try to put this thing out of your mind, the more you will remember it. But that isn't what it means to forget." Then I go on to explain that "to forget" means "not to hold it against the person who has wronged us." We may remember what others have done, but we treat them *as though they never did it.*

How is this possible? It is possible because of the cross, for there God treated His Son *as though He had done it!* Our experience of forgiveness from God makes it possible for us to forgive others.

Applying God's Truth:

1. Which of your sins stand out in your mind as those for which you are most thankful that God remembers no more?

2. Because God so readily forgives and forgets our confessed sins, how do you keep from taking His forgiveness for granted?

3. What are some recent situations in which you had the opportunity to forgive another person's offense against you, yet for some reason chose not to do so? Are you satisfied that you did the right thing, or do you need to reevaluate some of those decisions/attitudes?

Scripture: Read Hebrews 8:13

"By calling this covenant 'new,' He has made the first one obsolete; and what is obsolete and aging will soon disappear" (Heb. 8:13).

HAND IN HAND

The emphasis in the New Covenant is on God's "I will." The nation of Israel at Sinai said, "Everything the Lord has said we will do" (Ex. 24:3). But they did not obey God's words. It is one thing to *say*, "We will!" and quite another to do it. But the New Covenant does not depend on man's faithfulness to God but on God's faithful promise to man. The writer of Hebrews affirms God's "I will" on behalf of those who trust Jesus Christ. In fact, God's "I will" is stated three times in Hebrews 8:10 and six times in verses 8-12.

God led Israel out of Egypt the way a father would take a child by the hand and lead him. God gave Israel His holy Law for their own good, to separate them from the other nations, and to protect them from the sinful practices of the heathen. But the nation failed. God's responses to Israel's disobedience were to discipline them repeatedly and finally to send them into captivity.

God did not find fault with His covenant but with His people. The problem is not with the Law, but with our sinful natures, for by ourselves we cannot keep God's Law. The Law "made nothing perfect" (7:19) because it could not change any human heart. Only God's grace can do that.

Applying God's Truth:

1. In what ways does God lead you as a father might lead a child?

2. If God did not find fault with the "Old" Covenant, why did He provide a new one?

3. How do you think the Old Covenant "will soon disappear"?

Scripture: Read Hebrews 9:1-14

"The blood of goats and bulls . . . sanctify them so that they are outwardly clean. How much more, then, will the blood of Christ, who through the eternal Spirit offered himself unblemished to God, cleanse our consciences from acts that lead to death, so that we may serve the living God!" (Heb. 9:13-14)

INTERNAL CHANGES

The Old Covenant rituals could not change a person's heart. This is not to say that a worshiper did not have a spiritual experience if his heart trusted God, but it does mean that the emphasis was on the external cere-monial cleansing. So long as the worshiper obeyed the prescribed regula-tions, he was declared clean. It was "the purifying of the flesh," but not the cleansing of the conscience.

We learned from Hebrews 8 that the ministry of the New Covenant is *internal.* "I will put my laws in their minds and write them on their hearts" (8:10). This work is done by the Holy Spirit of God. But the Spirit could not dwell within us if Jesus Christ had not paid for our sins. Cleansing our consciences cannot be done by some external ceremony; it demands an inter-nal power. Because Jesus Christ is "unblemished," He was able to offer the perfect sacrifice.

Applying God's Truth:

1. How might you have felt as an Old Testament believer, using animal blood in your worship ceremonies? Why do you think blood was chosen as a symbol of worship?

2. How do you feel knowing that your religion still depends on blood—the blood of Jesus shed on your behalf? Do you ever have problems explain-ing this in your twentieth-century conversations?

3. To what extent are you certain that internal changes have taken place in your life?

Scripture: Read Hebrews 9:15-28

"For Christ did not enter a man-made sanctuary that was only a copy of the true one; he entered heaven itself, now to appear for us in God's presence" (Heb. 9:24).

BETTER THAN MAN-MADE

The New Covenant Christian has *reality!* We are not depending on a high priest on earth who annually visits the holy of holies in a temporary sanctuary. We depend on the heavenly High Priest who has entered once and for all into the eternal sanctuary. There He represents us before God, and He *always will.*

Beware of trusting anything for your spiritual life that is "man-made." It will not last. The tabernacle was replaced by Solomon's temple, and that temple was destroyed by the Babylonians. When the Jews returned to their land after the Captivity, they rebuilt their temple; and King Herod, in later years, expanded and embellished it. But the Romans destroyed that temple, and it has never been rebuilt.

Furthermore, since the genealogical records have been lost or destroyed, the Jews are not certain who can minister as priests. These things that are "man-made" are perishable, but the things not made with hands are eternal.

Applying God's Truth:

1. What are some man-made items you find valuable in your worship of God?

2 We know that *what* Jesus did as our High Priest is extremely important, but what is equally important about *where* He ministers?

3. What are some unseen, eternal things you value?

Scripture: Read Hebrews 10:1-18

"He waits for his enemies to be made his footstool, because by one sacrifice he has made perfect forever those who are being made holy" (Heb. 10:13-14).

A PERFECT STANDING

How do we know *personally* that we have a perfect standing before God? Because of the witness of the Holy Spirit through the Word (vv. 15-18). The witness of the Spirit is based on the work of the Son and is given through the words of Scripture. The writer (vv. 16-17) quoted Jeremiah 31:33-34, part of a passage he'd also quoted in Hebrews 8:7-12. The Old Covenant worshiper could not say that he "no longer felt guilty for [his] sins" (v. 2). But the New Covenant believer *can* say that his sins are remembered *no more*. There is "no longer any sacrifice for sin" (v. 18) and no more remembrance of sin!

I once shared a conference with a fine Christian psychiatrist whose lectures were very true to the Word. "The trouble with psychiatry," he told me, "is that it can only deal with symptoms. A psychiatrist can remove a patient's feelings of guilt, but he cannot remove the guilt. It's like a trucker loosening a fender on his truck so he won't hear the motor knock. A patient can end up feeling better, but have two problems instead of one!"

When a sinner trusts Christ, his sins are all forgiven, the guilt is gone, and the matter is completely settled forever.

Applying God's Truth:

1. Do you fully believe that you have a perfect standing before God? Why or why not?

2. In what specific ways do you feel you are being "made holy"?

3. Is it possible that you might be repeatedly asking forgiveness for a sin that God has already forgiven? If so, how can you put it behind you and move forward in your spiritual life?

Scripture: Read Hebrews 10:19-23

"Let us hold unswervingly to the hope we profess, for he who promised is faithful" (Heb. 10:23).

HANGING ON TO HOPE

The readers of this epistle were being tempted to forsake their confession of Jesus Christ by going back to the Old Covenant worship. The writer did not exhort them to hold on to their salvation because their security was in Christ and not in themselves (v. 25). Rather, he invited them to hold fast to "the hope we profess."

We have noted in our study of Hebrews that there is an emphasis on the glorious hope of the believer. God is "bringing many sons to glory" (2:10). Believers "share in the heavenly calling" (3:1) and therefore can rejoice in hope (3:6). Hope is one of the main themes of Hebrews 6. We are looking for Christ to return (9:28), and we are seeking that city that is yet to come (13:14).

When a believer has his hope fixed on Christ, and relies on the faithfulness of God, then he will not waver. Instead of looking back (as the Jews so often did), we should look ahead to the coming of the Lord.

Applying God's Truth:

1. How would you define "the hope [you] profess"?

2. If you became even more sure of the faithfulness of God than you are now, how might your spiritual life be affected?

3. If you knew for sure that Jesus would return two weeks from today, what would you want to do during the next two weeks? Are they things you should be doing *anyway*?

Scripture: Read Hebrews 10:24-39

"Let us consider how we may spur one another on toward love and good deeds. Let us not give up meeting together, as some are in the habit of doing, but let us encourage one another—and all the more as you see the Day approaching" (Heb. 10:24-25).

Maintaining Togetherness

Fellowship with God must never become selfish. We must also fellowship with other Christians in the local assembly. Apparently, some of the wavering believers had been absenting themselves from the church fellowship. It is interesting to note that the emphasis here is not on what a believer gets from the assembly, but rather on what he can *contribute* to the assembly. Faithfulness in church attendance encourages others and provokes them to love and good works.

One of the strong motives for faithfulness is the soon coming of Jesus Christ. In fact, the only other place the word translated *meeting together* (v. 25) is used in the New Testament is in 2 Thessalonians 2:1, where it's translated *gathered* and deals with the coming of Christ.

The three great Christian virtues are evidenced here: *faith* (Heb. 10:22), *hope* (v. 23), and *love* (v. 24). They are the fruit of our fellowship with God in His heavenly sanctuary.

Applying God's Truth:

1. How would you respond to someone who says, "I don't need to go to church. I can worship God just as well out by myself in nature"?

2. What are the primary benefits you receive from group worship? What do you contribute to the group?

3. How can you "spur" other people toward love and good deeds in a positive way—without "getting on their case"?

Scripture: Read Hebrews 11:1-5

"Faith is being sure of what we hope for and certain of what we do not see" (Heb. 11:1).

FAITH AND CONSEQUENCES

True biblical faith is *confident obedience to God's Word in spite of circumstances and consequences.* This faith operates quite simply. God speaks and we hear His Word. We trust His Word and act on it no matter what the circumstances are or what the consequences may be. The circumstances may be impossible, and the consequences frightening and unknown; but we obey God's Word just the same and believe He will do what is right and what is best.

The unsaved world does not understand true biblical faith, probably because it sees so little faith in action in the church today. The cynical editor H.L. Mencken defined faith as "illogical belief in the occurrence of the impossible." The world failed to realize that faith is only as good as its object, and the object of faith is God. Faith is not some "feeling" that we manufacture. It is our total response to what God has revealed in His Word.

The writer of Hebrews makes it clear that faith is a very practical thing (v. 3), in spite of what unbelievers say. Faith enables us to understand what God does. Faith enables us to see what others cannot see. As a result, faith enables us to do what others cannot do! Dr. J. Oswald Sanders put it perfectly: "Faith enables the believing soul to treat the future as present and the invisible as seen."

Applying God's Truth:

1. Now that you've read the author's definition of faith, how would you define it in your own words?

2. Based on your definition, what are some of the best ways to *increase* your faith?

3. On a scale of 1 (least) to 10 (most), to what extent do circumstances and consequences affect your level of faith?

Scripture: Read Hebrews 11:6-16

"Without faith it is impossible to please God, because anyone who comes to him must believe that he exists and that he rewards those who earnestly seek him" (Heb. 11:6).

FAITH LOOKS FORWARD

Faith looks to the future, for that is where the greatest rewards are found. The people named in this chapter (and those unnamed) did not receive "the things promised" (v. 13), but they had God's witness to their faith that one day they would be rewarded. God's purpose involves Old Testament saints as well as New Testament saints! One day all of us shall share that heavenly city that true saints look for by faith.

We today should give thanks for these saints of old, for they were faithful during difficult times, and yet *we* are the ones who have received the better blessing. They saw some of these blessings afar off, but we enjoy them today through Jesus Christ. If the saints of old had not trusted God and obeyed His will, Israel would have perished and the Messiah would not have been born.

Without faith it is impossible to please God. But this faith grows as we listen to His Word and fellowship in worship and prayer. Faith is possible to all kinds of believers in all kinds of situations. It is not a luxury for a few "elite saints." It is a necessity for all of God's people.

Lord, increase our faith!

Applying God's Truth:

1. When is your faith the strongest? When does it seem weakest?

2. Why is faith necessary to please God? Shouldn't obedience be enough in itself?

3. What specific steps can you take to increase your faith?

Scripture: Read Hebrews 11:17-30

"Abraham reasoned that God could raise the dead. . . . By faith Isaac blessed Jacob and Esau. . . . By faith Jacob, when he was dying, blessed each of Joseph's sons. . . . By faith Joseph, when his end was near, spoke about the exodus of the Israelites from Egypt" (Heb. 11:19-22).

ROLE MODELS

In Abraham, Isaac, Jacob, and Joseph, we have four generations of faith. These men sometimes failed, but they were devoted to God and trusted His Word. Isaac passed the promises and the blessings along to Jacob, and Jacob shared them with his twelve sons. Jacob was a pilgrim, for even as he was dying he leaned on his pilgrim staff (v. 21).

The faith of Joseph was certainly remarkable. After the way his family treated him, you would think he would have abandoned his faith; but instead, it grew stronger. Even the ungodly influence of Egypt did not weaken his trust in God. Joseph did not use his family, his job, or his circumstances as an excuse for unbelief.

We have to admire the faith of the patriarchs. They did not have a complete Bible, and yet their faith was strong. They handed God's promises down from one generation to another. In spite of their failures and testings, these men and women believed God and He bore witness to their faith. How much more faith you and I should have!

Applying God's Truth:

1. What biblical characters would you cite as having the greatest levels of faith? Why?

2. Who are you more like: Abraham, Isaac, Jacob, or Joseph? Why?

3. How do you think your own level of faith would have been affected if you had lived in the days prior to Jesus' life—if you only had had the promise of a Savior without the actual fulfillment of the promise?

Scripture: Read Hebrews 11:31-40

"By faith the prostitute Rahab, because she welcomed the spies, was not killed with those who were disobedient" (Heb. 11:31).

A CHANGE OF LIFESTYLE

R ahab was a prostitute, an unlikely person to put faith in the true God of Israel! *She was saved by grace* because the other inhabitants of the city were marked out for death. God in His mercy and grace permitted Rahab to live. But *she was saved by faith.* She protected the spies, put the cord in the window as directed (Josh. 2:15-21), apparently won her family to the true faith (2:13; 6:25), and in every way obeyed the Lord.

Not only was Rahab delivered from judgment, but she became a part of the nation of Israel. She married Salmon and gave birth to Boaz who was an ancestor of King David. Imagine a pagan prostitute becoming a part of the ancestry of Jesus Christ! That is what faith can do!

Rahab is certainly a rebuke to unsaved people who give excuses for not trusting Christ. "I don't know very much about the Bible" is an excuse I often hear. Rahab knew very little spiritual truth, but she acted on what she did know. "I am too bad to be saved!" is another excuse. But Rahab was a condemned heathen prostitute! She stands as one of the great women of faith in the Bible.

Applying God's Truth:

1. Do you know people similar to Rahab—with bad past or present reputations, yet a real and growing faith in God? How do most Christians relate to such people?

2. What do you think made Rahab different from all the other people in Jericho?

3. Can you think of any well-known people today who testify to pasts as bad or worse as Rahab's, yet who are dynamic models of Christian faith? What can you learn from such people?

Scripture: Read Hebrews 12:1-6

"Since we are surrounded by such a great cloud of witnesses, let us throw off every-thing that hinders and the sin that so easily entangles, and let us run with perse-verance the race marked out for us" (Heb. 12:1).

LOSING WEIGHT

A thletes used to wear training weights to help them prepare for events. No athlete would actually participate wearing the weights because they would slow him down. (The modern analogy is a baseball player who swings a bat with a heavy metal collar before he steps to the plate.) Too much weight would tax one's endurance.

What are the "weights" that we should remove so that we might win the race? Everything that hinders our progress. They might even be "good things" in the eyes of others. A winning athlete does not choose between the good and the bad; he chooses between the better and the best.

We should also get rid of "the sin that so easily entangles" (v. 1). While he does not name any specific sin, the writer was probably referring to the sin of unbelief. It was unbelief that kept Israel out of the Promised Land, and it is unbelief that hinders us from entering into our spiritual inheritance in Christ. The phrase "by faith" (or "through faith") is used twenty-one times in chapter 11, indicating that it is faith in Christ that enables us to endure.

Applying God's Truth:

1. What are some of the sins that are most likely to "entangle" you as you attempt to make spiritual progress?

2. What are some of the "weights" you are carrying—not necessarily sins, but things that may impede your spiritual growth?

3. What do you need to do to "throw off" the excess "weights" you may be carrying?

Scripture: Read Hebrews 12:7-29

"No discipline seems pleasant at the time, but painful. Later on, however, it produces a harvest of righteousness and peace for those who have been trained by it" (Heb. 12:11).

LOVE AND DISCIPLINE

No chastening at the time is pleasant either to the father or to his son, but the benefits are profitable. I am sure that few children believe it when their parents say, "This hurts me more than it hurts you." But it is true just the same. The Father does not enjoy having to discipline His children, but the benefits afterward make the chastening an evidence of His love.

What are some of the benefits? For one thing, there is "a harvest of righteousness." Instead of continuing to sin, the child strives to do what is right. There is also peace instead of war. The rebellion has ceased and the child is in a loving fellowship with the Father. Chastening also encourages a child to *exercise* in spiritual matters—the Word of God, prayer, meditation, witnessing, etc. All this leads to a new *joy*.

Of course, the important thing is how God's child responds to chastening. He can despise it or faint under it (v. 5), both of which are wrong. He should show reverence to the Father by submitting to His will (v. 9), using the experience to exercise himself spiritually.

Verses 12 and 13 sound like a coach's orders to his team. Lift up your hands. Strengthen those knees. Get those lazy feet on the track. On your mark, get set, GO.

Applying God's Truth:

1. When you think of "discipline," is it usually in a positive or negative context? What are some of the connotations of "discipline"?

2. Why do you discipline yourself in ways that may not be pleasant (dieting, exercise, etc.)? What are the spiritual parallels of such forms of self-discipline?

3. What is the connection between being chastened by God and experiencing joy? Can you give specific examples of this connection in your own life?

Scripture: Read Hebrews 13

"Keep your lives free from the love of money and be content with what you have, because God has said, 'Never will I leave you; never will I forsake you'" (Heb. 13:5).

CONTENTMENT THAT LASTS

A Christian couple was ministering to believers in Eastern Europe, behind the Iron Curtain. The couple had brought in Christian literature, blankets, and other necessary items. At the church gathering, the couple assured the believers that Christians in America were praying for believers in Eastern Europe.

"We are happy for that," one believer replied, "but we feel that Christians in America need more prayer than we do. We here in Eastern Europe are suffering, but you in America are very comfortable; and it is always harder to be a good Christian when you are comfortable."

The phrase "love of money" can be applied to a love for *more* of anything. Someone asked millionaire Bernard Baruch, "How much money does it take for a rich man to be satisfied?" Baruch replied, "Just a million more than he has." Covetousness is the desire for more, whether we need it or not.

Contentment cannot come from material things, for they can never satisfy the heart. Only God can do that. When we have God, we have all that we need. The material things of life can decay or be stolen, but God will never leave us or forsake us.

Applying God's Truth:

1. On a scale of 1 (least) to 10 (most), how content would you say you are with the things you have right now?

2. Are any signs of discontent evident in your life (such as worry, complaining, covetousness, etc.)? If so, how do you deal with them?

3. Create an antidote for discontent by completing this sentence: "The next time I begin to experience a sense of discontentment, I will remember that _____, and then I will _____."

PATIENCE

30 Daily Readings from the Book of Job

THE ONLY THING MANY OF US KNOW ABOUT PATIENCE IS HOW TO SPELL the word.

The Book of Job is the greatest book ever written on patience. Nobody in Bible history, except Jesus Christ, suffered more than Job, and because Job suffered, we can learn from him how to accept the tough experiences of life and profit from them. As you listen to Job's debates with his friends, and then hear the penetrating words of Jehovah, you can discover new depths of understanding about life and new facets of truth about yourself. Through it all, you can learn how to develop patience.

What life does *to* us depends on what life finds *in* us. The Book of Job challenges us to have faith in our hearts that the trials of life are appointments, not accidents, and that God does indeed work all things together for our good. When God puts us into the furnace, He keeps His eye on the clock and His hand on the thermostat, so we don't have to be afraid.

One more thing: whenever you ask God for patience, He usually sends trials. Be prepared. There are no shortcuts when it comes to building Christian character. But it's worth it to go through the furnace of suffering if, like Job, we can say "Though he slay me, yet will I hope in him!" (Job 13:15) When that's your testimony, you'll come out of the furnace as pure gold.

That's what happened to Job, and it can happen to us.

Scripture: Read James 5:11

"You have heard of Job's perseverance and have seen what the Lord finally brought about. The Lord is full compassion and mercy" (James 5:11).

READY TO SUFFER?

Many people have *heard* about Job and his trials, but not many people *understand* what those trials were all about and what God was trying to accomplish. Nor do they realize that Job suffered as he did so that God's people today might learn from his experiences how to be patient in suffering and endure to the end.

When I decided to write about Job, I said to my wife, "I wonder how much suffering we'll have to go through so I can write this book." Little did we realize the trials that God would permit us to experience! But we can testify that God is faithful, He answers prayer, and He always has a wonderful purpose in mind (Jer. 29:11).

You too may have to go through the furnace in order to study the Book of Job and really grasp its message. If so, don't be afraid! By faith, just say with Job, "He knows the way that I take; when he has tested me, I will come forth as gold" (Job 23:10). God fears no fire. Whatever we have that is burned up and left behind in the furnace wasn't worth having anyway.

As we study the Book of Job together, I trust that two things will be accomplished in your life: you will learn to be patient in your own trials, and you will learn how to help others in their trials. Your world is filled with people who need encouragement, and God may be preparing you for just that ministry. Either way, I hope this book helps you.

Applying God's Truth:

1. What are some current situations you are facing that are causing you to suffer?

2. On a scale of 1 (least) to 10 (most), how severely would you say you have suffered in the past? What events have caused the most intense suffering?

3. What do you hope to discover as you go through the Book of Job?

Scripture: Read Job 1:1-5

"In the land of Uz there lived a man whose name was Job. This man was blameless and upright; he feared God and shunned evil" *(Job 1:1).*

GRITTY INTEGRITY

Lord Byron was on target when he wrote: "Truth is always strange; stranger than fiction."

The Book of Job is not religious fiction. Job was a real person, not an imaginary character; both Ezekiel (14:14, 20) and James (5:11) attest to that. Because he was a real man who had real experiences, he can tell us what we need to know about life and its problems in this real world.

Job was "blameless and upright." He was not sinless, for nobody can claim that distinction; but he was complete and mature in character and "straight" in conduct. The word translated "blameless" is related to "integrity," another important word throughout the Book of Job. People with integrity are whole persons, without hypocrisy or duplicity. In the face of his friends' accusations and God's silence, Job maintained his integrity; and the Lord ultimately vindicated him.

The foundation for Job's character was the fact that he "feared God and shunned evil." To fear the Lord means to respect who He is, what He says, and what He does. It is not the cringing fear of a slave before a master but the loving reverence of a child before a father, a respect that leads to obedience. "The remarkable thing about fearing God," said Oswald Chambers, "is that when you fear God you fear nothing else, whereas if you do not fear God you fear everything else."

Applying God's Truth:

1. What things would you need to do before other people considered you blameless?

2. Can you think of a recent situation where you considered compromising your integrity? If not, can you think of any situation where you *might*?

3. Would you say that you fear God? Explain.

Scripture: Read Job 1:6-19

"Yet another messenger came and said, 'Your sons and daughters were feasting . . . when suddenly a mighty wind swept in from the desert and struck the four corners of the house. It collapsed on them and they are dead'" (Job 1:18-19).

FIRST, THE BAD NEWS

In one day, Job was stripped of his wealth. One after another, four frightened messengers reported that 500 yoke of oxen, 500 donkeys, and 3,000 camels were stolen in enemy raids; 7,000 sheep were struck by lightning and killed; and all ten of his children were killed in a windstorm.

Job knew *what* had happened, but he did not know *why* it had happened, and that is the crux of the matter. Because the author allows us to visit the throne room of heaven and hear God and Satan speak, we know who caused the destruction, and why he was allowed to cause it. But if we did not have this insight, we would probably take the same approach as Job's friends and blame Job for the tragedy.

Several important truths emerge from this scene, not the least of which is that *God is sovereign in all things*. He is on the throne of heaven, the angels do His will and report to Him, and even Satan can do nothing to God's people without God's permission. "The Almighty" is one of the key names for God in Job; it is used thirty-one times. From the outset, the writer reminds us that, no matter what happens in this world and in our lives, God is on the throne and has everything under control. We may not know until we get to heaven why God allowed certain things to happen. Meanwhile, we walk by faith and say with Job, "May the name of the Lord be praised" (v. 21).

Applying God's Truth:

1. If the devastating events of Job's life happened to you today, what do you think you would do? Be specific.

2. How would these events make you feel about God? (Be truthful.)

3. When you get to heaven, what is one thing you would like to ask God about?

Scripture: Read Job 1:20-22

"The Lord gave and the Lord has taken away; may the name of the Lord be praised" (Job 1:21).

WORST OF TIMES, WORSHIP TIMES

The hosts of heaven and of hell watched to see how Job would respond to the loss of his wealth and his children. He expressed his grief in a manner normal for that day, for God expects us to be human (1 Thes. 4:13). After all, even Jesus wept (John 11:35). But then Job worshiped God and uttered a profound statement of faith.

First, he looked back to his birth: "Naked I came from my mother's womb." Everything Job owned was given to him by God, and the same God who gave it had the right to take it away. Job simply acknowledged that he was a steward.

Then Job looked ahead to his death: "and naked I will depart." He would not return to his mother's womb, because that would be impossible. He would go to "Mother Earth," be buried, and turn to dust. Nothing that he acquired between his birth and death would go with him into the next world.

Finally, Job looked up and uttered a magnificent statement of faith: "The Lord gave and the Lord has taken away; may the name of the Lord be praised." Instead of cursing God, as Satan said Job would do, Job blessed the Lord! Anybody can say, "The Lord gave" or "The Lord has taken away"; but it takes real faith to say in the midst of sorrow and suffering, "May the name of the Lord be praised."

Applying God's Truth:

1. Do you think Job's worship during his great tragedy suggests that he was in denial of his situation? Explain.

2. Do you think Job's actions were appropriate? Why?

3. What are some less effective responses to tragedy that people use today?

Scripture: Read Job 2–3

"When Job's three friends . . . heard about all the troubles that had come upon him, they set out from their homes and met together by agreement to go and sympathize with him and comfort him" (Job 2:11).

THREE HEADS ARE NO BETTER THAN ONE

You will be spending a good deal of time with Job's three friends, so you had better get acquainted with them.

All three of the men were old (32:6), older than Job (15:10), but we assume that *Eliphaz* was the oldest. He is named first (2:11), he spoke first, and the Lord seems to have accepted him as the elder member of the trio (42:7). Eliphaz put great faith in tradition (15:18-19), and the God he worshiped was an inflexible lawgiver. He had a rigid theology that left little or no room for the grace of God.

Bildad must have been the second oldest of the three since he is named second and spoke after Eliphaz. In a word, Bildad was a *legalist*. For some reason, Bildad was sure that Job's children died because they also were sinners (8:4). The man seemed to have no feeling for his hurting friend.

Zophar was the youngest of the three and surely the most dogmatic. He speaks like a schoolmaster addressing a group of ignorant freshmen. "Know this!" is his unfeeling approach. He is merciless and tells Job that God was giving him far less than he deserved for his sins! (11:6) Interestingly enough, Zophar speaks to Job only twice. Either he decided he was unable to answer Job's arguments or felt that it was a waste of time trying to help Job.

All three men said some good and true things, as well as some foolish things; but they were of no help to Job because their viewpoint was too narrow. These men perfectly illustrate Dorothy Sayers' statement, "There's nothing you can't prove if your outlook is only sufficiently limited."

Applying God's Truth:

1. When you have serious problems, what three friends do you most trust for advice?

2. Do you have "friends" like Job's, who offer advice with little if any sensitivity? How do you respond to their advice?

3. What can *you* learn about being a friend from Eliphaz, Bildad, and Zophar?

Scripture: Read Job 4–5

"Then Eliphaz the Temanite replied: 'If someone ventures a word with you, will you be impatient? But who can keep from speaking?'" (Job 4:1-2)

A WORD FROM THE UNWISE

Job's three friends were silent for seven days (2:13), and Job later wished they had stayed that way (13:5). Then Eliphaz the Temanite answered Job. But what did he answer? The pain in Job's heart? No, he answered the words from Job's lips, *and this was a mistake*. A wise counselor and comforter must listen with the heart and respond to feelings as well as to words. You do not heal a broken heart with logic; you heal a broken heart with love. Yes, you must speak the truth, but be sure to speak the truth in love (Eph. 4:15).

Eliphaz's approach seems to start out positive enough, even gentle, but it was only honey to prepare Job for the bitterness that would follow. "Don't get upset, Job!" is what he was saying. "In the past your words have been a help to many people, and we want our words to be a help to you."

Never underestimate the power of words to encourage people in the battles of life. James Moffat translates Job 4:4, "Your words have kept men on their feet." The right words, spoken at the right time, and with the right motive, can make a tremendous difference in the lives of others. Your words can nourish those who are weak and encourage those who are defeated. But your words can also hurt those who are broken and only add to their burdens, so be careful what you say and how you say it.

Applying God's Truth:

1. What do you suppose Job's friends were thinking during their seven days of silence?

2. Can you think of a recent time when you responded to someone's *words* rather than his or her *feelings*? How might you have improved your response?

3. When was a time that you felt you had the right words, at the right time, and with the right motive—and helped or comforted someone a great deal?

Scripture: Read Job 6–8

"Then Bildad the Shuhite replied: 'How long will you say such things? Your words are a blustering wind'" (Job 8:1-2).

DEFENDING JUSTICE, FORGETTING LOVE

Your words are a blustering wind." Can you imagine a counselor saying that to a suffering individual who wanted to die? Bildad did; in fact, he used the same approach in his next speech (18:2). Job had poured out his grief and was waiting to hear a sympathetic word, but his friend said that Job's speech was just so much hot air.

There is a reason for Bildad's approach: he was so concerned about defending the justice of God that he forgot the needs of his friend. While Bildad's theology was correct—God *is* just—his application of that theology was wrong. Bildad was looking at only one aspect of God's nature—His holiness and justice—and had forgotten His love, mercy, and goodness. Yes, "God is light" (1 John 1:5); but don't forget that "God is love" (4:8, 16). His love is a holy love, and His holiness is exercised in love, even when He judges sin.

How are these two attributes of God reconciled? At the cross. When Jesus died for the sins of the world, the righteousness of God was vindicated, for sin was judged; but the love of God was demonstrated, for a Savior was provided. At Calvary, God is both "just and the one who justifies" (Rom. 3:24-26). God's law said, "The soul who sins is the one who will die" (Ezek. 18:4, 20); and God obeyed His own law in the sacrificing of His Son on the cross. In Christ's resurrection, the grace of God triumphed over sin and death, and all who repent of their sins and trust Jesus Christ will be saved.

Applying God's Truth:

1. What problems might people expect who focus too much on God's justice without considering His great love?

2. What problems might people expect who concentrate on God's love while excluding His holy justice?

3. What steps can you take to ensure that you maintain a sense of God's love *and* justice as you advise and console others?

Scripture: Read Job 9–10

"Though I were innocent, I could not answer him; I could only plead with my Judge for mercy" (Job 9:15).

AN OFFERING OF SUFFERING

In Job 9 and 10, Job asks three questions: (1) "How can I be righteous before God?" (9:1-13) (2) "How can I meet God in court?" (vv. 14-35) and (3) "Why was I born?" (10:1-22; see v. 18) You can see how these questions connect. Job is righteous, but he has to prove it. How can a mortal man prove himself righteous before God? Can he take God to court? But if God doesn't step in and testify on Job's behalf, what is the purpose of all this suffering? Why was Job even born?

Job could not understand what God was doing, *and it was important that he not understand.* Had Job known that God was using him as a weapon to defeat Satan, he could have simply sat back and waited trustfully for the battle to end. But as Job surveyed himself and his situation, he asked the same question the disciples asked when Mary anointed the Lord Jesus: "Why this waste?" (Mark 14:4) Before we criticize Job too severely, let's recall how many times we have asked that question ourselves when a baby has died or a promising young person was killed in an accident.

Nothing that is given to Christ in faith and love is ever wasted. The fragrance of Mary's ointment faded from the scene centuries ago, but the significance of her worship has blessed Christians in every age and continues to do so. Job was bankrupt and sick, and all he could give to the Lord was his suffering by faith; *but that is just what God wanted in order to silence the devil.*

Applying God's Truth:

1. What top three questions about life and God are *you* currently struggling with?

2. Can you think of an event in the past when you couldn't understand what God was doing (or why), but later were able to see His plan clearly?

3. Mary offered ointment. Job offered suffering. Can you think of something equally unusual or unique to offer God?

Scripture: Read Job 11

"If you put away the sin that is in your hand and allow no evil to dwell in your tent, then you will lift up your face without shame; you will stand firm and without fear" *(Job 11:14-15).*

ZOPHAR, SO GOOD?

Z ophar makes three accusations against Job: Job is guilty of sin (vv. 1-4); Job is ignorant of God (vv. 5-12); and Job is stubborn in his refusal to repent (vv. 13-20). "There is hope!" is Zophar's encouraging word to Job, and he described what Job could experience. But if Job wanted these blessings, he had to get them on Zophar's terms. Yes, there was hope, but it was hope with a condition attached to us: Job must repent and confess his sins (vv. 13-14). *Zophar is tempting Job to bargain with God so he can get out of his troubles.* This is exactly what Satan wanted Job to do!

"Does Job fear God for nothing?" Satan asked (1:9). Satan accused Job of having a "commercial faith" that promised prosperity in return for obedience. If Job had followed Zophar's advice, he would have played right into the hands of the enemy.

Job did not have a "commercial faith" that made bargains with God. He had a confident faith that said, "Though he slay me, yet will I hope in him" (13:15). That doesn't sound like a man looking for an easy way out of difficulties. "Job did not understand the Lord's reasons," said Charles Spurgeon, "but he continued to confide in His goodness." That is faith!

Applying God's Truth:

1. What have people recently accused you of? How did each accusation make you feel?

2. In what ways do people today attempt to bargain with God?

3. How would you feel in Job's place after hearing the accusations and advice of Zophar?

Scripture: Read Job 12–14

"Though he slay me, yet will I hope in him; I will surely defend my ways to his face" (Job 13:15).

APPEALING TO A HIGHER COURT

Job 13:13-17 is one of the greatest declarations of faith found anywhere in Scripture, but it must be understood in its context. Job is saying, "I will take my case directly to God and prove my integrity. I know I am taking my life in my hands in approaching God, because He is able to slay me. But if He doesn't slay me, it is proof that I am not the hypocrite you say I am." Later, Job will take an oath and challenge God to pass judgment (Job 27). To approach God personally was a great act of faith, but Job was so sure of his integrity that he would take his chances. After all, if he did nothing, he would die; and if he was rejected by God, he would die; but there was always the possibility that God would prove him right.

Why does Job want to meet God in court? So that God can once and for all state His "case" against Job and let Job know the sins in his life that have caused him to suffer so much. "Why should God pay so much attention to me?" asks Job. "He treats me like an enemy, but I'm just a weak leaf in the wind, a piece of chaff that is worth nothing. I'm a piece of rotting wood and a moth-eaten garment, yet God treats me like a prisoner of war and watches me every minute" (13:24-28). Job felt the time had come to settle the matter, even if it meant losing his own life in the process.

Applying God's Truth:

1. What do you think about Job's desire to meet God "in court"?

2. Have you ever felt so righteous and innocent that you would invite God to check you out personally? Explain.

3. What do you think motivated Job's actions: Desperation? Confidence? Or something else?

Scripture: Read Job 15

"All his days the wicked man suffers torment, the ruthless through all the years stored up for him" (Job 15:20).

You Get What You Deserve?

In his first speech, Eliphaz had described the blessings of the godly man (5:17-26); but now he describes the sufferings of the ungodly man. The problem with Eliphaz's statement about the judgment of the wicked is that *it is not always true in this life.* Many wicked people go through life apparently happy and successful, while many godly people experience suffering and seeming failure. It is true that *ultimately* the wicked suffer and the godly are blessed but, meanwhile, it often looks like the situation is reversed (Ps. 73; Jer. 12:1-4). Furthermore, God gives sunshine to the evil and the good and sends rain on the just and the unjust (Matt. 5:45). He is long-suffering toward sinners (2 Peter 3:9) and waits for His goodness to lead them to repentance (Rom. 2:4; Luke 15:17-19).

The greatest judgment God could send to the wicked in this life would be to *let them have their own way.* "They have their reward" (Matt. 6:2, 5, 16). The only heaven the godless will know is the enjoyment they have on earth in this life, and God is willing for them to have it. The only suffering the godly will experience is in this life, for in heaven there will be no pain or tears. Furthermore, the suffering that God's people experience now is working *for* them and will one day lead to glory (1 Peter 1:6-8; 5:10; 2 Cor. 4:16-18; Rom. 8:18). Eliphaz and his friends had the situation all confused.

Applying God's Truth:

1. Do you ever agree with Eliphaz's opinion, expressed in today's key verse? Why?

2. How many cases can you think of where a righteous person you know is experiencing major suffering? How about wicked people who seem to prosper?

3. The next time *you* suffer unfairly, what might you remember to help you endure the situation?

Scripture: Read Job 16–17

"If the only home I hope for is the grave . . . where then is my hope?" (Job 17:13, 15)

NOTHING LEFT TO LIVE FOR

Job's friends were against him and would not go to court and "post bond" for him (vv. 3-5). People treated Job as if he were the scum of the earth (v. 6). His body was only the shadow of what it had been (v. 7), and all of his plans had been shattered (v. 11). His friends would not change their minds and come to his defense (v. 10). In fact, they would not face his situation honestly, but they kept telling him that the light would soon dawn for him (v. 12). Is it any wonder that Job saw in death the only way of escape?

God did not answer Job's plea for death because He had something far better planned for him. God looked beyond Job's depression and bitterness and saw that he still had faith. When I was a young pastor, I heard an experienced saint say, "I have lived long enough to be thankful for unanswered prayer." At the time, I was shocked by the statement, but now that I have lived a few more years myself, I know what she was talking about. In the darkness of despair and the prison of pain, we often say things that we later regret, *but God understands all about it and lovingly turns a deaf ear to our words but a tender eye to our wounds.*

Applying God's Truth:

1. Have you ever felt that you had little if anything to live for? If so, what were the circumstances? If not, what's the worst you've ever felt (emotionally)?

2. How might Job's friends have affected his outlook in a more positive way?

3. Can you think of an unanswered prayer in your past that you're thankful for?

Scripture: Read Job 18

"The lamp of the wicked is snuffed out; the flame of his fire stops burning" (Job 18:5).

FEAR AS A MOTIVATOR

In Bildad's second speech, his weapon was *fear*. If the three friends could not reason with Job, or shame Job into repenting, perhaps they could frighten Job by describing what happens when wicked people die. However, Bildad made two mistakes when he gave this speech about the horrors of death. To begin with, he preached it to the wrong man, for Job was already a believer (1:1, 8). Second, he preached it with the wrong motive, for there was no love in his heart. Dr. R.W. Dale, the British preacher, once asked evangelist D.L. Moody if he ever used "the element of terror" in his preaching. Moody replied that he usually preached one sermon on heaven and one on hell in each of his campaigns, but that a "man's heart ought to be very tender" when preaching about the doom of the lost. Bildad did not have a very tender heart.

Though Bildad was talking to the wrong man and with the wrong motive, what he said about death should be taken seriously. Death is an enemy to be feared by all who are not prepared to die (1 Cor. 15:26), and the only way to be prepared is to trust Jesus Christ (John 5:24).

For the Christian believer, death means going home to the Father in heaven (John 14:1-6), falling asleep on earth and waking up in heaven (Acts 7:60; Phil. 1:21-23), entering into rest (Rev. 14:13), and moving into greater light (Prov. 4:18). None of the pictures Bildad used (Job 18:5-21) should be applied to those who have trusted the Lord for salvation.

Applying God's Truth:

1. Has anyone ever tried to use fear as a motivator to attempt to scare you into being a better person or better Christian? How well did the appeal work?

2. What are some other "motivators" people use with the wrong motives?

3. Think of your own recent interactions with friends and family members. Can you think of any instances where you have tried to influence others with improper motives or tactics?

Scripture: Read Job 19:1-20

"He has blocked my way so I cannot pass; he has shrouded my paths in darkness" (Job 19:8).

DARKNESS ON A DEAD-END STREET

Job saw himself as a traveler fenced in. Satan had complained that God had "walled in" Job and his family so that they were protected from trouble (1:9-12). Now Job is complaining because God has blocked his path, and he cannot move. Job could not see what lay ahead because God had shrouded the way with darkness.

At times God permits His children to experience darkness on a dead-end street where they don't know which way to turn. When this happens, *wait for the Lord to give you light in His own time.* Don't try to manufacture your own light or to borrow light from others.

Dr. Bob Jones, Sr. used to say, "Never doubt in the darkness what God has taught you in the light." In fact, what God teaches us in the light will become even more meaningful in the darkness.

"Oh, the unspeakable benediction of the 'treasures of darkness'!" wrote Oswald Chambers. "It is not the days of sunshine and splendor and liberty and light that leave their lasting and indelible effect upon the soul, but those nights of the Spirit in which, shadowed by God's hand, hidden in the dark cleft of some rock in a weary land, He lets the splendors of the outskirts of Himself pass before our gaze."

Applying God's Truth:

1. How do you tend to react when God chooses not to reveal what lies ahead for you?

2. On a scale of 1 (least) to 10 (most), how strong is your faith "in the darkness"? How could it be stronger?

3. What are some things you discover about God during difficult times that you might not otherwise notice?

Scripture: Read Job 19:21-29

"I know that my Redeemer lives, and that in the end he will stand upon the earth" (Job 19:25).

CARVED IN STONE

Why, in today's reading, did Job want his words to be recorded permanently? He thought he was going to die before God would vindicate him, and he wanted people to remember how he suffered and what he said. Bildad warned him, "The memory of [a wicked man] perishes from the earth" (18:17), and Job wanted his record to remain.

At this point, Job uttered another of his statements of faith that in this book punctuate his many expressions of grief and pain. It is significant that Job would go from the depths of despair to the heights of faith, and then back into the depths again. *This is often the normal experience of people experiencing great suffering.*

In spite of what some preachers say, very few people can maintain a constant high level of faith and courage in times of severe pain and trial. John Henry Jowett, at one time known as "the greatest preacher in the English-speaking world," wrote to a friend: "I wish you wouldn't think I am such a saint. You seem to imagine that I have no ups and downs, but just a level and lofty stretch of spiritual attainment with unbroken joy and equanimity. By no means! I am often perfectly wretched, and everything appears most murky" (*John Henry Jowett*, by Arthur Porrit, p. 290).

Job expressed confidence that, even if he died, he would still have a Redeemer who one day would exercise judgment on the earth. Furthermore, Job affirmed that he himself expected to live again and see his Redeemer! It was an affirmation of faith in the resurrection of the human body.

Applying God's Truth:

1. What things do you believe to be true about God so strongly that they could be recorded permanently—"carved in stone," so to speak?

2. Are you as open about the "lows" of your spiritual life as you are the "highs"? Do you think you *should* be?

3. What are the benefits of having the confidence that you have a living Redeemer?

Scripture: Read Job 20:1–21:6

"Listen carefully to my words; let this be the consolation you give me" (Job 21:2).

NOW EAR THIS

Listen to Job's appeal to his friends that they try to understand how he feels. "If you really want to console me, just keep quiet and listen" (v. 2, paraphrase). The Greek philosopher Zeno said, "The reason why we have two ears and only one mouth is that we may listen the more and talk the less." The friends thought their words would encourage Job, but he said that their silence would encourage him even more (13:13).

Job pointed out that his complaint was not against men but against God. Men had not caused his afflictions, and men could not take them away. If he was impatient, it was because God had not answered him (21:3). The longer God waited, the worse Job's situation became. "Look at me and be astonished; clap your hand over your mouth" (v. 5).

As Job contemplated what he was about to say, it stirred him to the depths (v. 6). This was no speech from "off the top of his head," for it had to do with the basic facts of life and death. If Job's friends were in his situation, they would see things differently and *say* things differently.

Applying God's Truth:

1. Can you think of someone to whom you could minister simply by *listening* to him or her?

2. Job's friends were trying to be helpful. Why don't you think Job appreciated their words?

3. How can you remember to show more empathy the next time you're in a position to advise or console someone?

Scripture: Read Job 21:7-34

"Their prosperity is not in their own hands, so I stand aloof from the counsel of the wicked" (Job 21:16).

LIFESTYLE ENVY

The saddest thing about the wicked is the way they leave God out of their lives and still prosper (vv. 14-15). The wicked take credit for their wealth, but Job acknowledged that everything comes from God (1:21). How, then, can Job's three friends classify him with the wicked?

We must face the disturbing fact that too many professed Christians actually admire and envy the lifestyle of the rich and famous. In one of his books, Dr. Kenneth Chafin tells about a pastor and deacon who were visiting prospects and stopped at a beautiful suburban home. The lawn looked like it was manicured, and two expensive cars sat in the driveway. Furthermore, the pastor and deacon could see the man of the house comfortably seated in his spacious living room, watching television. Everything about the place reeked of affluence. The deacon turned to his pastor and asked, "What kind of good news do we have for this fellow?"

In over forty years of ministry, I have performed many weddings and watched many young Christian couples get started in their homes. What a joy it has been to see homes where couples set the right priorities and resist the temptation to "follow the crowd" and live for material possessions. Unfortunately, some have lost their spiritual vision and succeeded in this world—without acknowledging the Lord. Alas, they have their reward.

Applying God's Truth:

1. Does anything ever cause you to be jealous of others? (Bigger homes? Better cars? Etc.)

2. How do you deal with twinges of jealousy when they come?

3. How do you think God feels when His people succumb to jealousy of others' material possessions?

Scripture: Read Job 22

"Is it for your piety that he rebukes you and brings charges against you? Is not your wickedness great? Are not your sins endless?" (Job 22:4-5)

THE SLANDERERS OF UZ

What should have been an encouraging discussion among friends had become an angry and painful debate. Instead of trying to calm things down, Eliphaz assumed the office of prosecuting attorney and turned the debate into a trial. It was three against one as Job sat on the ash heap and listened to his friends lie about him. According to the Jewish Talmud, "The slanderous tongue kills three: the slandered, the slanderer, and him who listens to the slander." At the ash heap in Uz, it was death all around!

Eliphaz first accused Job of the sin of pride (vv. 1-3). Job was acting as though his character and conduct were important to God and beneficial to Him in some way. Eliphaz's theology centered around a distant God who was the judge of the world but not the friend of sinners.

But Job's character and conduct *were* important to God, for *God was using Job to silence the devil*. Neither Job nor his three friends knew God's hidden plan, but Job had faith to believe that God was achieving some purpose in his life and would one day vindicate him. Furthermore, the character and behavior of God's people *are* important to the Lord because His people bring Him either joy or sorrow (1 Thes. 4:1; Heb. 11:5; Gen. 6:5-6; Ps. 37:23). He is not a passive, distant God who does not identify with His people, but the God who delights in them as they delight in Him (Ps. 18:19; Isa. 63:9; Heb. 4:14-16).

Applying God's Truth:

1. How do you tend to react when people make false accusations against you?

2. How do you handle those times when you *know* you're right, but are outnumbered by people who disagree with you?

3. Can you think of how any unpleasant circumstances you're currently facing might be part of God's "hidden plan"?

Scripture: Read Job 23–24

"He knows the way that I take; when he has tested me, I will come forth as gold" *(Job 23:10).*

THE GREATER THE HEAT, THE PURER THE GOLD

God knew where Job was—in the furnace! But it was a furnace of God's appointment, not because of Job's sin, and God would use Job's affliction to purify him and make him a better man. This is not the only answer to the question, "Why do the righteous suffer?" but it is one of the best, and it can bring the sufferer great encouragement.

Scripture often uses the image of a furnace to describe God's purifying ministry through suffering (Isa. 48:10; Deut 4:20; Ps. 66:10). The image is also used in 1 Peter 1:6-7 and 4:12 of believers going through persecution.

When God puts His own people into the furnace, He keeps His eye on the clock and His hand on the thermostat. He knows how long and how much. We may question why He does it to begin with, or why He doesn't turn down the heat or even turn it off, but our questions are only evidences of unbelief. Job 23:10 is the answer: "He knows the way that I take; when he has tested me, I will come forth as gold." *Gold does not fear the fire.* The furnace can only make the gold purer and brighter.

Applying God's Truth:

1. Before today's reading, what would you have said if a friend asked, "Why do you think good people are allowed to suffer?"

2. Do you try to avoid the heat of "God's furnace," or do you allow hard times to purify you? Give some examples.

3. Do you trust God *completely* to protect you during your "furnace experiences"? Why or why not?

Scripture: Read Job 25–26

"These are but the outer fringe of his works; how faint the whisper we hear of him! Who then can understand the thunder of his power?" (Job 26:14)

ON THE FRINGE

Bildad's speech in Job 25 is the shortest in the book and focuses on God's power (vv. 1-3) and justice (vv. 4-6). It is disturbing to see how Job's friends speak so knowingly about God when, in the end, God revealed that they really didn't know what they were talking about. Too often, those who say the most about God know the least about God.

Job first rebuked Bildad for giving him no help (26:1-4). Then Job extolled the greatness of God (vv. 5-13). The three friends must have listened impatiently because they already knew the things Job was talking about, *but they hadn't drawn the right conclusion from them.* Because they saw God's handiwork in nature, they thought they knew all about God, and therefore they could explain God to Job.

Job said that just the opposite was true (v. 14). What we see of God in creation is but the fringes of His ways, and what we hear is but a whisper of His power! Knowing a few facts about the creation of God is not the same as knowing truths about the God of Creation.

The fourteenth-century British spiritual writer Richard Rolle said, "He truly knows God perfectly that finds Him incomprehensible and unable to be known." The more we learn about God, the more we discover how much more there is to know! Beware of people who claim to know all about God, for their claim is proof they know neither God nor themselves.

Applying God's Truth:

1. How do you respond to people who claim to speak for God, yet obviously don't reflect His love or knowledge?

2. Think of everything you *do* know about God. What percentage of His fullness do you think your knowledge would comprise?

3. What are some things you could do to: (1) know God more completely, and (2) better represent Him to others?

Scripture: Read Job 27–28

"The fear of the Lord—that is wisdom, and to shun evil is understanding" (Job 28:28).

THE BEGINNING OF WISDOM

The first step toward true wisdom is a reverent and respectful attitude toward God, which also involves a humble attitude toward ourselves. Personal pride is the greatest barrier to spiritual wisdom. "When pride comes, then comes disgrace, but with humility comes wisdom" (Prov. 11:2).

The next step is to ask God for wisdom (James 1:5) and make diligent use of the means He gives us for securing His wisdom, especially knowing and doing the Word of God (Matt. 7:21-29). It is not enough merely to study; we must also obey what God tells us to do (John 7:17). As we walk by faith, we discover the wisdom of God in the everyday things of life. Spiritual wisdom is not abstract; it is very personal and very practical.

As we fellowship with other believers in the church and share with one another, we can learn wisdom. Reading the best books can also help us grow in wisdom and understanding. The important thing is that we focus on Christ, for He is our wisdom (1 Cor. 1:24) and in Him is hidden "all the treasures of wisdom and knowledge" (Col. 2:3). The better we know Christ and the more we become like Him, the more we will walk in wisdom and understand the will of the Lord. We must allow the Holy Spirit to open the eyes of our heart so we can see God in His Word and understand more of the riches we have in Christ (Eph. 1:15-23).

Applying God's Truth:

1. In what ways is personal pride a potential barrier for your own accumulation of spiritual wisdom?

2. What are some *specific* situations for which you need to ask God for additional wisdom?

3. Can you think of any good *human* resources to help provide wisdom for the situations you've listed?

Scripture: Read Job 29

"How I long for the months gone by, for the days when God watched over me" (Job 29:2).

GONE BUT NOT FORGOTTEN

J ob had opened his defense by saying that he wished he had never been born (Job 3). Now he closed his defense by remembering the blessings he and his family had enjoyed prior to his crisis. This is a good reminder that we should try to see life in a balanced way. Yes, God permits us to experience difficulties and sorrows, but God also sends victories and joys. "Shall we accept good from God, and not trouble?" (2:10) Charles Spurgeon said that too many people write their blessings in the sand but engrave their sorrows in marble.

"How I long for the months gone by, for the days when God watched over me!" When we are experiencing trials, it's natural for us to long for "the good old days"; but our longing will not change our situation. Someone has defined "the good old days" as "a combination of a bad memory and a good imagination." In Job's case, however, his memory was accurate, and "the good old days" really were good.

There is a ministry in memory if we use it properly. In days of disappointment, it's good to "remember the deeds of the Lord . . . remember your miracles of long ago" (Ps. 77:11). But the past must be a rudder to guide us and not an anchor to hold us back. If we try to duplicate today what we experienced yesterday, we may find ourselves in a rut that robs us of maturity.

Applying God's Truth:

1. Have you ever wished you had never been born? If yes, what caused your feelings?

2. What are some potential drawbacks to being nostalgic and thinking about "the good old days"?

3. How can your memory be a "ministry" to you or someone else?

Scripture: Read Job 30

"In his great power God becomes like clothing to me; he binds me like the neck of my garment. He throws me into the mud, and I am reduced to dust and ashes" (Job 30:18-19).

MUD WRESTLING WITH GOD

Job experienced sufferings similar to those of our Lord Jesus Christ. In the daytime, Job endured unbearable suffering; and at night, God wrestled with him, made his clothing like a straitjacket, and threw him in the mud. Every night, God wrestled with Job; and Job lost.

Job prayed to God. He even stood up and cried out for deliverance, but his prayers were unanswered (v. 20). Instead of God's hand bringing help, it only attacked Job ruthlessly and tossed him about like a feather in a storm (vv. 21-22). Job begged for his life, but death seemed inevitable (1:23).

Job had faithfully helped others in their need (29:12-17), but now nobody would help him. They wouldn't weep with him or even touch him. He was treated like a leper who might contaminate them, or like a condemned man whom God might destroy at any time. It just wasn't wise to get too close.

Where were the people that Job had helped? Surely some of them would have wanted to show their appreciation by encouraging their benefactor in his time of need. But nobody came to his aid. Mark Twain wrote, "If you pick up a starving dog and make him prosperous, he will not bite you. This is the principal difference between a dog and a man." But according to missionary doctor Wilfred Grenfell, "The service we render for others is really the rent we pay for our room on this earth."

Applying God's Truth:

1. Has it ever seemed that God must have some kind of personal grudge against you?

2. After you help others, but they neglect to help you in return, how is your attitude toward service affected? (Do you allow the negligence of others to affect *your* ministry?)

3. Are you as honest about your feelings toward God as Job is in 30:18-23? Why or why not?

Scripture: Read Job 31–32:1

"So these three men stopped answering Job, because he was righteous in his own eyes" *(Job 32:1)*.

ELI-WHO?

J ob was silent. He had ended his defense and given oath that he was not guilty of the sins he had been accused of by his friends. Job had challenged God either to vindicate him or pass sentence on him.

Job's three friends were silent, appalled that Job had dared to speak so boldly *to* God and *about* God.

God was silent. No fire came from heaven, and no voice spoke in divine wrath. The silence was God's eloquent witness to the three friends that they were wrong in what they had said both about Job and about God.

However, in the crowd around the ash heap, one person was not silent. It was Elihu, a man so unknown that his full pedigree had to be given so people could identify him (v. 2). While Elihu said some of the same things as the other speakers, his purpose was different from theirs. He was not trying to prove that Job was a sinner, but that Job's view of God was wrong. Elihu introduced a new truth into the debate: that God sends suffering, not necessarily to punish us for our sins, but to keep us from sinning (33:18, 24) and to make us better persons (36:1-15). Paul would have agreed with the first point (2 Cor. 12:7-10) and the writer of Hebrews with the second (Heb. 12:1-11).

Applying God's Truth:

1. After Job had debated his three friends and poured his heart out to God, how do you think he felt when he heard silence rather than answers?

2. How would you have felt in his place to discover that yet another person had opinions to offer—and that he was just getting started?

3. Even though Elihu was making valid observations, do you think Job was taking them to heart? Why or why not?

Scripture: Read Job 32:2–33

"But Elihu . . . became very angry with Job for justifying himself rather than God" (*Job 32:2*).

SOUNDS AND SILENCE

Four times we are told that Elihu was angry. He was angry at the three friends for not refuting Job, and he was angry at Job for justifying himself rather than God. Job claimed that God was wrong, and the three friends couldn't prove that Job was wrong! Bildad, Zophar, and Eliphaz had given up the cause (v. 15) and were waiting for God to come and deal personally with Job (vv. 12-13). Elihu was disgusted at their failure.

"It is easy to fly into a passion—anybody can do that," wrote Aristotle. "But to be angry with the right person to the right extent and at the right time and with the right object and in the right way—that is not easy, and it is not everyone who can do it."

Elihu promised Job that God would radically alter his situation if only he would humble himself. It would be like a new birth! (33:25) He would once more enjoy prayer and fellowship with God (v. 26). He could confess his sins and admit that God had punished him far less than he deserved (v. 27). Job would move out of the darkness into the light and gladly bear witness of God's redemption (v. 28).

Verses 31-33 suggest that Elihu wanted Job's response, but at the same time Elihu wanted Job to keep quiet! Elihu was filled to the brim with his subject and didn't want to stop talking. But Job didn't reply because he was waiting for God to speak. Job had already stated his case and thrown down the gauntlet. What Elihu thought about him or said to him made little difference to Job.

Job had taken his case to a much higher court, and when Elihu finishes speaking, the Judge will appear.

Applying God's Truth:

1. Do you think anger ever affects your ministry to others? In what specific ways?

2. When was the last time you felt you were angry "with the right person to the right extent and at the right time and with the right object and in the right way"?

3. Is it easy for you to ignore someone who is very angry? What do you think Job's lack of response to Elihu indicated about his mind-set?

Scripture: Read Job 34–35

"Listen to me, you men of understanding. Far be it from God to do evil, from the Almighty to do wrong" (Job 34:10).

DEFENDING GOD

Theology ("the science of God") used to be called "the queen of sciences" because it deals with the most important knowledge we can have, the knowledge of God. Theology is a necessary science, but it is also a difficult science; for it is our attempt to know the Unknowable (Rom. 11:33-36). God has revealed Himself in creation, in providence, in His Word, and supremely in His Son; but our understanding of what God has revealed may not always be clear.

"The essence of idolatry," wrote A.W. Tozer, "is the entertainment of thoughts about God that are unworthy of Him" (*The Knowledge of the Holy*, Harper and Row, p. 11). So, whoever attempts to explain and defend the Almighty must have the humble heart of a worshiper; for "knowledge puffs up, but love builds up" (1 Cor. 8:1).

As you read Elihu's speeches, you get the impression that he was not growing; he was swelling. You also get the impression that his listeners' minds were wandering, because he kept exhorting them to listen carefully (Job 33:1, 31, 33; 34:2, 10, 16).

Yet Elihu emphasized that God is sovereign and the Book of Job magnifies the sovereignty of God. From the very first chapter, it is obvious that God is in control; for even Satan is told what he can and cannot do. During the debate, it appears that God is absent, but He is aware of how Job feels and what Job and his friends say. Elihu was right on target: God is sovereign and cannot do wrong.

Applying God's Truth:

1. What are some questions of theology that have come up in your interactions with skeptics or people of other faiths?

2. Do you know religious people who are "all theory and no practicality"? How might people avoid such a problem?

3 Even though Elihu was "right on target," do you think Job benefited from his words? Why or why not?

Scripture: Read Job 36–37

"How great is God—beyond our understanding! The number of his years is past finding out" (Job 36:26).

A HELPFUL, BUT OVERLOOKED, MINISTRY

Elihu urged Job to catch a new vision of the greatness of God and start praising Him (vv. 22-25). God wants to teach us through our sufferings (v. 22), and one evidence that we are learning our lessons is that we praise and thank Him, even for trials. "Glorify Him for His mighty works for which He is so famous" (v. 24, TLB). "Praise changes things" just as much as "prayer changes things."

With all his verbosity and lack of humility, Elihu did say some good things that Job needed to hear. Elihu's use of rhetorical questions in 37:14-18 prepared Job for the series of questions Jehovah would ask him in Job 38–41. Unlike the three friends, Elihu assessed Job's problem accurately: Job's *actions* may have been right—he was not the sinner his three friends described him to be—but his *attitudes* were wrong. He was not the "saint" Job saw himself to be. Job was slowly moving toward a defiant, self-righteous attitude that was not at all healthy. It was this "know-it-all" attitude that God exposed and destroyed when He appeared to Job and questioned him.

So, even though God said nothing about Elihu, the man did have a helpful ministry to Job. Unfortunately, Job wouldn't accept it.

Applying God's Truth:

1. What are some things you will *always* be able to praise God for—even when everything seems to be going wrong?

2. Can you think of anyone who has been trying—sincerely—to minister to you in some way, only to have you ignore his or her efforts? What can you do to begin to show appreciation?

3. What are some good actions you've performed lately where your attitudes weren't quite as good as they should have been?

Scripture: Read Job 38–41

"Then the Lord answered Job out of the storm" (Job 38:1).

GOD RESPONDS

We prefer that God speak to us in the sunshine, but sometimes He must speak out of the storm. Experiencing this majestic demonstration of God's power made Job very susceptible to the message God had for him. God's address to Job centered on His works in nature and consisted of seventy-seven questions interspersed with divine commentary relating to the question. The whole purpose of this interrogation was to make Job realize his own inadequacy and inability to meet God as an equal and defend his cause.

"Summon me, and I will answer," Job had challenged God, "or let me speak, and you reply" (Job 13:22). God had now responded to Job's challenge.

Job was sure that his speeches had been filled with wisdom and knowledge, but God's first question put an end to that delusion: "Who is this that darkens my counsel with words without knowledge?" (Job 38:2) *The Living Bible* paraphrases it, "Why are you using your ignorance to deny my providence?" God didn't question Job's integrity or sincerity; He only questioned Job's ability to explain the ways of God in the world. Job had spoken the truth about God (42:7), but his speeches had lacked humility. Job thought he knew about God, but he didn't realize how much he *didn't* know about God. Knowledge of our own ignorance is the first step toward true wisdom.

Applying God's Truth:

1. When was the last time God "spoke" to you through His nature or creation?

2. Job and his friends had debated God's will for a long time. How do you suppose they felt when God eventually began to speak for Himself?

3. If "knowledge of our own ignorance is the first step toward true wisdom," have you taken a giant step, a medium step, or a baby step? Explain.

Scripture: Read Job 42:1-6

"Then Job replied to the Lord: 'I know that you can do all things. . . . Therefore I despise myself and repent in dust and ashes" (Job 42:1-2, 6).

FROM SINNER TO SERVANT

Job knew he was beaten. There was no way he could argue his case with God. Quoting God's very words (vv. 3-4), Job humbled himself before the Lord and acknowledged His power and justice in executing His plans (v. 2). Then Job admitted that his words had been wrong and that he had spoken about things he didn't understand (v. 3). Job withdrew his accusations that God was unjust and not treating him fairly. He realized that whatever God does is right and man must accept it by faith.

Job told God, "I can't answer Your questions! All I can do is confess my pride, humble myself, and repent." Until now, Job's knowledge of God had been indirect and impersonal, but that was changed. Job had met God personally and seen himself to be but "dust and ashes."

"The door of repentance opens into the hall of joy," said Charles Spurgeon, and it was true for Job. In the climax of the book, Job the sinner became Job the servant of God. How did Job serve God? By enduring suffering and not cursing God, and thereby silencing the devil! Suffering in the will of God is a ministry that God gives to a chosen few.

Applying God's Truth:

1. When you realize you are wrong about something, how quick are you to repent?

2. In terms of percentages, how much of your own transformation from sinner to servant of God do you think is complete?

3. Do you know anyone for whom you think suffering is a "ministry"? What can you do to encourage such people?

Scripture: Read Job 42:7-16

"After Job had prayed for his friends, the Lord made him prosperous again and gave him twice as much as he had before" (Job 42:10).

GOD AS AUTHOR

Job ended up with twice as much as he had before. He had twenty children, ten with God and ten in his home. (He and his wife were also reunited.) Friends and relatives brought money for a "restoration fund," which Job must have used for purchasing breeders, and eventually, Job had twice as much livestock as before. He was once again a wealthy man.

But we must not misinterpret this final chapter and conclude that every trial will end with all problems solved, all hard feelings forgiven, and everybody "living happily ever after." It just doesn't always happen that way! This chapter assures us that, no matter what happens to us, *God always writes the last chapter*. Therefore, we don't have to be afraid. We can trust God to do what is right, no matter how painful our situation might be.

But Job's greatest blessing was not the regaining of his health and wealth or the rebuilding of his family and circle of friends. His greatest blessing was *knowing God better and understanding His working in a deeper way*. "In the whole story of Job," wrote G. Campbell Morgan, "we see the patience of God and endurance of man. When these act in fellowship, the issue is certain. It is that of the coming forth from the fire as gold, that of receiving the crown of life" (*The Answers of Jesus to Job*, Baker, p. 117).

No matter what God permits to come into our lives, He always has His "afterward." He writes the last chapter—and that makes it worth it all.

Applying God's Truth:

1. Would you say that Job's story had a happy ending? Why or why not?

2. Do you think you can learn to know God better without going through the depth of suffering that Job experienced? Explain.

3. Think back to the things you were suffering with as you began reading through Job. How, if at all, has your perspective changed in regard to your problems?

WISDOM

30 Daily Readings from the Book of 1 Corinthians

W E LIVE IN THE MIDST OF A "KNOWLEDGE EXPLOSION" SO INCREDIBLE that even the experts can't keep up with all the developments in their fields. More and more, people are having to specialize, and the specialists have to depend on each other.

Knowledge abounds, but wisdom languishes. Wisdom is the right use of knowledge. Knowledge has to do with *facts*, but wisdom thrives on *truths*. Knowledge prepares you to make a living, but wisdom enables you to make a life. Our world is rich in knowledge and poor in wisdom, and, tragically enough, the world doesn't know where wisdom is found.

According to the Apostle Paul, true wisdom is found in Jesus Christ. When Paul wrote the letter we call 1 Corinthians, he wrote it for a group of Christians who were trying to mix Christian wisdom and pagan philosophy, the "wisdom of God" and the "wisdom of this world." Paul showed them how foolish they were in this attempt.

Paul explains in this letter what true wisdom is, how to get it, and how to use it to the glory of God and the building up of His church. If you want to "be wise," there's a price to pay, *but the price to pay for being foolish is even greater*!

First Corinthians is a letter about real people with real problems, a letter that magnifies Jesus Christ, the cross, and the wisdom of God in Christ. It's a letter we all need to study today.

So, don't just get smart. Be wise.

Scripture: Read 1 Corinthians 1:1-3

"To the church of God in Corinth and to those sanctified in Christ Jesus and called to be holy, together with all those everywhere who call on the name of our Lord Jesus Christ" (1 Cor. 1:2).

PROBLEMS IN THE CHURCH

Jesus, yes! The church, no!" Remember when that slogan was popular among young people in the '60s? They certainly could have used it with sincerity in Corinth back in A.D. 56, because the local church there was in serious trouble. Sad to say, the problems did not stay within the church family; they were known by the unbelievers outside the church.

To begin with, the church at Corinth was a *defiled* church. Some of its members were guilty of sexual immorality; others got drunk; still others were using the grace of God to excuse worldly living. It was also a *divided* church, with at least four different groups competing for leadership (v. 12). This meant it was a *disgraced* church. Instead of glorifying God, it was hindering the progress of the Gospel.

How did this happen? The members of the church permitted the sins of the city to get into the local assembly. Corinth was a polluted city, filled with every kind of vice and worldly pleasure. It was also a proud, philosophical city, with many itinerant teachers promoting their speculations.

Any time you have proud people, depending on human wisdom, adopting the lifestyle of the world, you are going to have problems.

Applying God's Truth:

1. In what ways is your church like the church at Corinth? How is it different?

2. How is your church influenced by the problems of the city where it is located?

3. What, personally, do you hope to accomplish by reading through the Book of 1 Corinthians?

Scripture: Read 1 Corinthians 1:4-17

"I appeal to you, brothers, in the name of our Lord Jesus Christ, that all of you agree with one another so that there may be no divisions among you and that you may be perfectly united in mind and thought" (1 Cor. 1:10).

DIVIDED LOYALTIES

A Christian photographer friend told me about a lovely wedding that he "covered." The bride and groom came out of the church, heading for the limousine, when the bride suddenly left her husband and ran to a car parked across the street! The motor was running and a man was at the wheel, and off they drove, leaving the bridegroom speechless. The driver of the "get-away car" turned out to be an old boyfriend of the bride, a man who had boasted that "he could get her any time he wanted her." Needless to say, the husband had the marriage annulled.

When a man and woman pledge their love to each other, they are set apart for each other; and any other relationship outside of marriage is sinful. Just so, the Christian belongs completely to Jesus Christ; he is set apart for Him and Him alone. But he is also a part of a worldwide fellowship, the church, "all those everywhere who call on the name of our Lord Jesus Christ" (v. 2). A defiled and unfaithful believer not only sins against the Lord, but he also sins against his fellow Christians.

Applying God's Truth:

1. Can you identify any ways that your church has deserted Jesus to pursue worldly interests?

2. On a personal level, are there any activities you need to give up in order to follow Jesus more completely?

3. How can the sin of one person affect the church as a whole?

Scripture: Read 1 Corinthians 1:18-31

"God chose the foolish things of the world to shame the wise; God chose the weak things of the world to shame the strong" (1 Cor. 1:27).

LOW AND MIGHTY

God chose the foolish, the weak, the lowly, and the despised to show the proud world their need and His grace. The lost world admires birth, social status, financial success, power, and recognition. But none of these things can guarantee eternal life.

The message and miracle of God's grace in Jesus Christ utterly puts to shame the high and mighty people of this world. The wise of this world cannot understand how God changes sinners into saints, and the mighty of this world are helpless to duplicate the miracle. God's "foolishness" confounds the wise; God's "weakness" confounds the mighty!

The annals of church history are filled with the accounts of great sinners whose lives were transformed by the power of the Gospel. In my own ministry, as in the ministry of most pastors and preachers, I have seen amazing things take place that the lawyers and psychologists could not understand. We have seen delinquent teenagers become successful students and useful citizens. We have seen marriages restored and homes reclaimed, much to the amazement of the courts.

And why does God reveal the foolishness and the weakness of this present world system, even with its philosophy and religion? "So that no one may boast before him" (v. 29). Salvation must be wholly of grace; otherwise, God cannot get the glory.

Applying God's Truth:

1. Can you think of a recent lesson you've learned from someone most people would consider foolish, weak, or lowly?

2. What is an amazing act of God you've witnessed lately that "confounds" those who are wise and/or powerful?

3. Are you content with being perceived by others as foolish and weak? Explain.

Scripture: Read 1 Corinthians 2:1-5

"I resolved to know nothing while I was with you except Jesus Christ and him crucified" (1 Cor. 2:2).

MIXED MESSAGES

My wife was at the wheel of our car as we drove to Chicago, and I was in the copilot's seat reading the page proofs of another author's book that a publisher had asked me to review. Occasionally I would utter a grunt, and then a groan, and finally I shook my head and said, "Oh, no! I can't believe it!"

"I take it you don't like the book," she said. "Something wrong with it?"

"You bet there is!" I replied. "Just about everything is wrong with it, because this man does not know what the message of the Gospel really is!"

There was a time, however, when that author had been faithful to the Gospel. But over the years, he had begun to take a philosophical (and, I fear, political) approach to the Gospel. The result was a hybrid message that was no Gospel at all.

It is worth noting that when Paul ministered in Corinth, he obeyed our Lord's commission and preached the Gospel. What had happened at Corinth is happening in churches today: men are mixing philosophy (man's wisdom) with God's revealed message, and this is causing confusion and division. Different preachers have their own "approach" to God's message, and some even invent their own vocabulary! Paul urged his readers to return to the fundamentals of the Gospel message.

Applying God's Truth:

1. In what ways do some people try to combine ungodly philosophies with the truth of the Gospel?

2. In what ways do some people try to combine a political agenda with the truth of the Gospel?

3. How can you stay focused on "Jesus Christ and Him crucified" without getting bogged down in politics and philosophy?

Scripture: Read 1 Corinthians 2:6-10

" 'No eye has seen, no ear has heard, no mind has conceived what God has prepared for those who love him'—but God has revealed it to us by his Spirit" (1 Cor. 2:9-10).

SALVATION: A UNITED EFFORT

Our salvation involves all three Persons in the Godhead. You cannot be saved apart from the Father's electing grace, the Son's loving sacrifice, and the Spirit's ministry of conviction and regeneration. It is not enough to say, "I believe in God." What God? Unless it is "the God and Father of our Lord Jesus Christ" (Eph. 1:3), there can be no salvation.

This Trinitarian aspect of our salvation helps us to understand better some of the mysteries of our salvation. Many people get confused (or frightened) when they hear about election and predestination. As far as the Father is concerned, I was saved when He chose me in Christ before the foundation of the world (Eph. 1:4); but I knew nothing about that the night I was saved! It was a hidden part of God's wonderful eternal plan.

As far as God the Son is concerned, I was saved when He died for me on the cross. He died for the sins of the whole world, yet the whole world is not saved. This is where the Spirit comes in: as far as the Spirit is concerned, I was saved on May 12, 1945 at a Youth for Christ rally where I heard Billy Graham (then a young evangelist) preach the Gospel. It was then that the Holy Spirit applied the Word to my heart, I believed, and God saved me.

Applying God's Truth:

1. In what ways did you observe the activity of each member of the Godhead in regard to your salvation?

2. What would you consider a "hidden part of God's wonderful plan" for your own life?

3. Why do you think God allows salvation to be such a "mystery" to us?

Scripture: Read 1 Corinthians 2:11-16

"This is what we speak, not in words taught us by human wisdom but in words taught by the Spirit, expressing spiritual truths in spiritual words" (1 Cor. 2:13).

SPEAKING THE LANGUAGE

Each of our four children has a different vocation. We have a pastor, a nurse, an electronics designer, and a secretary in a commercial real estate firm. Each of the children had to learn a specialized vocabulary in order to succeed. The only one I really understand is the pastor.

The successful Christian learns the vocabulary of the Spirit and makes use of it. He knows the meaning of justification, sanctification, adoption, propitiation, election, inspiration, and so forth. In understanding God's vocabulary, we come to understand God's Word and God's will for our lives. If the engineering student can grasp the technical terms of chemistry, physics, or electronics, why should it be difficult for Christians, taught by the Spirit, to grasp the vocabulary of Christian truth?

Yet I hear church members say, "Don't preach doctrine. Just give us heart-warming sermons that will encourage us!" Sermons based on what? If they are not based on doctrine, they will accomplish nothing! "But doctrine is so dull!" people complain. Not if it is presented the way the Bible presents it. Doctrine to me is exciting! What a thrill to be able to study the Bible and let the Spirit teach us "the deep things of God" (v. 10).

Applying God's Truth:

1. How would you define the Christian concept of justification? Sanctification? Adoption? Propitiation? Election? Inspiration?

2. If your understanding of Christian doctrine isn't what you want it to be, what are some of your better options to learn what you want to know?

3. As you learn "the vocabulary of the Spirit," do you foresee any potential problems with *using* Christian "lingo"? Explain.

DAY 7 / WISDOM

Scripture: Read 1 Corinthians 3:1-9

"I gave you milk, not solid food, for you were not yet ready for it. Indeed, you are still not ready. You are still worldly" (1 Cor. 3:2-3).

WATCH YOUR DIET

What are the marks of maturity? For one thing, you can tell the mature person by *his diet*. As I write this chapter, we are watching our grandson and our granddaughter grow up. Becky is still being nursed by her mother, but Jonathan now sits at the table and uses his little cup and (with varying degrees of success) his tableware. As children grow, they learn to eat different food. They graduate from milk to meat.

What is the difference? The usual answer is that "milk" represents the easy things in the Word, while "solid food" (or "meat") represents the hard doctrines. But I disagree with that traditional explanation, and my proof is Hebrews 5:10-14. That passage seems to teach that "milk" represents what Jesus Christ did on earth, while "solid food" concerns what He is doing now in heaven. The writer of Hebrews wanted to teach his readers about the present heavenly priesthood of Jesus Christ, but his readers were so immature, he could not do it.

It is not difficult to determine a believer's spiritual maturity, or immaturity, if you discover what kind of "diet" he enjoys. The immature believer knows little about the present ministry of Christ in heaven. He knows the *facts* about our Lord's life and ministry on earth, but not the *truths* about His present ministry in heaven. He lives on "Bible stories" and not Bible doctrines. He has no understanding of 1 Corinthians 2:6-7.

Applying God's Truth:

1. What food(s) would you say best represent(s) your current spiritual "diet"? Why?

2. If "milk" represents what Jesus did on earth and "meat" represents what He is doing now in heaven, which "food group" are you more familiar with? How can you get a better "balanced diet"?

3. Can you give a personal example about someone who knows spiritual "facts," but not necessarily "truths"?

Scripture: Read 1 Corinthians 3:10-23

"Do not deceive yourselves. If any one of you thinks he is wise by the standards of this age, he should become a 'fool' so that he may become wise" (1 Cor. 3:18).

SECRETS OF CHURCH SUCCESS

Young ministers often asked Dr. Campbell Morgan the secret of his pulpit success. Morgan replied, "I always say to them the same thing—work; hard work; and again, work!" Morgan was in his study at 6 o'clock each morning, digging treasures out of the Bible. You can find wood, hay, and straw (v. 12) in your backyard, and it will not take too much effort to pick it up. But if you want gold, silver, and jewels, *you have to dig for them.* Lazy preachers and Sunday School teachers will have much to answer for at the Judgment Seat of Christ—and so will preachers and teachers who *steal* materials from others instead of studying and making it their own.

It comes as a shock to some church members that you cannot manage a local church the same way you run a business. This does not mean we should not follow good business principles, but the operation is totally different. There is a wisdom of this world that works for the world, but it will not work for the church.

The world depends on promotion, prestige, and the influence of money and important people. The church depends on prayer, the power of the Spirit, humility, sacrifice, and service. The church that imitates the world may seem to succeed in time, but it will turn to ashes in eternity.

Applying God's Truth:

1. What would you say best describes the type of "building" you've been doing on the spiritual foundation that Jesus has laid: straw, hay, wood, precious stones, silver, or gold? Explain.

2. What successful business principles do you think would work for the church? Which ones won't?

3. In what ways do you try to help your church be the best it can be?

Scripture: Read 1 Corinthians 4:1-13

"It seems to me that God has put us apostles on display at the end of the procession, like men condemned to die in the arena. We have been made a spectacle to the whole universe, to angels as well as to men" (1 Cor. 4:9).

NO PLACE FOR PRIDE

There is no place for pride in the ministry. If a truly great leader like Paul considered himself "on display at the end of the procession," where does this leave the rest of us? Church members are wrong when they measure ministers other than by the standards God has given. They are also wrong when they boast about their favorite preachers. This is not to say that faithful servants cannot be recognized and honored, but in all things, God must be glorified (1 Thes. 5:12-13).

Paul was a fool according to the standards of men. Had he remained a Jewish rabbi, he could have attained great heights in the Jewish religion (Gal. 1:14). Or had he sided with the Jewish legalists in the Jerusalem church and not ministered to the Gentiles, he could have avoided a great deal of persecution (Acts 15; 21:17ff).

The Corinthians were wise in their own eyes, but they were actually fools in the sight of God. By depending on the wisdom and the standards of the world, they were acting like fools. The way to be spiritually wise is to become a fool in the eyes of the world (1 Cor. 3:18). I often find myself quoting those words of martyred Jim Elliot: "He is no fool who gives what he cannot keep to gain what he cannot lose."

Applying God's Truth:

1. What specific ways can you think of that pride has damaged the church as a whole? How about your local church?

2. Do you think congregation members help contribute to the pride of some preachers? How might this potential problem be kept to a minimum?

3. What are some things you "cannot keep"? What are the things you "cannot lose"?

Scripture: Read 1 Corinthians 4:14-21

"The kingdom of God is not a matter of talk but of power" (1 Cor. 4:20).

DISCIPLINE VERSUS DISOBEDIENCE

A child's will must be broken, but not destroyed. Until a colt is broken, it is dangerous and useless, but once it learns to obey, it becomes gentle and useful. Pride is a terrible thing in the Christian life and in the church. The yeast of sin (5:6-8) had made the Corinthians "puffed up," even to the point of saying, "Paul will not come to us! His bark is worse than his bite!" (See 2 Cor. 10:8-11.)

Paul had been patient with their disobedience, but now he warned them that the time had come for discipline. Paul was not like the tolerant modern mother who shouted at her spoiled son, "This is the last time I'm going to tell you for the last time!"

A faithful parent must discipline his children. It is not enough to teach them and be an example before them; he must also punish them when they rebel and refuse to obey. Paul would have preferred to come with meekness and deal with their sins in a gentle manner, but their own attitude made this difficult. They were puffed up—and even proud of their disobedience! (1 Cor. 5:1-2)

The contrast in this paragraph is between *speech* and *power*, words and deeds. The arrogant Corinthians had no problem "talking big," the way children often will do, but they could not back up their talk with their "walk." Their religion was only in words. Paul was prepared to back up his "talk" with power, with deeds that would reveal their sins and God's holiness.

Applying God's Truth:

1. At what point did you move from needing to be disciplined by others into taking responsibility for self-discipline?

2. How does lack of self-discipline among its members cause problems in *today's* church?

3. In what specific area(s) is it hardest to discipline yourself? How can you persevere even though it is difficult?

Scripture: Read 1 Corinthians 5

"It is actually reported that there is sexual immorality among you, and of a kind that does not occur even among pagans: A man has his father's wife. And you are proud!" (1 Cor. 5:1-2)

SHAPE UP OR SHIP OUT

The people at Corinth were puffed up. They were boasting of the fact that their church was so "open-minded" that even fornicators could be members in good standing! The sin in question was a form of incest: a professed Christian (and a member of the church) was living with his stepmother in a permanent alliance. Since Paul does not pass judgment on the woman (vv. 9-13), we assume that she was not a member of the assembly and probably not even a Christian. This kind of sin was condemned by the Old Testament Law as well as by the laws of the Gentile nations. Paul shamed the church by saying, "Even the unsaved Gentiles don't practice this kind of sin!"

While Christians are not to judge one another's motives or ministries, we are certainly expected to be honest about each other's conduct. In my own pastoral ministry, I have never enjoyed having to initiate church discipline, but since it is commanded in the Scriptures, we must obey God and set personal feelings aside.

Paul described here an official church meeting at which the offender was dealt with according to divine instructions. Public sin must be publicly judged and condemned. The sin was not to be "swept under the rug"; for, after all, it was known far and wide even among the unsaved who were outside the church.

Applying God's Truth:

1. If you had been a member of the assembly at Corinth, how do you think you would have been affected by the blatant sin within the church?

2. What issues in today's church might attract similar attention from the secular world?

3. Do you have guidelines to help determine whether to: (1) Dismiss a problem as a "weaker brother" issue; (2) Forgive the sin and ignore it; or (3) See it as a danger and confront the person? If not, do you *need* guidelines?

Scripture: Read 1 Corinthians 6:1-8

"The very fact that you have lawsuits among you means you have been completely defeated already. Why not rather be wronged? Why not rather be cheated?" (1 Cor. 6:7)

LOSS SUITS

The church at Corinth was rapidly losing its testimony in the city. Not only did the unsaved know about the immorality in the assembly, but they were also aware of the lawsuits involving members of the church. Not only were there sins of the flesh, but also sins of the spirit.

Paul detected three tragedies in this situation. First, *the believers were presenting a poor testimony to the lost.* Even the unbelieving Jews dealt with their civil cases in their own synagogue courts. To take the problems of Christians and discuss them before the "unjust" and "unbelievers" was to weaken the testimony of the Gospel.

Second, *the congregation had failed to live up to its full position in Christ.* Since the saints will one day participate in the judgment of the world and even of fallen angels, they ought to be able to settle their differences here on earth. The Corinthians boasted of their great spiritual gifts. Why, then, did they not use them in solving their problems?

There was a third tragedy: *the members suing each other had already lost.* Even if some of them won their cases, they had incurred a far greater loss in their disobedience to the Word of God. Better to lose money or possessions than to lose a brother and lose your testimony beside.

Applying God's Truth:

1. Do you think Paul's plea for Christians to avoid lawsuits between each other still applies? Why?

2. On a scale of 1 (least) to 10 (most), how much anger do you feel when someone takes advantage of you? How might the number eventually be lower?

3. Rather than secular lawsuits, what are some other options Christians today could pursue when they feel wronged by a fellow believer?

Scripture: Read 1 Corinthians 6:9-20

"Flee from sexual immorality. All other sins a man commits are outside his body, but he who sins sexually sins against his own body" (1 Cor. 6:18).

THE BEST SEX

There is certainly excitement and enjoyment in sexual experience outside of marriage, *but there is not enrichment.* Sex outside of marriage is like a man robbing a bank: he gets something, but it is not his and he will one day pay for it. Sex within marriage can be like a person putting money into a bank: there is safety, security, and he will collect dividends.

Paul referred to the creation account to explain the seriousness of sexual sin. When a man and woman join their bodies, *the entire personality is involved.* There is a much deeper experience, a "oneness" that brings with it deep and lasting consequences. Paul warned that sexual sin is the most serious sin a person can commit against his body, for it involves the whole person.

Paul did not suggest that being joined to a harlot was the equivalent of marriage, for marriage also involves *commitment.* When two people pledge their love and faithfulness to each other, they lay a strong foundation on which to build. Marriage protects sex and enables the couple, committed to each other, to grow in this wonderful experience.

In my pastoral counseling, I have had to help married couples whose relationship was falling apart because of the consequences of premarital sex, as well as extramarital sex. The harvest of sowing to the flesh is sometimes delayed, but it is certain (Gal. 6:7-8). How sad it is to live with the consequences of *forgiven* sin.

Applying God's Truth:

1. In what ways is sex *enriched* through marriage? Explain.

2. How is premarital or extramarital sex a sin "against one's own body"?

3. Can you think of some specific situations where sexual sin was forgiven, yet the person(s) involved still had to "live with the consequences"?

Scripture: Read 1 Corinthians 7:1-24

"The wife's body does not belong to her alone but also to her husband. In the same way, the husband's body does not belong to him alone but also to his wife" (1 Cor. 7:4).

A BETTER YIELD

As in all things, the spiritual must govern the physical; for our bodies are God's temples. The husband and wife may abstain from sex in order to devote their full interest to prayer and fasting (7:5), but they must not use this as an excuse for prolonged separation. Paul is encouraging Christian partners to be "in tune" with each other in matters both spiritual and physical.

Not only did the church ask about celibacy, but they also asked Paul about divorce. If divorce does occur, the parties should remain unmarried or seek reconciliation. It has been my experience as a pastor that when a husband and wife are yielded to the Lord, and when they seek to please each other in the marriage relationship, the marriage will be so satisfying that neither partner would think of looking elsewhere for fulfillment.

"There are no sex problems in marriage," a Christian counselor once told me, "only personality problems with sex as one of the symptoms." The present frightening trend of increased divorces among Christians (and even among the clergy) must break the heart of God.

Applying God's Truth:

1. For what reasons do you think married couples begin to withhold sex from each other? What are the potential consequences of doing so?

2. What signs do you detect in today's society that suggest husbands and wives aren't yielding to each other (and God) as they should?

3. What advice would you offer a Christian couple on the brink of divorce?

Scripture: Read 1 Corinthians 7:25-40

"A woman is bound to her husband as long as he lives. But if her husband dies, she is free to marry anyone she wishes, but he must belong to the Lord" (1 Cor. 7:39).

MAKING MARRIAGE LAST

It is God's will that the marriage union be permanent, a lifetime commitment. There is no place in Christian marriage for a "trial marriage," nor is there any room for the "escape-hatch attitude: "If the marriage doesn't work, we can always get a divorce."

For this reason, marriage must be built on something sturdier than good looks, money, romantic excitement, and social acceptance. There must be Christian commitment, character, and maturity. There must be a willingness to grow, to learn from each other, to forgive and forget, to minister to one another.

Paul closed the section by telling the widows that they were free to marry, but the man "must belong to the Lord" (v. 39). This means that they must not only marry believers, but marry in the will of God. Paul's counsel was that they remain single, but he left the decision to them.

God has put "walls" around marriage, not to make it a prison, but to make it a safe fortress. The person who considers marriage a prison should not get married. When two people are lovingly and joyfully committed to each other—and to their Lord—the experience of marriage is one of enrichment and enlargement. They grow together and discover the richness of serving the Lord as a "team" in their home and church.

Applying God's Truth:

1. Based on personal observations, what would you say are the most common reasons for divorce?

2. Now, thinking of the couples you know who have been together for a long time, what do you see as the "secrets" of a strong marriage?

3. In what ways do you feel people today take marriage (and remarriage) too lightly?

Scripture: Read 1 Corinthians 8

"We know that we all possess knowledge. Knowledge puffs up, but love builds up" *(1 Cor. 8:1).*

PUFFY "I"S AND "KNOW"S

L ove and knowledge must go together. It has well been said, "Knowledge without love is brutality, but love without knowledge is hypocrisy." Paul's great concern was that the strong saints help the weaker saints to grow and to stop being weak saints. Some people have the false notion that the *strong* Christians are the ones who live by rules and regulations and who get offended when others exercise their freedom in Christ, but such is not the case. It is the *weak* Christians who must have the security of law and who are afraid to use their freedom in Christ. It is the weak Christians who are prone to judge and criticize stronger believers and to stumble over what they do. This, of course, makes it difficult for the strong saints to minister to their weaker brothers and sisters.

It is here that love enters the picture, for "love builds up" and puts others first. When spiritual knowledge is used in love, the stronger Christian can take the hand of the weaker Christian and help him to stand and walk so as to enjoy his freedom in Christ. *You cannot force-feed immature believers and transform them into giants.* Knowledge must be mixed with love; otherwise, the saints will end up with "big heads" instead of enlarged hearts.

Applying God's Truth:

1. Do you know anyone who has "knowledge without love"? How about "love without knowledge"? How do you relate to such people?

2. How has someone used a combination of love and knowledge to make you a stronger Christian?

3. How are *you* using love and knowledge to help weaker Christians? Can you think of other people you know who could use some help?

Scripture: Read 1 Corinthians 9:1-18

"What then is my reward? Just this: that in preaching the gospel I may offer it free of charge, and so not make use of my rights in preaching it" (1 Cor. 9:18).

NOT IN IT FOR THE MONEY

It is unfortunate when the ministry of the Gospel is sometimes hindered by an overemphasis on money. The unsaved world is convinced that most preachers and missionaries are only involved in "religious rackets" to take money from innocent people. No doubt there are religious "racketeers" in the world today, people who "use" religion to exploit others and control them. We would certainly not agree with their purposes or their practices. We must make sure that nothing we do in our own ministry gives the impression that we are of their number.

A wrong attitude toward money has hindered the Gospel from the earliest days of the church. Simon the magician thought he could buy the gift of the Spirit with money (Acts 8:18-24). Ananias and Sapphira loved money more than they loved the truth, and God killed them (Acts 5).

For eighteen fruitful years, Dr. H.A. Ironside pastored Moody Church in Chicago. I recall the first time I heard him announce an offering. He said, "We ask God's people to give generously. If you are not a believer in Jesus Christ, we do not ask you to give. We have a gift for you—eternal life through faith in Christ!" He made it clear that the offering was for believers, lest the unsaved in the congregation stumble over money and then reject the Gospel.

Applying God's Truth:

1. What are some misperceptions about the church formed by people who witness "religious racketeers"?

2. Do you think money should *ever* be discussed publicly at church? To what extent?

3. How can money propel the cause of the Gospel? How can it become a hindrance?

Scripture: Read 1 Corinthians 9:19-27

"Run in such a way as to get the prize. Everyone who competes in the games goes into strict training. They do it to get a crown that will not last; but we do it to get a crown that will last forever" (1 Cor. 9:24-25).

RUN FOR YOUR (SPIRITUAL) LIFE

An athlete must be disciplined if he is to win the prize. Discipline means giving up the good and the better for the best. The athlete must watch his diet as well as his hours. He must smile and say "No, thank you" when people offer him fattening desserts or invite him to late-night parties. There is nothing wrong with food or fun, but if they interfere with your highest goals, then they are hindrances and not helps.

The Christian does not run the race in order to get to heaven. He is in the race because he has been saved through faith in Jesus Christ. Only Greek citizens were allowed to participate in the games, and they had to obey the rules both in their training and in their performing. Any contestant found breaking the training rules was automatically disqualified. The famous Indian athlete, Jim Thorpe, had to return his Olympic gold medals because the committee discovered he had previously played on a professional team.

In order to give up his rights and have the joy of winning lost souls, Paul had to discipline himself. That is the emphasis of 1 Corinthians 9: Authority (rights) must be balanced by discipline. If we want to serve the Lord and win His reward and approval, we must pay the price.

Applying God's Truth:

1. In what ways has your spiritual life been like a race so far?

2. What do you expect to "win" when you get to the "finish line"?

3. Though "discipline" is often used in a negative context, how is it a positive attribute in sports and spiritual development?

Scripture: Read 1 Corinthians 10

" *'Everything is permissible'—but not everything is beneficial. 'Everything is permissible'—but not everything is constructive. Nobody should seek his own good, but the good of others"* (1 Cor. 10:23-24).

INCONSISTENTLY CONSISTENT

Paul probably appeared inconsistent to those who did not understand his principles of Christian living. At times, he would eat what the Gentiles were eating. At other times, he would eat only "kosher" food with the Jews. But instead of being inconsistent, he was actually living *consistently* by the principles he laid down in these chapters of 1 Corinthians.

A weather vane seems inconsistent, first pointing in one direction and then in another. But a weather vane is always consistent: it always points toward the direction where the wind is blowing. That is what makes it useful.

As Christians we *do* have freedom. This freedom was purchased for us by Jesus Christ, so it is very precious. Freedom comes from knowledge: "You will know the truth, and the truth will set you free" (John 8:32). However, knowledge must be balanced by love; otherwise, it will tear down instead of build up.

The way we use our freedom and relate to others indicates whether we are mature in Christ. Strong and weak Christians need to work together in love to edify one another and glorify Jesus Christ.

Applying God's Truth:

1. Can you think of ways that obedience to God's commands may have made you appear inconsistent to other people from time to time?

2. Do you find it more comfortable to have hard and fast rules for behavior, or the freedom to be somewhat inconsistent? Explain.

3. In what ways can Christian freedom be misused if we aren't careful?

Scripture: Read 1 Corinthians 11:1-16

"I want you to realize that the head of every man is Christ, and the head of the woman is man, and the head of Christ is God" (1 Cor. 11:3).

ORDER IN THE CHURCH

E astern society at this time was very jealous over its women. Except for the temple prostitutes, the women wore long hair and, in public, wore a covering over their heads. (Paul did not use the word *veil*, i.e., a covering over the face. The woman put her regular shawl over her head, and this covering symbolized her submission and purity.) For the Christian women in the church to appear in public without the covering, let alone to pray and share the Word, was both daring and blasphemous.

Paul sought to restore order by reminding the Corinthians that God had made a difference between men and women, that each had a proper place in God's economy. There were also appropriate customs that symbolized these relationships and reminded both men and women of their correct places in the divine scheme. Paul did not say, or even hint, that *difference* meant *inequality* or *inferiority*. If there is to be peace in the church, then there must be some kind of order; and order of necessity involves rank. However, *rank* and *quality* are two different things. The captain has a higher rank than the private, but the private may be a better man.

Applying God's Truth:

1. What are some of the expectations for the men and women in your church that help ensure order?

2. Considering that the worship service is only an hour or so out of a week, do you think it's wrong to submit your personal feelings to achieve order? Explain.

3. If someone feels inferior or unequal at church, what are his or her options?

Scripture: Read 1 Corinthians 11:17-34

"A man ought to examine himself before he eats of the bread and drinks of the cup" (*1 Cor. 11:28*).

WHOSE SUPPER IS THIS, ANYWAY?

Since the beginning of the church, it was customary for the believers to eat together. It was an opportunity for fellowship and for sharing with those who were less privileged. No doubt they climaxed this meal by observing the Lord's Supper.

The "agape feast" (from the Greek word for *love*) was part of the worship at Corinth, but some serious abuses had crept in. For one thing, there were various cliques in the church and people ate with their own "crowd" instead of fellowshipping with the whole church family.

Another fault was selfishness: the rich people brought a great deal of food for themselves while the poorer members went hungry. And some of the members were even getting drunk.

Of course, the divisions at the dinner were but evidence of the deeper problems in the church. The Corinthians thought they were advanced believers, when in reality they were but little children. Paul did not suggest that they abandon the feast, but rather that they restore its proper meaning. The "agape feast" should have been an opportunity for edification, but they were using it as a time for embarrassment.

Applying God's Truth:

1. Do you recognize any of these early church problems (or similar ones) in your own church "fellowships"?

2. What would you suggest to make your church meetings more edifying for all people involved?

3. How might your "regular" meetings bring more glory to God?

Scripture: Read 1 Corinthians 12

"If one part [of the body] suffers, every part suffers with it; if one part is honored, every part rejoices with it" *(1 Cor. 12:26).*

BODY BUILDING

Diversity in the body is an evidence of the wisdom of God. Each member needs the other members, and no member can afford to become independent. When a part of the human body becomes independent, you have a serious problem that could lead to sickness and even death. In a healthy human body, the various members cooperate with each other and even compensate for each other when a crisis occurs. The instant any part of the body says to any other part, "I don't need you!" it begins to weaken and die and create problems for the whole body.

A famous preacher was speaking at a ministers' meeting, and he took time before and after the meeting to shake hands with the pastors and chat with them. A friend asked him, "Why take time for a group of men you may never see again?" The world-renowned preacher smiled and said, "Well, I may be where I am because of them! Anyway, if I didn't need them on the way up, I might need them on the way down!" No Christian servant can say to any other servant, "My ministry can get along without you!"

Applying God's Truth:

1. In terms of a human body, what "part" would you say you are in the church? Why?

2. What is a recent situation where you suffered because someone else did? When have you rejoiced because someone else was joyful?

3. Who are some people you've been trying to "get along without" whom you might ought to start to work *with* instead?

Scripture: Read 1 Corinthians 13

"If I give all I possess to the poor and surrender my body to the flames, but have not love, I gain nothing" (1 Cor. 13:3).

NOT ENOUGH LOVE?

It was Jonathan Swift, the satirical author of *Gulliver's Travels*, who said, "We have just enough religion to make us hate, but not enough to make us love one another." Spiritual gifts, no matter how exciting and wonderful, are useless and even destructive if they are not ministered in love. In all three of the "body" passages in Paul's letters, there is an emphasis on love. The main evidence of maturity in the Christian life is a growing love for God and for God's people, as well as a love for lost souls. It has well been said that love is the "circulatory system" of the body of Christ.

Few chapters in the Bible have suffered more misinterpretation and misapplication than 1 Corinthians 13. Divorced from its context, it becomes "a hymn to love" or a sentimental sermon on Christian brotherhood. Many people fail to see that Paul was still dealing with the Corinthians' problems when he wrote these words: the abuse of the gift of tongues, division in the church, envy of others' gifts, selfishness (remember the lawsuits?), impatience with one another in the public meetings, and behavior that was disgracing the Lord.

The only way spiritual gifts can be used creatively is when Christians are motivated by love.

Applying God's Truth:

1. Can you think of people who try to use spiritual gifts without being loving as well? What do you think of their ministries?

2. Do you think love is sweet and natural, or difficult and rare? Explain.

3. Of all of your current relationships and situations, where would you say love is *most* needed?

Scripture: Read 1 Corinthians 14:1-25

"Follow the way of love and eagerly desire spiritual gifts" (1 Cor. 14:1).

DO YOU UNDERSTAND?

A ministry that does not build up will tear down, no matter how "spiritual" it may seem. When we explain and apply the Word of God to individual lives, we have a ministry of edification. In this section, Paul repeatedly shows concern for *understanding*. It is not enough for the minister to impart information to people; the people must *receive* it if it is to do them any good. The seed that is received in the good ground is the seed that bears fruit, but this means that there must be an *understanding* of the Word of God (Matt. 13:23). If a believer wants to be edified, he must prepare his heart to receive the Word (1 Thes. 2:13). Not everybody who *listens* really *hears*.

The famous Congregationalist minister, Dr. Joseph Parker, preached at an important meeting and afterward was approached by a man who criticized a minor point in the sermon. Parker listened patiently to the man's criticism, and then asked, "And what *else* did you get from the message?" This remark simply withered the critic, who then disappeared into the crowd. Too often we are quick to judge the sermon instead of allowing the Word of God to judge us.

Applying God's Truth:

1. In what ways have people "built you up" this week? What opportunities did they miss?

2. When have you recently been guilty of listening without hearing?

3. What are three things you can do to try to be a more understanding person from now on? Specifically, how can you better understand people who don't agree with you on the issue of speaking in tongues?

Scripture: Read 1 Corinthians 14:26-35

"God is not a God of disorder but of peace" (1 Cor. 14:33).

GROUP CONSIDERATION

We must use the Word of God to test every message that we hear, asking the Spirit to guide us. There are false teachers in the world and we must beware. But even true teachers and preachers do not know everything and sometimes make mistakes. Each listener must evaluate the message and apply it to his own heart.

Our public meetings are more formal than those of the early church, so it is not likely that we need to worry about the order of the service. But in our more informal meetings, we need to consider one another and maintain order. I recall being in a testimony meeting where a woman took forty minutes telling a boring experience and, as a result, destroyed the spirit of the meeting.

Evangelist D.L. Moody was leading a service and asked a man to pray. Taking advantage of his opportunity, the man prayed on and on. Sensing that the prayer was killing the meeting instead of blessing it, Moody spoke up and said, "While our brother finishes his prayer, let us sing a hymn!" Those who are in charge of public meetings need to have discernment—and courage.

Applying God's Truth:

1. If you were a professional church consultant, what objective suggestions would you give your pastor for how to improve your church worship services?

2. Do people at your church tend to abuse the privilege of participating in public worship? Do you think they should be tolerated or confronted? Why?

3. In what ways do you think your church leaders need to have clearer discernment? Additional courage?

Scripture: Read 1 Corinthians 14:36-40

"Everything should be done in a fitting and orderly way" (1 Cor. 14:40).

A TONGUES SUMMARY

It might be helpful to summarize what Paul wrote about the gift of tongues. It is the God-given ability to speak in a known language with which the speaker was not previously acquainted. The purpose was not to win the lost, but to edify the saved. Not every believer had this gift, nor was this gift an evidence of spirituality or the result of a "baptism of the Spirit."

Only three persons were permitted to speak in tongues in one meeting, and they had to do so in order and with interpretation. If there was no interpreter, they had to keep silent. Prophecy is the superior gift, but tongues were not to be despised if they were exercised according to Scripture.

When the foundational work of the apostles and prophets ended, it would seem that the gifts of knowledge, prophecy, and tongues would no longer be needed. "Where there are tongues, they will be stilled" (13:8). Certainly God could give this gift today if He pleased, but I am not prepared to believe that every instance of tongues is divinely energized. Nor would I go so far as to say that all instances of tongues are either satanic or self-induced.

It is unfortunate when believers make tongues a test of fellowship or spirituality. That in itself would alert me that the Spirit would not be at work. Let's keep our priorities straight and major on winning the lost and building the church.

Applying God's Truth:

1. Do you have any questions about the gift of tongues? If so, where can you go to find answers?

2. What do you think 1 Corinthians 13:8 means: "Where there are tongues, they will be stilled"?

3. Why do you think Paul gave so many instructions regarding the proper procedures for speaking in tongues?

Scripture: Read 1 Corinthians 15:1-28

"[Jesus] appeared to James, then to all the apostles, and last of all he appeared to me also, as to one abnormally born. For I am the least of the apostles and do not even deserve to be called an apostle" (1 Cor. 15:7-9).

PAUL'S WITNESS

One of the greatest witnesses of the Resurrection was Paul himself, for as an unbeliever he was soundly convinced that Jesus was dead. The radical change in his life—a change which brought him persecution and suffering—is certainly evidence that the Lord had indeed been raised from the dead. Paul made it clear that his salvation was purely an act of God's grace, but that grace worked in and through him as he served the Lord.

At this point, Paul's readers would say, "Yes, we agree that *Jesus* was raised from the dead." Then Paul would reply, "If you believe that, then you must believe in the resurrection of *all* the dead!" Christ came as a man, truly human, and experienced all that we experienced, except that He never sinned. If there is no resurrection, then Christ was not raised. If He was not raised, there is no Gospel to preach. If there is no Gospel, then you have believed in vain and you are still in your sins! If there is no resurrection, then believers who have died have no hope. We shall never see them again!

The conclusion is obvious: Why be a Christian if we have only suffering in this life and no future glory to anticipate? (In vv. 29-34, Paul expanded this idea.) The resurrection is not just important; it is "of first importance" (v. 3), because all that we believe hinges upon it.

Applying God's Truth:

1. Is the resurrection of the dead "of first importance" to you? Give an example.

2. What would you tell a friend who asked, "How do you think you're going to be different after your resurrection?"

3. Can people look at the changes you've made in your life and see God's grace? Why or why not?

Scripture: Read 1 Corinthians 15:29-58

"Thanks be to God! He gives us the victory through our Lord Jesus Christ" *(1 Cor. 15:57)*.

VICTORY: NOW AND LATER

The heavenly kingdom is not made for the kind of bodies we now have, bodies of flesh and blood. So when Jesus returns, the bodies of living believers will instantly be transformed to be like His body (1 John 3:1-3), and the dead believers shall be raised with new glorified bodies. Our new bodies will not be subject to decay or death.

Sigmund Freud, the founder of psychiatry, wrote: "And finally there is the painful riddle of death, for which no remedy at all has yet been found, nor probably ever will be." Christians have victory *in* death and *over* death! Why? Because of the victory of Jesus Christ in His own resurrection. Jesus said: "Because I live, you also will live" (John 14:19).

We share the victory *today*. The literal translation of 1 Corinthians 15:57 is, "But thanks be to God *who keeps on giving us the victory* through our Lord Jesus Christ." We experience "the power of his resurrection" (Phil. 3:10). First Corinthians 15:58 is Paul's hymn of praise to the Lord as well as his closing admonition to the church. Because of the assurance of Christ's victory over death, we know that nothing we do for Him will ever be wasted or lost. We can be steadfast in our service, unmovable in suffering, abounding in ministry to others, because we know our labor is not in vain.

Applying God's Truth:

1. What are your fears and concerns about death?

2. In what ways has Jesus provided victory in regard to the things you just listed?

3. In what other areas do you need to experience victory? What steps do you need to take toward more complete victory in your spiritual struggles?

Scripture: Read 1 Corinthians 16:1-9

"On the first day of every week, each one of you should set aside a sum of money in keeping with his income, saving it up, so that when I come no collections will have to be made" (1 Cor. 16:2).

DOCTRINE AND DUTY

It is unfortunate when Christian ministries lose their testimony because they mismanage funds entrusted to them. Every ministry ought to be businesslike in its financial affairs. Paul was very careful not to allow anything to happen that would give his enemies opportunity to accuse him of stealing funds (2 Cor. 8:20-21).

This explains why Paul encouraged the *churches* to share in the offering and to select dependable representatives to help manage it. Paul was not against *individuals* giving personally; in this chapter he named various individuals who assisted him personally. This no doubt included helping him with his financial needs. But generally speaking, Christian giving is church-centered. Many churches encourage their members to give designated gifts through the church treasury.

It is interesting that Paul mentioned the offering just after his discussion about the resurrection. There were no "chapter breaks" in the original manuscripts, so the readers would go right from Paul's hymn of victory into his discussion about money. Doctrine and duty go together; so do worship and works. Our giving is "not in vain" because our Lord is alive. It is His resurrection power that motivates us to give and to serve.

Applying God's Truth:

1. What connection do you see between Jesus' resurrection and your giving to the church?

2. What procedures does your church have to make sure money is not mismanaged?

3. Do you think monetary giving is all that is required of us, or do you think Paul's guidelines might apply to other kinds of giving as well? Explain.

Scripture: Read 1 Corinthians 16:10-24

"Be on your guard; stand firm in the faith; be men of courage; be strong. Do everything in love" (1 Cor. 16:13-14).

IN CONCLUSION . . .

Paul's closing words need not detain us. The "holy kiss" (v. 20) was a common mode of greeting, the men kissing the men and the women kissing the women. If Paul were writing to Western churches, he would say, "Shake hands with one another."

Paul usually dictated his letters and then took the pen and added his signature. He also added his "benediction of grace" as a mark that the letter was authentic. The word *anathema* (v. 22, KJV) is Aramaic and means "accursed." Not to love Christ means not to believe in Him, and unbelievers are accursed (John 3:16-21). The word *maran-atha* is Greek and means "our Lord comes" or (as a prayer) "our Lord, come!" If a person loves Jesus Christ, he will also love His appearing (2 Tim. 4:8).

Paul had been stern with the Corinthian believers, but he closed his letter by assuring them of his love. After all, wounds from a friend can be trusted (Prov. 27:6).

Paul has shared a great deal of spiritual wisdom with us. May we receive it with meekness and put it into practice to the glory of God!

Applying God's Truth:

1. Does your church have a special or unique type of greeting? If not, do you think it could use one?

2. If you had been a first-century Christian reading this epistle for the first time, what questions do you think you might have had for Paul?

3. What three things have you learned (or been reminded of) from 1 Corinthians that you think are most noteworthy?

ENCOURAGEMENT

30 Daily Readings from the Book of 2 Corinthians

W HY?"
That's the easiest question to ask and the hardest to answer. Why do people suffer? Why do our best laid plans fall apart? Why do the people we love make life difficult for us? Why doesn't God answer prayer and change our circumstances? Why can't life be easier?

Why, Lord? And why *me*?

We live in difficult days and they aren't about to get easier. Each stage of life brings with it special joys and challenges, and also special trials and sorrows. Nobody is exempt from the battles of life.

Though he lived centuries ago, the Apostle Paul knew a great deal about the problems and the difficulties people go through today. Human nature and human problems haven't really changed that much since Paul wrote the letter we call 2 Corinthians. His theme? "Be encouraged! It's always too soon to quit!"

This is the most intimate letter Paul ever wrote. In it, he bares his heart and tells us some of the difficult experiences he went through and how the Lord gave him the encouragement he needed day after day. Paul didn't just *endure* the trials of life, nor did he selfishly try to *escape* them. Instead, he learned how to *enlist* them to build a life that triumphed over pain and problems and brought glory to God.

Your daily study of this ancient letter can help you follow Paul's example and trust Paul's God, the God who still says, "My grace is sufficient for you" (2 Cor. 12:9). Paul can show you how to make your difficulties work *for* you and not against you.

Our English word *discourage* means "without heart." When Christ is Lord of your life, He can put into your heart the courage you need to face life with its problems and be a victor, not a victim.

No matter what the feelings within you or the circumstances around you or the pressures against you, *you can be encouraged!* And you can encourage others.

Scripture: Read 2 Corinthians 1:1-5

"Praise be to the God and Father of our Lord Jesus Christ, the Father of compassion and the God of all comfort, who comforts us in all our troubles, so that we can comfort those in any trouble with the comfort we ourselves have received from God" (2 Cor. 1:3-4).

GOD IS IN CONTROL

Paul began his letter with a doxology. He certainly could not sing about his circumstances, but he could sing about the God who is in control of all circumstances. Paul had learned that praise is an important factor in achieving victory over discouragement and depression.

In 2 Corinthians Paul praised God for *present* blessings, for what God was accomplishing then and there. During the horrors of the Thirty Years' War, Pastor Martin Rinkart faithfully served the people in Eilenburg, Saxony. He conducted as many as forty funerals a day, a total of over 4,000 during his ministry. Yet out of this devastating experience, he wrote a "table grace" for his children which today we use as a hymn of thanksgiving":

> Now thank we all our God,
> With heart and hands and voices,
> Who wondrous things hath done,
> In whom His world rejoices!

Whatever the Father did for Jesus when He was ministering on earth, He is able to do for us today. We are dear to the Father because His Son is dear to Him, and we are citizens of "the kingdom of the Son he loves" (Col. 1:13). We are precious to the Father, and He will see to it that the pressures of life will not destroy us.

Applying God's Truth:

1. As you begin this book, what reasons do you have to offer thanksgiving and praise?

2. For what are you seeking comfort today?

3. What might you need to do to better comprehend the love that God has for you?

Scripture: Read 2 Corinthians 1:6-7

"Our hope for you is firm, because we know that just as you share in our sufferings, so also you share in our comfort" (2 Cor. 1:7).

LEADING THE WAY

One of my favorite preachers is Dr. George W. Truett, who pastored First Baptist Church of Dallas, Texas for nearly fifty years. In one of his sermons, he told about an unbelieving couple whose baby died suddenly. Dr. Truett conducted the funeral and later had the joy of seeing them both trust Jesus Christ.

Many months later, a young mother lost her baby, and again, Dr. Truett was called to bring her comfort. Nothing he shared with her seemed to help her. But at the funeral service, the newly converted mother stepped to the girl's side and said, "I passed through this, and I know what you are passing through. God called me, and through the darkness I came to Him. He has comforted me, and He will comfort you!"

Dr. Truett said, "The first mother did more for the second mother than I could have done, maybe in days and months; for the first young mother had traveled the road of suffering herself."

We do not need to experience exactly the same trials in order to be able to share God's encouragement. If we have experienced God's comfort, then we can "comfort those in any trouble" (v. 4b). Of course, if we have experienced similar tribulations, they can help us identify better with others and know better how they feel; but our experiences cannot alter the comfort of God. That remains sufficient and efficient no matter what our own experiences may have been.

Applying God's Truth:

1. Can you recall a similar instance in your life or the life of a friend or family member that caused you to question God's love or doubt His power? How did you deal with your feelings?

2. Which do you tend to share with others more frequently: your sufferings, or a sense of comfort? Why?

3. Does your faith in God tend to change based on the amount of comfort you feel? Explain.

Scripture: Read 2 Corinthians 1:8-24

"In our hearts we felt the sentence of death. But this happened that we might not rely on ourselves but on God, who raises the dead" (2 Cor. 1:9).

SPECIAL SUFFERINGS

God permits trials to come. There are ten basic words for suffering in the Greek language, and Paul used five of them in this letter. There are some sufferings that we endure simply because we are human and subject to pain; but there are other sufferings that come because we are God's people and want to serve Him.

We must never think that trouble is an accident. For the believer, everything is a divine appointment. God encourages us in all our tribulations by teaching us from His Word that it is He who permits trials to come. He encourages us further by reminding us that *He is in control of trials* (v. 9). Paul was weighed down like a beast of burden with a load too heavy to bear. But God knew just how much Paul could take, and He kept the situation under control.

We do not know what the specific "trouble" was, but it was great enough to make Paul think he was going to die. Whether it was peril from his many enemies, serious illness, or special satanic attack, we do not know, but we do know that God controlled the circumstances and protected His servant. Paul may have despaired of life, but God did not despair of Paul.

Applying God's Truth:

1. How do you feel toward God when you encounter some kind of suffering?

2. Can you think of past personal trials where, looking back, you can see why God permitted them to happen?

3. What are some of your most pressing current trials? What can you do to ensure that you remain focused on God during these times?

Scripture: Read 2 Corinthians 2:1-11

"If you forgive anyone, I also forgive him. And what I have forgiven—if there was anything to forgive—I have forgiven in the sight of Christ for your sake, in order that Satan might not outwit us" (2 Cor. 2:10-11).

TO LIVE BELOW WITH SAINTS WE KNOW

I have often quoted an anonymous rhyme that perfectly describes one of the most frequent problems we have as the people of God:

> To live above with saints we love,
> Will certainly be glory!
> To live below with saints we know,
> Well, that's another story!

One of the members of the Corinthian church caused Paul a great deal of pain. We are not sure if this is the same man Paul wrote about in 1 Corinthians 5, the man who was living in open fornication, or if it was another person, someone who publicly challenged Paul's apostolic authority. Paul had made a quick visit to Corinth to deal with this problem (2 Cor. 12:14; 13:1) and had also written a painful letter to them about the situation. In all of this, he revealed a compassionate heart.

Paul could have exercised his apostolic authority and commanded the people to respect him and obey him, but he preferred to minister with patience and love. Love always considers the feelings of others and seeks to put their good ahead of everything else.

When I was a child, I didn't always appreciate the discipline that my parents gave me. But now that I look back, I can thank God that they loved me enough to hurt me and hinder me from harming myself. Now I understand what they really meant when they said, "This hurts us more than it hurts you."

Applying God's Truth:

1. When people offend you, are you quick to "reveal a compassionate heart"? If not, what is your usual course of action?

2. On a scale of 1 (least) to 10 (most), how much of each of the following qualities do you normally exhibit in a conflict situation: Love? Patience? Logic? Force? Empathy?

3. How do you think Satan tends to work through our personal conflicts?

Scripture: Read 2 Corinthians 2:12-17

"Thanks be to God, who always leads us in triumphal procession in Christ and through us spreads everywhere the fragrance of the knowledge of him" (2 Cor. 2:14).

JOIN THE PARADE

Paul was sure that God *was leading him in triumph*. The picture here is that of the "Roman Triumph," the special tribute that Rome gave to their conquering generals. If a commander-in-chief won a complete victory over the enemy on foreign soil, and if he killed at least 5,000 enemy soldiers and gained new territory for the Emperor, then that commander-in chief was entitled to a Roman triumph. The processional would include the commander riding in a golden chariot, surrounded by his officers. The parade would also include a display of the spoils of battle, as well as the captive enemy soldiers. The Roman priests would also be in the parade, carrying burning incense to pay tribute to the victorious army.

Jesus Christ, our great commander-in-chief, came to foreign soil (this earth) and completely defeated the enemy (Satan). Instead of killing 5,000 persons, He gave life to more than 5,000 persons—to 3,000 plus at Pentecost and to another 2,000 plus shortly after Pentecost (Acts 2:41; 4:4). Jesus Christ claimed the spoils of battle—lost souls who had been in bondage to sin and Satan. What a splendid victory!

The victorious general's sons would walk behind their father's chariot, sharing in his victory; and that is where believers are today—following in Christ's triumph. We do not fight for victory; we fight *from* victory. Neither in Asia nor in Corinth did the situation look like victory to Paul, but he believed God—and God turned defeat into victory.

Applying God's Truth:

1. List some reasons you have to feel triumphant today.

2. Does it *feel* as if you're on the winner's side in your spiritual battle, or do you have to accept it by faith?

3. What battles are you fighting on your own? How do you need God's help?

Scripture: Read 2 Corinthians 3:1-6

"You show that you are a letter from Christ, the result of our ministry, written not with ink but with the Spirit of the living God, not on tablets of stone but on tablets of human hearts" (2 Cor. 3:3).

WRITTEN ON THE HEART

When God gave the Law, He wrote it on the tables of stone, and those tables were placed in the ark of the covenant. Even if the Israelites could read the two tables, this experience would not change their lives. The Law is an external thing, and people need an *internal* power if their lives are to be transformed. The legalist can admonish us with his "Do this!" or "Don't do that!" But he cannot give us the power to obey. If we do obey, often it is not from the heart—and we end up worse than before!

The ministry of grace changes the heart. The Spirit of God uses the Word of God and writes it on the heart. The Corinthians were wicked sinners when Paul came to them, but his ministry of the Gospel of God's grace completely changed their lives. (See 1 Cor. 6:9-11.) Their experience of God's grace certainly meant more to them than the letters of commendation carried by the false teachers. The Corinthian believers were lovingly written on Paul's heart, and the Spirit of God had written the truth on their hearts, making them "living epistles of Christ."

The test of ministry is changed lives, not press releases or statistics. It is much easier for the legalist to boast, because he can "measure" his ministry by external standards. The believer who patiently ministers by the Spirit of God must leave the results with the Lord. How tragic that the Corinthians followed the boastful Judaizers and broke the heart of the man who had rescued them from judgment.

Applying God's Truth:

1. Since you are a "letter from Christ," what would you say is the message that is written on the tablet of your human heart?

2. Can you think of any "external" religious rules you follow because of obligation rather than genuine gratitude or worship?

3. In what way(s) do you attempt to measure your ministry as a Christian?

Scripture: Read 2 Corinthians 3:7-11

"If what was fading away came with glory, how much greater is the glory of that which lasts!" (2 Cor. 3:11)

GLORY: PAST AND PRESENT

Paul wrote at a period in history when the ages were overlapping. The New Covenant of grace had come in, but the temple services were still being carried on and the nation of Israel was still living under Law. In A.D. 70, the city of Jerusalem and the temple would be destroyed by the Romans, and that would mark the end of the Jewish religious system.

The Judaizers wanted the Corinthian believers to go back under the Law, to "mix" the two Covenants. "Why go back to that which is temporary and fading away?" Paul asked. "Live in the glory of the New Covenant, which is getting greater and greater." The glory of the Law is but the glory of past history, while the glory of the New Covenant is the glory of present experience.

The glory of the Law was fading in Paul's day, and today that glory is found only in the records in the Bible. The nation of Israel has no temple or priesthood. If they did build a temple, there would be no Shekinah glory dwelling in the holy of holies. The Law of Moses is a religion with a most glorious past, but it has no glory today. The light is gone; all that remain are the shadows (Col. 2:16-17).

But the ministry of grace is internal (2 Cor. 3:1-3); it brings life (vv. 4-6), and it involves increasing glory (vv. 7-11).

Applying God's Truth:

1. Do you know people who try to focus more on Old Testament Law (rules and regulations) than the New Covenant of grace? How do they do this?

2. What are some temporal things that people try to "glory" in?

3. In your own life, do you tend to dwell more on the "light" of past accomplishments than in the here-and-now? Explain.

Scripture: Read 2 Corinthians 3:12-18

"Now the Lord is the Spirit, and where the Spirit of the Lord is, there is freedom" *(2 Cor. 3:17)*

LAW AND LEGALISM

The result of Old Covenant ministry is bondage; but the result of New Covenant ministry is freedom in the Spirit. Legalism keeps a person immature, and immature people must live by rules and regulations (see Gal. 4:1-7). God wants His children to obey, not because of an external code (the Law), but because of internal character. Christians do not live under the Law, but this does not mean that we are lawless! The Spirit of God writes the Word of God on our hearts, and we obey our Father because of the new life He has given us within.

The lure of legalism is still with us. False cults prey on professed Christians and church members, as did the Judaizers in Paul's day. We must learn to recognize false cults and reject their teachings. But there are also Gospel-preaching churches that have legalistic tendencies and keep their members immature, guilty, and afraid. They spend a great deal of time dealing with the externals, and they neglect the cultivation of the inner life. They exalt standards and they denounce sin, but they fail to magnify the Lord Jesus Christ. Sad to say, in some New Testament churches we have an Old Testament ministry.

Paul said that his own ministry was triumphant (2 Cor. 1–2) and glorious (chap. 3). The two go together. When your ministry involves the glory of God—you cannot quit!

Applying God's Truth:

1. What are some evidences of "freedom in the Spirit" that you've observed in your life?

2. How do you prevent legalistic thinking from affecting your spiritual freedom?

3. How might your personal ministry become more triumphant? More glorious?

Scripture: Read 2 Corinthians 4:1-6

"Since through God's mercy we have this ministry, we do not lose heart" *(2 Cor. 4:1).*

MOTIVATION FOR MINISTRY

The way you look at your ministry helps to determine how you will fulfill it. If you look on serving Christ as a burden instead of a privilege, you will be a drudge and do only what is required of you. Some people even look upon service as a punishment from God. When Paul considered the fact that he was a minister of Jesus Christ, he was overwhelmed by the grace and mercy of God.

His positive attitude toward the ministry kept him from being a quitter. He confessed to the Corinthians that his trials in Asia had almost brought him to despair (1:8). In spite of his great gifts and vast experience, Paul was human and subject to human frailties. But how could he lose heart when he was involved in such a wonderful ministry? Would God have entrusted this ministry to him so that he might fail? Of course not! With the divine calling came the divine enabling; he knew that God would see him through.

A discouraged Methodist preacher wrote to the great Scottish preacher, Alexander Whyte, to ask his counsel. Should he leave the ministry? "Never think of giving up preaching!" Whyte wrote to him. "The angels around the throne envy you your great work!" That was the kind of reply Paul would have written, the kind of reply all of us need to ponder whenever we feel our work is in vain.

Applying God's Truth:

1. Under what circumstance are you most prone to "give up" spiritually?

2. How might it help you to dwell on God's mercy during times when it becomes difficult to keep going?

3. On a scale of 1 to 10, where 1 = Burden and 10 = Privilege, where would you rate your feelings toward your personal ministry?

Scripture: Read 2 Corinthians 4:7-18

"We have this treasure in jars of clay to show that this all-surpassing power is from God and not from us" (2 Cor. 4:7).

HIDDEN TREASURE

Sometimes God permits our vessels to be jarred so that some of the treasure will spill out and enrich others. Suffering reveals not only the weakness of man but also the glory of God. Paul presented a series of paradoxes in this paragraph: earthen vessels—power of God; the dying Jesus—the life of Jesus; death working—life working. The natural mind cannot understand this kind of spiritual truth and therefore cannot understand why Christians triumph over suffering.

Not only must we focus on the treasure and not on the vessel, but we must also focus on the Master and not on the servant. If we suffer, it is for Jesus' sake. If we die to self, it is that the life of Christ might be revealed in us. If we go through trials, it is so that Christ might be glorified. And all of this is for the sake of others. As we serve Christ, death works in us—but life works in those to whom we minister.

Dr. John Henry Jowett said, "Ministry that costs nothing, accomplishes nothing." He was right. A pastor friend and I once heard a young man preach an eloquent sermon, but it lacked something. "There was something missing," I said to my friend, and he replied, "Yes, and it won't be there until his heart is broken. After he has suffered awhile, he will have a message worth listening to."

Applying God's Truth:

1. Think of yourself as a vessel that carries the treasure of God, and then try to describe yourself in such terms (large or small, strong or fragile, new or antique, etc.).

2. When was the last time you felt "jarred" significantly—to the point of almost breaking? How did you handle the situation?

3. When most people look at your life, what do you think they see: yourself, or the treasure you contain? Why?

Scripture: Read 2 Corinthians 5:1-10

"We are always confident and know that as long as we are at home in the body we are away from the Lord" (2 Cor. 5:6).

MOBILE HOMES

The people of God can be found in one of two places: either in heaven or on earth (Eph. 3:15). None of them is in the grave, in hell, or in any "intermediate place" between earth and heaven. Believers on earth are "at home in the body," while believers who have died are "absent from the body." Believers on earth are "absent from the Lord," while believers in heaven are "present with the Lord."

Because he had this kind of confidence, Paul was not afraid of suffering and trials, or even of dangers. He was willing to "lose his life" for the sake of Christ and the ministry of the Gospel. He walked by faith and not by sight. He looked at the eternal unseen, not the temporal seen (4:18). Heaven was not simply a *destination* for Paul: it was a *motivation*. Like the heroes of faith in Hebrews 11, he looked for the heavenly city and governed his life by eternal values.

Paul had courage for the conflict and would not lose heart. He had a glorious ministry that transformed lives. He had a valuable treasure in the earthen vessel of his body, and he wanted to share that treasure with a bankrupt world. He had a confident faith that conquered fear, and he had a future hope that was both a destination and a motivation. No wonder Paul was "more than conqueror"! (Rom. 8:37) Every believer in Jesus Christ has these same marvelous possessions and can find through them courage for the conflict.

Applying God's Truth:

1. To what extent would you say you are so confident of heaven that no problem on earth will significantly concern you?

2. How might heaven become more of a motivation for you, and not just a destination?

3. On a scale of 1 to 10, where 1 = "Living by sight" and 10 = "Living by faith," where would you say you are right now?

Scripture: Read 2 Corinthians 5:11-15

"He died for all, that those who live should no longer live for themselves but for him who died for them and was raised again" (2 Cor. 5:15).

DYING TO LIVE

It has well been said, "Christ died our death for us that we might live His life for Him." If a lost sinner has been to the cross and been saved, how can he spend the rest of his life in selfishness?

In 1858, Frances Ridley Havergal visited Germany with her father who was getting treatment for his afflicted eyes. While in a pastor's home, she saw a picture of the Crucifixion on the wall, with the words under it: "I did this for thee. What hast thou done for Me?" Quickly she took a piece of paper and wrote a poem based on that motto, but she was not satisfied with it, so she threw the paper into the fireplace. The paper came out unharmed! Later, her father encouraged her to publish it; and we sing it today to a tune composed by Philip P. Bliss.

> I gave My life for thee,
> My precious blood I shed,
> That thou might'st ransomed be,
> And quickened from the dead.
> I gave, I gave, My life for thee,
> What hast thou given for Me?

Christ died that we might live *through* Him and *for* Him, and that we might live *with* Him. Because of Calvary, believers are going to heaven to live with Christ forever!

Applying God's Truth:

1. Think back a year. Are you "living for Christ" more effectively today than you did then, less effectively, or about the same? Why?

2. Make a mental list of all the things Christ has done for you—both generally and specifically.

3. List the ways you are living for yourself and compare that list to the ways you are living for Christ. Where do your primary interests lie?

Scripture: Read 2 Corinthians 5:16-21

"We are therefore Christ's ambassadors, as though God were making his appeal through us. We implore you on Christ's behalf: Be reconciled to God" *(2 Cor. 5:20).*

REPRESENTING THE KING

Since Christians in this world are the ambassadors of Christ, this means that the world is in rebellion against God. He has sent His ambassadors into the world to declare peace, not war. We represent Jesus Christ (4:5; John 20:21). If sinners reject us and our message, it is Jesus Christ who is actually rejected. What a great privilege it is to be heaven's ambassadors to the rebellious sinners of this world!

When I was a young pastor, it used to embarrass me somewhat to make visits and confront people with the claims of Christ. Then it came to me that I was a privileged person, an ambassador of the King of kings! There was nothing to be embarrassed about. In fact, the people I visited should have been grateful that one of Christ's ambassadors came to see them.

God has not declared war on the world; at the cross He declared peace. But one day, He *will* declare war; and then it will be too late for those who have rejected the Savior (2 Thes. 1:3-10). Satan is seeking to tear everything apart in this world, but Christ and His church are involved in the ministry of reconciliation, bringing things back together again, and back to God.

Ministry is not easy. If we are to succeed, we must be motivated by the fear of the Lord, the love of Christ, and the commission that He has given to us. What a privilege it is to serve Him!

Applying God's Truth:

1. Create what you think would be a good job description for an "ambassador of Christ."

2. What are some potential drawbacks of being an ambassador?

3. Who are some people to whom you might become an ambassador of Christ—people who might not hear the Gospel from anyone else?

Scripture: Read 2 Corinthians 6

"We commend ourselves in every way: in great endurance; in troubles, hardships and distresses; in beatings, imprisonments and riots; in hard work, sleepless nights, and hunger . . . having nothing, and yet possessing everything" (2 Cor. 6:4-5, 10).

AN ATTITUDE OF GRATITUDE

What a price Paul paid to be faithful in his ministry! And yet how little the Corinthians really appreciated all he did for them. They brought sorrow to his heart, yet he was "always rejoicing" in Jesus Christ (v. 10). He became poor that they might become rich (see 1 Cor. 1:5; 2 Cor. 8:9). The word translated *poor* means "the complete destitution of a beggar."

Was Paul wrong in appealing for their appreciation? I don't think so. Too many churches are prone to take for granted the sacrificial ministry of pastors, missionaries, and faithful church officers. Paul was not begging for praise, but he was reminding his friends in Corinth that his ministry to them had cost him dearly.

Of course, in all of this personal testimony, Paul was refuting the malicious accusations of the Judaizers. How much had *they* suffered for the people of Corinth? What price had *they* paid for their ministry? Like most "cultists" today, these false teachers stole another man's converts; they did not seek to win the lost themselves.

It has well been said, "If you want to find gratitude, look in the dictionary." Are we showing gratitude to those who have ministered to us?

Applying God's Truth:

1. What are some sacrifices you've made for others lately that didn't seem to be appreciated? How did you feel?

2. How careful are you to show gratitude for the good things other people do for *you*?

3. Can you think of some negative personal experiences (sacrifices) you've faced that turned out to be very beneficial for other people?

Scripture: Read 2 Corinthians 7

"Since we have these promises, dear friends, let us purify ourselves from every-thing that contaminates body and spirit, perfecting holiness out of reverence for God" (2 Cor. 7:1).

A SEPARATE PEACE

God blesses those who separate themselves from sin and unto the Lord. Because of God's gracious promises, we have some spiritual responsibil-ities. We must cleanse ourselves once and for all of anything that defiles us. It is not enough to ask God to cleanse us; we must clean up our own lives and get rid of those things that make it easy for us to sin. No believer can leg-islate for any other believer; each one knows the problems of his own heart and life.

Too often Christians deal with symptoms and not causes. We keep con-fessing the same sins because we have not gotten to the root of the trouble and "purified ourselves." Perhaps there is something that "contaminates"—a filth-iness of the flesh that feeds the old nature (Rom. 13:14). Or it may be filthi-ness of the spirit, an attitude that is sinful. The prodigal son was guilty of sins of the flesh, but his "moral" elder brother was guilty of sins of the spirit. He could not even get along with his own father. (See Luke 15:11-21.)

But cleansing ourselves is only half of the responsibility; we must also be "perfecting holiness out of reverence for God" (2 Cor. 7:1). This is a con-stant process as we grow in grace and knowledge (2 Peter 3:18).

Applying God's Truth:

1. Can you think of spiritual "symptoms" you frequently deal with that might suggest a deeper root problem?

2. What are some ways that you can consciously separate yourself from sin-ful things?

3. Do you work hard at remaining separate from sin, or do you just hope that God will remove your temptations some day?

Scripture: Read 2 Corinthians 8:1-7

"We want you to know about the grace that God has given the Macedonian churches. Out of the most severe trial, their overflowing joy and their extreme poverty welled up in rich generosity" (2 Cor. 8:1-2).

GRACE GIVING

When you have experienced the grace of God in your life, you will not use difficult circumstances as an excuse for not giving. In my first pastorate, we had a great need for a new church building, but some of the people opposed a building program because of the "economic situation." Apparently the steel mills were planning to go on strike, and the refineries were going to shut down, and the railroads were having problems . . . and it seemed like a risky time to build. But there were enough people who believed in "grace giving" so that the church did erect a new sanctuary—in spite of the strikes, shutdowns, layoffs, and other economic problems. Grace giving means giving in spite of circumstances.

It is possible to give generously but not give enthusiastically. "The preacher says I should give until it hurts," said a miserly church member, "but for me, it hurts just to think about giving!" The Macedonian churches needed no prompting or reminding, as did the church at Corinth. They were more than willing to share in the collection. In fact, *they begged to be included!* (v. 4) How many times have you heard a Christian beg for somebody to take an offering?

Grace not only frees us from our sins, but it frees us from ourselves. The grace of God will open your heart *and your hand.* Your giving is not the result of cold calculation, but of warmhearted jubilation!

Applying God's Truth:

1. What are the most common reasons you hear people use for not giving more to their church?

2. In what ways do you think giving is related to God's grace in one's life?

3. What three adjectives best describe your attitude toward giving?

Scripture: Read 2 Corinthians 8:8-9

"You know the grace of our Lord Jesus Christ, that though he was rich, yet for your sakes he became poor, so that you through his poverty might become rich" *(2 Cor. 8:9).*

A "POOR" EXAMPLE

In what ways was Jesus rich? Certainly He was rich in His Person, for He is eternal God. He is rich in His possessions and in His position as King of kings and Lord of lords. He is rich in His power, for He can do anything. Yet, in spite of the fact that He had all these riches—and more—*He became poor.*

The tense of the verb indicates that it is His incarnation, His birth at Bethlehem, that is meant here. He united Himself to mankind and took upon Himself a human body. He left the throne to become a servant. He laid aside all His possessions so that He did not even have a place to lay His head. His ultimate experience of poverty was when He was made sin for us on the cross. Hell is eternal poverty, and on the cross Jesus Christ became the poorest of the poor.

Why did He do it? That we might become rich! This suggests that we were poor before we met Jesus Christ, and we were—totally bankrupt. But now that we have trusted Him, we share in all of His riches! We are now the children of God, "heirs of God and coheirs with Christ" (Rom. 8:17). Since this is true, *how can we refuse to give to others?* He became poor to make us rich! Can we not follow His example?

Applying God's Truth:

1. How might your becoming poorer (financially) help someone else become richer (spiritually)?

2. Why do you think Jesus chose to live a human life of poverty when He could just as easily have led a sinless but wealthy life?

3. In your opinion, how closely related are a person's giving habits and his or her spiritual maturity?

Scripture: Read 2 Corinthians 8:10-24

"Last year you were the first not only to give but also to have the desire to do so. Now finish the work, so that your eager willingness to do it may be matched by your completion of it" (2 Cor. 8:10-11).

HEART GIFTS

Grace giving must come from a willing heart; it cannot be coerced or forced. During my years of ministry, I have endured many offering appeals. I have listened to pathetic tales about unbelievable needs. I have forced myself to laugh at old jokes that were supposed to make it easier for me to part with my money. I have been scolded, shamed, and almost threatened, and I must confess that none of these approaches has ever stirred me to give more than I planned to give. In fact, more than once I gave less because I was so disgusted with the worldly approach. (However, I have never gotten like Mark Twain, who said that he was so sickened by the long appeal that he not only did not give what he planned to give but he took a bill out of the plate!)

We must be careful here not to confuse *willing* with *doing*, because the two must go together. If the willing is sincere and in the will of God, then there must be "a completion of it" (v. 11; Phil. 2:12-13). Paul did not say that *willing* was a substitute for *doing*, because it is not. But if our giving is motivated by grace, we will give more willingly, and not because we have been forced to give.

God sees the "heart gift" and not the "hand gift." If the heart wanted to give more, but was unable to do so, God sees it and records it accordingly. But if the hand gives more than the heart wants to give, God records what is in the heart, no matter how big the offering in the hand might be.

Applying God's Truth:

1. What fund-raising techniques are most offensive to you? Which, if any, do you endorse?

2. Do you think pastors ought to spend much time discussing giving to the church? Why?

3. Do you think giving is an ongoing priority for most people, or do they tend to give in spurts? Why?

Scripture: Read 2 Corinthians 9:1-5

"I thought it necessary to urge the brothers to visit you in advance and finish the arrangements for the generous gift you had promised. Then it will be ready as a generous gift, not as one grudgingly given" (2 Cor. 9:5).

PROMPTING WITHOUT PRESSURING

Apparently, Paul did not see anything wrong or unspiritual about asking people to promise to give. He did not tell them how much they had to promise, but he did expect them to keep their promise. Notice the words that Paul used as he wrote about the collection. It was a "service to the saints" (v. 1) and "a generous gift" (v. 5). Was Paul perhaps hinting that the Corinthians give more than they had planned?

However, Paul was careful not to put on any pressure. He wanted their gift to be "a generous gift, not as one grudgingly given." High-pressure offering appeals do not belong to grace giving.

Our greatest encouragement for giving is that it pleases the Lord, but there is nothing wrong with practicing the kind of giving that provokes others to give. This does not mean that we should advertise what we do as individuals because that kind of practice would violate one of the basic principles of giving: give secretly to the Lord (Matt. 6:1-4). However, Paul was writing to *churches*, and it is not wrong for congregations to announce what they have given collectively. If our motive is to boast, then we are not practicing grace giving. But if our desire is to provoke others to share, then God's grace can work through us to help others.

Applying God's Truth:

1. To what extent do you need to be prompted from time to time to give to your church?

2. If giving is to be done willingly, out of generosity, do you think it's improper to ask people to give? Why?

3. What are some ways to inspire people to give without having to ask them?

Scripture: Read 2 Corinthians 9:6-15

"Remember this: Whoever sows sparingly will also reap sparingly, and whoever sows generously will also reap generously" (2 Cor. 9:6).

WAITING FOR THE HARVEST

As we sow, we are enriched and we enrich others (v. 11). The farmer reaps immediate physical benefits as he works in his field, but he has to wait for the harvest. The Christian who is motivated by grace reaps the blessings of personal enrichment in his or her own life and character, and this enrichment benefits others. The final result is glory to God as others give thanks to Him. Paul was careful to point out that grace giving does not bring credit to us; it brings thanksgiving to God. We are but channels through whom God works to meet the needs of others.

God enriches us so that we may give even more bountifully. One of the joys of grace giving is the joy of giving more and more. Everything we have—not just our income—belongs to God, is given to God, and is used by God to accomplish His work. We are enriched in everything with Him and with others. As a pastor, I have watched young Christians lay hold of these principles of grace giving and start to grow. It has been a great joy to see them trust God as their giving is motivated by grace.

Grace giving means that we really believe that God is the great giver, and we use our material and spiritual resources accordingly. You simply cannot outgive God!

Applying God's Truth:

1. Recall some personal examples that illustrate the sowing/reaping principle of 2 Corinthians 9:6.

2. When you give to the church, to what extent do you want to see definite (and perhaps immediate) results?

3. Do you think we see most of the "harvest" of our giving? Why?

Scripture: Read 2 Corinthians 10:1-6

"The weapons we fight with are not the weapons of the world. On the contrary, they have divine power to demolish strongholds. We . . . take captive every thought to make it obedient to Christ" (2 Cor. 10:4-5).

WALLS OF RESISTANCE

There are walls of resistance in the minds of people, and these walls must be pulled down. What are these "mental walls"? Reasonings that are opposed to the truth of God's Word. Pride of intelligence that exalts itself. Paul was not attacking intelligence, but intellectualism, the high-minded attitude that makes people think they know more than they really do. Paul faced this "wisdom of men" when he founded the church (1 Cor. 1:18ff), and it had surfaced again with the coming of the Judaizers.

Paul's attitude of humility was actually one of his strongest weapons, for pride plays right into the hands of Satan. The meek Son of God had far more power than Pilate (see John 19:11), and He proved it. Paul used spiritual weapons to tear down the opposition—prayer, the Word of God, love, the power of the Spirit at work in his life. He did not depend on personality, human abilities, or even the authority he had as an apostle. However, he was ready to punish the offenders, if necessary, once the congregation had submitted to the Lord.

Many believers today do not realize that the church is involved in warfare, and those who do understand the seriousness of the Christian battle do not always know how to fight the battle. They try to use human methods to defeat demonic forces, and these methods are doomed to fail.

Applying God's Truth:

1. What are some of the "strongholds" that have positioned themselves in your life?

2. What are some spiritual "weapons" you may not be utilizing as well as you could? How could you use them more effectively?

3. What other "weapons" have you been using that simply haven't been getting the job done?

Scripture: Read 2 Corinthians 10:7-11

"Even if I boast somewhat freely about he authority the Lord gave us for building you up rather than pulling you down, I will not be ashamed of it" (2 Cor. 10:8).

MATURE AUTHORITY

In my many years of ministry, I have never ceased to be amazed at how some local churches treat their pastors. If a man shows love and true humility, they resist his leadership and break his heart. The next pastor will be a "dictator" who "runs the church"—and he gets just what he wants. And the people love him and brag about him! Our Lord was treated the same way, so perhaps we should not be surprised.

The opponents in the church were accusing Paul of not being a true apostle; for, if he were a true apostle, he would show it by using his authority. On the other hand, if Paul had "thrown his weight around," they would have found fault with that. No matter what course Paul took, they were bound to condemn him. This is what happens when church members are not spiritually minded, but evaluate ministry from a worldly viewpoint.

How a Christian uses authority is an evidence of his spiritual maturity and character. An immature person *swells* as he uses his authority, but a mature person *grows* in the use of authority, and others grow with him. The wise pastor, like the wise parent, knows when to wait in loving patience and when to act with determined power. It takes more power to wait than to strike. A mature person does not use authority to *demand* respect, but to *command* respect. Mature leaders suffer while they wait to act, while immature leaders act impetuously and make others suffer.

Applying God's Truth:

1. Do you think your pastor gets fair treatment from most congregation members? What problems, if any, do you detect?

2. How do you think pastors feel when they, like Paul, are forced to defend their ministries to insensitive accusers?

3. When you are in authority, do you tend to *command* respect or *demand* it?

Scripture: Read 2 Corinthians 10:12-18

"It is not the one who commends himself who is approved, but the one whom the Lord commends" (2 Cor. 10:18).

TEST TIME

How does God approve our work? By testing it. The word *approved* in verse 18 means "to approve by testing." There is a future testing at the Judgment Seat of Christ (1 Cor. 3:10ff), but there is also a present testing of the work that we do. God permits difficulties to come to local churches in order that the work might be tested and approved.

Over the years, I have seen ministries tested by financial losses, the invasion of false doctrine, the emergence of proud leaders who want to "run the church," and the challenge of change. Some of the churches have fallen apart and almost died because the work was not spiritual. Other ministries have grown because of the trials and have become purer and stronger, and, through it all, God was glorified.

Certainly our ministries must keep records and issue reports, but we must not fall into the "snare of statistics" and think that numbers are the only measurement of ministry. Each situation is unique, and no ministry can honestly be evaluated on the basis of some other ministry. The important thing is that we are where God wants us to be, doing what He wants us to do so that He might be glorified. Motive is as much a part of God's measurement of our work as is growth. If we are seeking to glorify and please God alone, and if we are not afraid of His evaluation of our hearts and lives, then we need not fear the estimates of men or their criticisms.

"Let him who boasts boast in the Lord" (2 Cor. 10:17).

Applying God's Truth:

1. What do you think of people who tend to commend themselves a lot? Why?

2. Do you think your church is ever in danger of falling into the "snare of statistics"? If so, in what ways?

3. What are some ways that God has recently "tested" *your* work? What were the results?

Scripture: Read 2 Corinthians 11:1-15

"I will keep on doing what I am doing in order to cut the ground from under those who want an opportunity to be considered equal with us in the things they boast about" *(2 Cor. 11:12).*

HOMEWARD BOUND

Paul had not used any devious tricks to catch the believers by surprise, attack them, or rob them. Both in his preaching of the Gospel and his handling of finances, he was open and honest. In my own travels, I have seen situations in local churches that have broken my heart. I have seen congregations show little or no appreciation to faithful pastors who were laboring sacrificially to see the church grow. Some of these men were underpaid and overworked, yet the churches seemed to have no love for them. However, their successors were treated like kings!

I once heard Dr. W.A. Criswell tell about the faithful missionary couple who returned to the United States on the same ship that brought Teddy Roosevelt home from a safari in Africa. Many reporters and photographers were on the dock, waiting to see Roosevelt and interview him and take pictures, but nobody was on hand to welcome home the veteran missionaries who had spent their lives serving Christ in Africa.

That evening, in their modest hotel room, the couple reviewed their arrival in New York City, and the husband was somewhat bitter.

"It isn't fair," he said to his wife. "Mr. Roosevelt comes home from a hunting trip, and the whole country is out to meet him. We get home after years of service, and nobody was there to greet us."

But his wife had the right answer: *"Honey, we aren't home yet."*

Applying God's Truth:

1. How do you feel when you hear others try to justify themselves by comparing themselves to other people when they have no genuine actions to back their claims? How do you think Paul felt?

2. Can you think of any current injustices in your own church were one person or group is being glorified when someone else is doing much more work?

3. In what ways are your own efforts being overlooked by others? How do you respond in such situations?

Scripture: Read 2 Corinthians 11:16-33

"I have labored and toiled and have often gone without sleep; I have known hunger and thirst and have often gone without food; I have been cold and naked. Besides everything else, I face daily the pressure of my concern for all the churches" *(2 Cor. 11:27-28).*

WHY BOTHER?

In my own limited itinerant ministry, I have had the convenience of automobiles and planes, and yet I must confess that travel wears me out. How much more difficult it was for Paul! No wonder he was filled with weariness and pain. He often had to go without food, drink, and sleep, and sometimes he lacked sufficient clothing to keep himself warm.

While any other traveler could have suffered these things, Paul endured them because of his love for Christ and the church. His greatest burden was not *around* him, but *within* him: the care of all the churches. Why did he care so much? Because he identified with the believers (v. 29). Whatever happened to "his children" touched his own heart, and he could not abandon them.

Paul climaxed this narration of his sufferings by telling of his humiliating experience at Damascus, when he—the great apostle—was smuggled out of the city in a basket let over the wall! (vv. 32-33) Would any of the Judaizers ever tell a story like that? Of course not! Even when Paul did narrate his sufferings, he was careful that Christ was glorified, and not Paul. May we never take for granted the sacrifices that others have made so that we might enjoy the blessings of the Gospel today.

Applying God's Truth:

1. What are some ways that you've suffered for the good of your church?

2. Think of all the people actively involved in your church. Can you think of anyone being overlooked who could use a note or word of encouragement?

3. If you and your fellow church members were willing to suffer a little more for the good of the church as a whole, what might be some of the results?

Scripture: Read 2 Corinthians 12:1-6

"I know a man in Christ who fourteen years ago was caught up to the third heaven. . . . And I know that this man . . . was caught up to Paradise. He heard inexpressible things, things that man is not permitted to tell" (2 Cor. 12:2-4).

A SECRET AND A THORN

The interesting thing is that Paul kept quiet about this experience of heaven for fourteen years! During those years, he was buffeted by a "thorn in the flesh" (v. 7), and perhaps people wondered why he had such a burdensome affliction. The Judaizers may have adopted the views of Job's comforters and said, "This affliction is a punishment from God." (Actually, it was a *gift* from God.) Some of Paul's good friends may have tried to encourage him by saying, "Cheer up, Paul. One day you'll be in heaven!" Paul could have replied, "That's why I have this thorn—I *went* to heaven!"

God honored Paul by granting him visions and revelations, and by taking him to heaven, but He honored him further by permitting him to hear "inexpressible things" while he was in heaven. He overheard the divine secrets that are shared only in heaven. These things could be spoken by God and by beings in heaven, but they could not be spoken by men.

Such an honor as this would have made most people very proud. Instead of keeping quiet for fourteen years, they would have immediately told the world and become famous. But Paul did not become proud. He simply told the truth—it was not empty boasting—and let the facts speak for themselves. His great concern was that nobody rob God of the glory.

Applying God's Truth:

1. Has anything astonishing ever happened in your Christian life?

2. When you tell others of the things God has done for you, how do you ensure that God gets the glory for those things (rather than having others simply think *you've* become a better person)?

3. How do you accept all the things God has done for you without becoming proud?

Scripture: Read 2 Corinthians 12:7-8

"To keep me from becoming conceited because of these surpassingly great revelations, there was given me a thorn in my flesh, a messenger of Satan, to torment me" (2 Cor. 12:7).

OPTIONS FOR SUFFERING

When God permits suffering to come to our lives, there are several ways we can deal with it. Some people become bitter and blame God for robbing them of freedom and pleasure. Others just "give up" and fail to get any blessing out of the experience because they will not put any courage into the experience. Still others grit their teeth and put on a brave front, determined to "endure to the very end." While this is a courageous response, it usually drains them of the strength needed for daily living; and after a time, they may collapse.

Was Paul sinning when he prayed to be delivered from Satan's buffeting? I don't think so. It is certainly a normal thing for a Christian to ask God for deliverance from sickness and pain. God has not *obligated* Himself to heal every believer whenever he prays, but He has encouraged us to bring our burdens and needs to Him. Paul did not know whether this "thorn in the flesh" was a temporary testing from God, or a permanent experience he would have to learn to live with.

There are those who want us to believe that an afflicted Christian is a disgrace to God. "If you are obeying the Lord and claiming all that you have in Christ," they say, "then you will never be sick." I have never found that teaching in the Bible. It is true that God promised the Jews special blessing and protection under the Old Covenant (Deut. 7:12ff), but He never promised the New Testament believers freedom from sickness or suffering.

Applying God's Truth:

1. Do you have any type of ailment you consider a "thorn" from God?

2. Why do you think God sometimes allows His people to endure chronic physical suffering?

3. What guidelines do you use to determine when to be persistent in prayer and when to accept something as a "thorn"?

Scripture: Read 2 Corinthians 12:9-21

"I will boast all the more gladly about my weaknesses, so that Christ's power may rest on me. . . . For when I am weak, then I am strong" (2 Cor. 12:9-10).

RISING ABOVE SUFFERING

God does not give us His grace simply that we might "endure" our sufferings. God's grace should enable us to *rise above* our circumstances and feelings and cause our afflictions to work *for us* in accomplishing positive good. God wants to build our character so that we are more like our Savior.

What benefits did Paul receive because of his suffering? For one thing, he experienced the power of Christ in his life. God transformed Paul's weakness into strength. The word translated *rest* means "to spread a tent over." Paul saw his body as a frail tent (5:1ff), but the glory of God had come into that tent and transformed it into a holy tabernacle.

Something else happened to Paul: he was able to glory in his infirmities. This does not mean that he preferred pain to health, but rather that he knew how to turn his infirmities into assets. What made the difference? The grace of God *and* the glory of God. He "delighted" in these trials and problems, not because he was psychologically unbalanced and enjoyed pain, but because he was suffering for the sake of Jesus Christ. He was glorifying God by the way he accepted and handled the difficult experiences of life.

"It is a greater thing to pray for pain's conversion than its removal," wrote P.T. Forsyth, and this is true. Paul won the victory, not by substitution, but by transformation. He discovered the sufficiency of the grace of God.

Applying God's Truth:

1. What effect should God's grace have on the "thorns" in your life?

2. Paraphrase Paul's statement in verse 10 as if you were answering a friend's query: "How can weakness be a strength?"

3. How might your spiritual life be different if you focused more on "converting" pain than having God completely remove it?

Scripture: Read 2 Corinthians 13:1-10

"He is not weak in dealing with you, but is powerful among you. For to be sure, he was crucified in weakness, yet he lives by God's power" *(2 Cor. 13:3-4).*

DECEPTIVE STRENGTH

Let Paul prove he is a true apostle!" said his opponents. Paul's reply was, "Like Jesus Christ, I am strong when it appears I am weak." On the cross, Jesus Christ manifested weakness; but the cross is still "the power of God" (1 Cor. 1:18). By the standards of the world, both Jesus and Paul were weak, but by the standards of the Lord, both were strong. It is a wise and mature worker who knows when to be "weak" and when to be "strong" as he deals with the discipline problems in the local church.

A pastor friend of mine, now in heaven, had a quiet manner of delivery in the pulpit, and a similar approach in his personal ministry. After hearing him preach, a visitor said, "I kept waiting for him to start preaching!" She was accustomed to hearing a loud preacher who generated more heat than light. But my friend built a strong church because he knew the true standards for ministry. He knew how to be "weak in Christ" and also how to be "strong."

How do people measure the ministry today? By a powerful oratory or biblical content? By Christian character or what the press releases say? Too many Christians follow the world's standards when they evaluate ministries; instead, they need to pay attention to God's standards.

Applying God's Truth:

1. What are some ways that Jesus was strong when He appeared weak?

2. Do you think some of your own strengths are interpreted by others as weaknesses? If so, in what ways?

3. Would you say your personal ministry generates more "heat" or "light"?

Scripture: Read 2 Corinthians 13:11-14

"Aim for perfection, listen to my appeal, be of one mind, live in peace. And the God of love and peace will be with you" (2 Cor. 13:11).

BE (AND STAY) ENCOURAGED

Our God is the "God of love and peace." Can the outside world tell that from the way we live and the way we conduct the business of the church? "Behold how they love one another!" was what the lost world said about the early church, but it has been a long time since the church has earned that kind of commendation.

The Corinthian believers then, and all believers now, desperately needed the blessings of grace, love, and communion. The Judaizers then, and the cultists today, emphasize law instead of grace, exclusiveness instead of love, and independence rather than communion (fellowship). The competition in the Corinthian church, resulting in divisions, would have been solved if the people had only lived by God's grace and love.

The church is a miracle, and it can be sustained only by the miracle ministry of God. No amount of human skill, talents, or programs can make the church what it ought to be. Only God can do that. If each believer is depending on the grace of God, walking in the love of God, and participating in the fellowship of the Spirit, not walking in the flesh, then he will be a part of the answer and not a part of the problem. He will be *living* this benediction—and being a benediction to others! Ask God to make you that kind of Christian.

Be encouraged—and then encourage others.

Applying God's Truth:

1. If a stranger monitored your words and actions for a week, do you think he or she would think you serve "a God of love and peace"?

2. What things do you do to try to build unity with other believers?

3. What three things could someone do for you (or say to you) that would encourage you most?

MATURITY

30 Daily Readings from the Book of James

There is a vast difference between age and maturity. Not everybody who grows old grows up.

Age is a quantity of time; maturity is a quality of experience. Age happens automatically: those who have the most birthdays live the longest. But maturity isn't automatic; you have to work at it.

Mature people have more life and enjoy more of life, especially the Christian life. God didn't save us from our sins in order to keep us infants in His family. He saved us so we would grow up and become more like Jesus Christ. Only then can we glorify Him and serve others. It is a tough world we live in, and you can't make it successfully without maturity.

Mature Christians aren't learners, always depending on somebody else to bail them out and carry them through. Instead, they're leaders who trust Christ to give them the encouragement and enablement they need for the demands of life. Through Jesus Christ, they can face life courageously and make it work for them, not against them.

For mature Christians, life isn't a playground in which babies fight over toys; it's a battleground where great moral issues must be defended. You can't send babies into battle. That's why God is challenging you and me to be mature, to develop the kind of Christian character that can stand the test.

The Epistle of James is about maturity, Christian maturity. It describes the characteristics of mature Christians and explains how they got that way. James also explains the important role that trials play in a maturing life, and he shows you how to keep your life in balance. (Infants are prone to stumble.) He even devotes an entire chapter to the question, "Why can't people get along with each other?"

All of us are either a part of the problem or a part of the answer. Mature Christians—and that can include *you*—are part of the answer.

Scripture: Read James 1:1

"James, a servant of God and of the Lord Jesus Christ, to the twelve tribes scattered among the nations: Greetings" (James 1:1).

MEET THE AUTHOR

James, the brother of our Lord, seems to be the most likely candidate for author of this letter. (By "brother," of course, I mean half-brother. Joseph was not our Lord's father since He was conceived by the Holy Spirit of God.)

James and the other brothers did not believe in Jesus during His earthly ministry (John 7:1-5 and Mark 3:31-35). Yet we find our Lord's brethren in the Upper Room praying with the disciples (Acts 1:14). What effected the change from unbelief to faith? First Corinthians 15:7 indicates that Jesus appeared to James after His resurrection! This convinced James that Jesus truly was the Savior, and he, in turn, shared this knowledge about Jesus with the other brothers.

James became the leader of the church in Jerusalem. Paul called him "a pillar" (Gal. 2:9). It was James who moderated the church conference described in Acts 15. He must have been a deeply spiritual man to gain the leadership of the Jerusalem church in so short a time. His stature is seen in Acts 15, where he was able to permit all the factions to express themselves, and then bring peace by drawing a conclusion based on the Word of God.

Applying God's Truth:

1. Have you ever been amazed at the accomplishments of a family member or close friend? How do you think James felt to discover that his brother was actually the Savior of the world?

2. An encounter with the resurrected Jesus turned James' life around. In what ways has your life changed due to your discoveries about who Jesus really is?

3. What are some of your goals as you read through these devotions from the Book of James?

Scripture: Read James 1:2

"Consider it pure joy, my brothers, whenever you face trials of many kinds" *(James 1:2)*.

GREAT EXPECTATIONS

Outlook determines outcomes, and attitude determines action. God tells us to expect trials. The believer who expects his Christian life to be easy is in for a shock. Because we are God's *scattered* people (v. 1) and not His *sheltered* people, we must experience trials. We cannot always expect everything to go our way. Some trials come simply because we are human—sickness, accidents, disappointments, even seeming tragedies. Other trials come because we are Christians. Satan fights us, the world opposes us, and this makes for a life of battle.

My wife and I once visited a world-famous weaver and watched his men and women work on the looms. I noticed that the undersides of the rugs were not very beautiful: the patterns were obscure and the loose ends of the yarn dangled. "Don't judge the worker or the work by looking at the wrong side," our guide told us. In the same way, we are looking at the wrong side of life; only the Lord sees the finished pattern. Let's not judge Him or His work from what we see today. His work is not finished yet!

Applying God's Truth:

1. What are some of the more severe trials you are facing right now?

2. How many of your trials can you honestly say you are facing with "pure joy"? How might you be able to glean more joy out of your less-than-desirable circumstances?

3. Do you tend to think God is uncaring or unfair when you have to experience unpleasant or undesired circumstances? Why?

Scripture: Read James 1:3

"You know that the testing of your faith develops perseverance" (James 1:3).

ON TRIAL

The only way the Lord can develop patience and character in our lives is through trials. Endurance cannot be attained by reading a book, listening to a sermon, or even praying a prayer. We must go though the difficulties of life, trust God, and obey Him. The result will be patience and character. Knowing this, we can face trials joyfully. We know that the end result will bring glory to God.

This fact explains why studying the Bible helps us grow in patience (Rom. 15:4). As we read about Abraham, Joseph, Moses, David, and even our Lord, we realize that God has a purpose in trials. God fulfills His purposes as we trust Him. There is no substitute for an understanding mind. Satan can defeat the ignorant believer, but he cannot overcome the Christian who knows his Bible and understands the purposes of God.

Applying God's Truth:

1. How does an athlete develop perseverance on a physical level? How do we develop *spiritual* perseverance?

2. What Bible character do you think best demonstrates perseverance? Why? What can you learn from him or her?

3. Rather than complain the next time your faith is tested, what are some other options you might try instead?

Scripture: Read James 1:4

"Perseverance must finish its work so that you may be mature and complete, not lacking anything" (*James 1:4*).

A COMMON PROBLEM

As you read the Epistle of James, you discover that the Jewish Christians were having some problems in their personal lives and in their church fellowship. For one thing, they were going through difficult testings. They were also facing temptations to sin. Some of the believers were catering to the rich, while others were being robbed by the rich. Church members were competing for offices in the church, particularly teaching offices.

One of the major problems in the church was a failure on the part of many to live what they professed to believe. Furthermore, the tongue was a serious problem, even to the point of creating wars and divisions in the assembly. Worldliness was another problem. Some of the members were disobeying God's Word and were sick physically because of it, and some were straying away from the Lord and the church.

But James was not discussing an array of miscellaneous problems. All of these problems had a common cause: *spiritual immaturity.* These Christians simply were not growing up. This gives us a hint as to the basic theme of this letter: *the marks of maturity in the Christian life.*

Applying God's Truth:

1. On a scale of 1 (least) to 10 (most), what would you say is your current level of spiritual maturity? Why?

2. Think back to your life one year ago. How have you matured spiritually since that time?

3. What is the significance of perseverance in the development of spiritual maturity?

Scripture: Read James 1:5-11

"If any of you lacks wisdom, he should ask God, who gives generously to all without finding fault, and it will be given to him" *(James 1:5).*

WISDOM IN ACTION

Wisdom is the right use of knowledge. All of us know people who are educated fools: they have brilliant academic records, but they cannot make the simplest decisions in life. I once met a gifted professor on a seminary campus, and he was wearing two hats!

Why do we need wisdom when we are going through trials? Why not ask for strength, or grace, or even deliverance? For this reason: *we need wisdom so we will not waste the opportunities God is giving us to mature.* Wisdom helps us understand how to use these circumstances for our good and God's glory.

An associate of mine, a gifted secretary, was going through great trials. She had had a stroke, her husband had gone blind, and then he had to be taken to the hospital where (we were sure) he would die. I saw her in church one Sunday and assured her that I was praying for her.

"What are you asking God to do?" she asked, and her question startled me.

"I'm asking God to help you and strengthen you," I replied.

"I appreciate that," she said, "but pray about one more thing. Pray that I'll have the wisdom not to waste all of this!"

She knew the meaning of James 1:5.

Applying God's Truth:

1. How would you define *wisdom* from a biblical perspective to a friend who might ask?

2. What are some problems you are facing today for which you need to request God's wisdom?

3. Since God "gives [wisdom] generously to all without finding fault," why do you think so many Christians are confused as to His will for their lives?

Scripture: Read James 1:12-15

"When tempted, no one should say, 'God is tempting me.' For God cannot be tempted by evil, nor does he tempt anyone; but each one is tempted when, by is own evil desire, he is dragged away and enticed" (James 1:13-14).

BEWARE THE HOOK

No temptation appears as temptation; it always seems more alluring than it really is. James used two illustrations from the world of sports to prove his point. *Dragged away* carries with it the idea of the baiting of a trap, and *enticed* in the original Greek means "to bait a hook." The hunter and the fisherman have to use bait to attract and catch their prey. No animal is deliberately going to step into a trap and no fish will knowingly bite at a naked hook. The idea is to *hide* the trap and the hook.

Temptation always carries with it some bait that appeals to our natural desires. The bait not only attracts us, but it also hides the fact that yielding to the desire will eventually bring sorrow and punishment. It is the bait that is the exciting thing.

When Jesus was tempted by Satan, He always dealt with the temptation on the basis of the Word of God. Three times He said, "It is written." From the human point of view, turning stones into bread to satisfy hunger is a sensible thing to do, but not from God's point of view. When you know the Bible, you can detect the bait and deal with it decisively. This is what it means to walk by faith and not by sight.

Applying God's Truth:

1. Are there certain areas where you seem more prone to temptation than other areas? What are they, and how do you try to deal with recurring temptations in those particularly vulnerable areas?

2. How would you differentiate between the fact that God allows testings of our faith (1:3), yet never tempts us (1:13)?

3. If someone wanted to tempt you to do wrong, what "bait" should he or she use? Whenever you see this bait, have you trained yourself to look for the "hook" as well?

Scripture: Read James 1:16-18

"Every good and perfect gift is from above, coming down from the Father of the heavenly lights, who does not change like shifting shadows" (James 1:17).

BRIGHT FORECAST

There are no shadows with the Father of Lights. It is impossible for God to change. He cannot change for the worse because He is holy; He cannot change for the better because He is already perfect. The light of the sun varies as the earth changes, but the sun itself is still shining. If shadows come between us and the Father, He did not cause them. He is the unchanging God. This means that we should never question His love or doubt His goodness when difficulties come or temptations appear.

The first barrier against temptation is a negative one: the judgment of God. The second barrier is positive: the goodness of God. A fear of God is a healthy attitude, but the love of God must balance it. We can obey Him because He may chasten us; or we can obey Him because He has already been so generous to us, and because we love Him for it.

The next time you are tempted, meditate on the goodness of God in your life. If you think you need something, wait on the Lord to provide it. Never toy with the devil's bait. One purpose for temptation is to teach us patience. David was tempted twice to kill King Saul and hasten his own coronation, but he resisted the temptation and waited for God's time.

Applying God's Truth:

1. Do you ever wish God would give you something *better* than what you have received from Him? If so, what do you think James would say about such thinking?

2. What are some things that occasionally get between you and God and tend to form "shadows"?

3. Are you completely, totally convinced of the absolute goodness of God? If not, what might you do to get a clearer perspective of His goodness?

Scripture: Read James 1:19-20

"Everyone should be quick to listen, slow to speak, and slow to become angry, for man's anger does not bring about the righteous life that God desires" (*James 1:19-20*).

TWO TO ONE

We have two ears and one mouth, which ought to remind us to listen more than we speak. Too many times we argue with God's Word, if not audibly, at least in our hearts and minds.

Do not get angry at God or His Word. "A patient man has great understanding, but a quick-tempered man displays folly" (Prov. 14:29). Many church fights are the result of short tempers and hasty words. There is a godly anger against sin, and if we love the Lord, we must hate sin. But man's anger does not produce God's righteousness. In fact, anger is just the opposite of the patience God wants to produce in our lives as we mature in Christ.

I once saw a poster that read, "Temper is such a valuable thing, it is a shame to lose it!" It is temper that helps to give steel its strength. The person who cannot get angry at sin does not have much strength to fight it. James warns us against getting angry at God's Word because it reveals our sins to us. Like the man who broke the mirror because he disliked the image in it, people rebel against God's Word because it tells the truth about them and their sinfulness.

Applying God's Truth:

1. When was the last time you became really angry? Do you think the situation would have been different if you had been quicker to listen and slower to speak?

2. In what ways do people tend to get angry at others in an attempt to "bring about the righteous life that God desires"?

3. If anger isn't a good solution to such situations, what are some better ones?

Scripture: Read James 1:21

"Get rid of all moral filth and the evil that is so prevalent, and humbly accept the word planted in you, which can save you" (James 1:21).

CROP FAILURE?

James saw the human heart as a garden; if left to itself, the soil would produce only weeds. He urged us to "pull out the weeds" and prepare the soil for the "implanted Word of God." He gives the picture of a garden overgrown with weeds that cannot be controlled. It is foolish to try to receive God's Word into an unprepared heart.

How do we prepare the soil of our hearts for God's Word? First, by confessing our sins and asking the Father to forgive us. Then, by meditating on God's love and grace and asking Him to "plow up" any hardness in our hearts. Finally, we must have an attitude of meekness. When you receive the Word with humility, you accept it, do not argue with it, and honor it as the Word of God. You do not try to twist it to conform it to your thinking.

If we do not receive the implanted Word, then we are deceiving ourselves. Christians who like to argue various "points of view" may be only fooling themselves. They think that their "discussions" are promoting spiritual growth, when in reality they may only be cultivating the weeds.

Applying God's Truth:

1. What are some of the "weeds" you've eliminated from your life since becoming a Christian? Do they tend to try to grow back, or have you pulled them up by the roots?

2. What are some other weeds with which you're still trying to deal?

3. In preparing your heart to receive God's Word, what do you find most difficult to do?

Scripture: Read James 1:23-27

"Anyone who listens to the word but does not do what it says is like a man who looks at his face in a mirror and, after looking at himself, goes away and immediately forgets what he looks like" (James 1:23-24).

THROUGH THE LOOKING GLASS

The main purpose for owning a mirror is to be able to see yourself and make yourself look as clean and neat as possible. As we look into the mirror of God's Word, we see ourselves as we really are. James mentions several mistakes people make as they look into God's mirror.

First, they merely glance at themselves. They do not carefully study themselves as they read the Word. Many sincere believers read a chapter of the Bible each day, but it is only a religious exercise and they fail to profit from it personally. Their conscience would bother them if they did not have their daily reading, when actually their conscience should bother them *because they read the word carelessly.*

The second mistake is that *they forget what they see.* If they were looking deeply enough into their hearts, what they would see would be unforgettable.

Mistake number three is: *they fail to obey what the Word tells them to do.* They think that hearing is the same as doing, and it is not. We Christians enjoy substituting reading for doing, or even talking for doing.

If we are to use God's mirror profitably, then we must gaze into it carefully and with serious intent. No quick glances will do. We must examine our own hearts and lives in the light of God's Word. This requires time, attention, and sincere devotion. Five minutes with God each day will never accomplish a deep spiritual examination.

Applying God's Truth:

1. How do you think your life would be different if mirrors had never been invented?

2. In your own experience, which of the three mistakes do you tend to make most frequently?

3. How might you need to restructure your devotional times in order to look more intently into the mirror of God's Word?

Scripture: Read James 2:1-4

"My brothers, as believers in our glorious Lord Jesus Christ, don't show favoritism" (*James 2:1*).

OUTER APPEARANCES

The religious experts in Christ's day judged Him by their human standards, and they rejected Him. He came from the wrong city, Nazareth of Galilee. He was not a graduate of their accepted schools. He did not have the official approval of the people in power. He had no wealth. His followers were a nondescript mob and included publicans and sinners. *Yet he was the very glory of God.*

Sad to say, we often make the same mistakes. When visitors come into our churches, we tend to judge them on what we see outwardly rather than what they are inwardly. Dress, color of skin, fashion, and other superficial things carry more weight than the fruit of the Spirit that may be manifest in their lives. We cater to the rich because we hope to get something out of them, and we avoid the poor because they embarrass us. Jesus did not do this, and He cannot approve of it.

How do we practice the deity of Christ in our human relationships? It is really quite simple: *look at everyone through the eyes of Christ.* If the visitor is a Christian, we can accept him because Christ lives in him. If he is not a Christian, we can receive him because Christ died for him. It is Christ who is the link between us and others, and he is a link of love. The basis for relationship with others is the person and work of Jesus Christ. Any other basis is not going to work.

Applying God's Truth:

1. Have you ever been a victim of discrimination? In what ways? Have you ever experienced *spiritual* discrimination?

2. Can you think of ways your church may tend to show favoritism to certain individuals or groups? Is there anything you can do about it?

3. Try this experiment: Attempt to see the next three people you come into contact with as you think Jesus would see those people. Make a mental note of any new observations you discover.

Scripture: Read James 2:5-9

"If you really keep the royal law found in Scripture, 'Love your neighbor as your-self,' you are doing right. But if you show favoritism, you sin and are convicted by the law as lawbreakers" (James 2:8-9).

LAW AND LOVE

Showing respect of persons can lead a person into disobeying all of God's Law. Take any one of the Ten Commandments and you will find ways of breaking it if you respect a person's social or financial status. Respect of persons could make you lie, for example. It could lead to idolatry (getting money out of the rich), or even mistreatment of one's parents. Once we start acting on the basis of respecting persons and rejecting God's Word, we are heading for trouble. And we need not break *all* of God's Law to be guilty. There is only one Lawgiver, and all of His Laws are from His mind and heart. If I disobey one law, I am capable of disobeying all of them; and by rebelling, I have already done so.

Christian love does not mean that I must *like* a person and agree with him on everything. I may not like his vocabulary or his habits, and I may not want him for an intimate friend. *Christian love means treating others the way God has treated me.* It is an act of the will, not an emotion that I try to manufacture. The motive is to glorify God. The means is the power of the Spirit within. As I act in love toward another, I may find myself drawn more and more to him, and I may see in him (through Christ) qualities that before were hidden to me.

Applying God's Truth:

1. What are some excuses you've heard people give to justify disobedience to God's clear commands?

2. Can you identify any ways in which your own "respect of persons" somehow interferes with your spiritual commitment?

3. Do you think it is possible to love someone you don't particularly like? Explain.

Scripture: Read James 2:10-13

"Speak and act as those who are going to be judged by the law that gives freedom, because judgment without mercy will be shown to anyone who has not been merciful. Mercy triumphs over judgment!" *(James 2:12-13)*

LICENSE AND LIBERTY

L iberty does not mean license. License (doing whatever I want to do) is the worst kind of bondage. Liberty means the freedom to be all that I can be in Jesus Christ. License is confinement; liberty is fulfillment.

The Word is called "the law that gives freedom" because God sees our hearts and knows what we would have done had we been free to do so. The Christian student who obeys only because the school has rules is not really maturing. What will he do when he leaves the school? God's Word can change our hearts and give us the desire to do God's will, so that we obey from inward compulsion and not outward constraint.

There is one obvious message to this section: our beliefs should control our behavior. If we really believe that Jesus is the Son of God, and that God is gracious, His Word is true, and one day He will judge us, then our conduct will reveal our convictions. Before we attack those who do not have orthodox doctrine, we must be sure that we practice the doctrines we defend. Jonah had wonderful theology, but he hated people and was angry with God (Jonah 4).

One of the tests of the reality of our faith is how we treat other people. Can we pass the test?

Applying God's Truth:

1. In what ways does mercy triumph over judgment?

2. What are some ways that you exercise your Christian liberty? Do you ever catch yourself trying to use a spiritual "license" to do something you shouldn't?

3. If a stranger observed your behavior for a week, do you think he or she could accurately determine your beliefs? Explain.

Scripture: Read James 2:14-19

"What good is it, my brothers, if a man claims to have faith but has no deeds? Can such faith save him?" (James 2:14)

DEAD FAITH

People with dead faith substitute words for deeds. They know the correct vocabulary for prayer and testimony, and can even quote the right verses from the Bible, but their walk does not measure up to their talk. They think that their words are as good as works, and they are wrong.

James gave a simple illustration in verses 15-16. A poor believer came into a fellowship without proper clothing and in need of food. The person with dead faith noticed the visitor and saw his needs, but he did not do anything to meet the needs. All he did was say a few pious words! "Go, I wish you well; keep warm and well fed." But the visitor went away just as hungry and naked as he came in.

As believers, we have an obligation to help meet the needs of people, no matter who they may be. "As we have opportunity, let us do good to all people, especially to those who belong to the family of believers" (Gal. 6:10). "I tell you the truth, whatever you did for one of the least of these brothers of mine, you did for me" (Matt. 25:40). To help a person in need is an expression of love, and faith works by love.

Applying God's Truth:

1. When was the last time you needed action from a person and received only words instead? How did you feel?

2. Do you think James is discounting the importance of faith by emphasizing actions so much? Why or why not?

3. Can you think of a time recently when *you* might have acted to help someone, yet settled for some kind of verbal affirmation instead? How can you prevent this from becoming a habit?

Scripture: Read James 2:20-26

"As the body without the spirit is dead, so faith without deeds is dead" *(James 2:26)*.

DYNAMIC FAITH

Faith is only as good as its object. The man in the jungle bows before an idol of stone and trusts it to help him, but he receives no help. No matter how much faith a person may generate, if it is not directed at the right object, it will accomplish nothing. "I believe" may be the testimony of many sincere people, but the big question is, "In whom do you believe? What do you believe?" We are not saved by *faith in faith*; we are saved by faith in Christ as revealed in His Word.

Dynamic faith is based on God's Word, and it involves the whole man. The whole person plays a part in true saving faith. The mind understands the truth, the heart desires the truth, and the will acts upon the truth. The men and women of faith named in Hebrews 11 were people of action: God spoke and they obeyed. Again, faith is not believing in spite of evidence; faith is obeying in spite of consequence.

True saving faith *leads to action*. Dynamic faith is not intellectual contemplation or emotional consternation; it leads to obedience on the part of the will. And this obedience is not an isolated event: it continues throughout the whole life. It leads to works.

Applying God's Truth:

1. List several things or people that you have faith in, and then rate them from "Most reliable" to "Least reliable."

2. When was a time recently when you had the faith to "obey in spite of consequence"? What happened as a result?

3. Do you think most people are capable of increasing their actions for God without increasing their faith? What do you think would be likely to happen as a result?

Scripture: Read James 3:1-6

"The tongue also is a fire, a world of evil among the parts of the body. It corrupts the whole person, sets the whole course of his life on fire, and is itself set on fire by hell" (James 3:6).

IT ONLY TAKES A SPARK

I was visiting the used bookstores along Charing Cross Road in London, and I remarked to a clerk that there were not as many stores as I expected. "There's a reason for that," he replied. "One night during World War II, the incendiary bombs hit and the fires destroyed at least a million books!"

On another occasion, a friend was taking my wife and me on a tour of the beautiful forests in California, and we came to an ugly section that was burned out. Not only was the face of nature scarred, but millions of dollars of valuable timber had been wiped out. "Somebody's lit cigarette," my friend commented as we drove past the blackened earth.

A fire can begin with just a small spark, but it can grow to destroy a city. A fire reportedly started in the O'Leary barn in Chicago at 8:30 P.M., October 8, 1871; and because that fire spread, over 100,000 people were left homeless, 17,500 buildings were destroyed, and 300 people died. It cost the city over $400,000,000.

Our words can start fires. In some churches, there are members or officers who cannot control their tongues, and the result is destruction. Let them move out of town or be replaced in office, and a beautiful spirit of harmony and love takes over.

Applying God's Truth:

1. In what ways have you experienced the destructive "fire" of someone else's harsh or insensitive words?

2. When was the last time you started a "four-alarm" verbal fire of your own? What started it, and what were the results?

3. Since the tongue is a fire, what qualities might you need to have at your disposal as a "spiritual fire extinguisher"?

Scripture: Read James 3:7-8

"No man can tame the tongue. It is a restless evil, full of deadly poison" (James 3:8).

TONGUE TAMING

Not only is the tongue like a fire, but it is also like a dangerous animal. It is restless and cannot be ruled, and it seeks its prey and then pounces and kills. My wife and I once drove through a safari park, admiring the animals as they moved about in their natural habitat. But there were warning signs posted all over the park: DO NOT LEAVE YOUR CAR! DO NOT OPEN YOUR WINDOWS! Those "peaceful" animals were capable of doing great damage, and even killing.

Some animals are poisonous, and some tongues spread poison. The deceptive thing about a poison is that it works secretly and slowly, and then it kills. How many times has some malicious person injected a bit of poison into the conversation, hoping it would spread and finally get to the person he or she wanted to hurt? As a pastor, I have seen poisonous tongues do great damage to individuals, families, classes, and entire churches. Would you turn hungry lions or angry snakes loose in your Sunday morning service? Of course not! But unruly tongues accomplish the same results.

James reminds us that animals can be tamed; and, for that matter, fire can be tamed. When you tame an animal, you get a worker instead of a destroyer. When you control fire, you generate power. The tongue cannot be tamed by man, but it can be tamed by God.

Applying God's Truth:

1. Based on your words during the past week, to what kind of animal(s) might you accurately compare your tongue?

2. Why is controlling our words particularly important in the context of church services?

3. In what ways do you think God "tames the tongue"? Do you think He can do so without our cooperation?

Scripture: Read James 3:9-12

"Out of the same mouth come praise and cursing. My brothers, this should not be" *(James 3:10).*

MIXED MESSAGES

If you and I are going to have tongues that delight, then we must meet with the Lord each day and learn from Him. We must get our "spiritual roots" deep into His Word. We must pray and meditate and permit the Spirit of God to fill our hearts with God's love and truth.

But James issued a warning: a fountain cannot give forth two kinds of water, and a tree cannot bear two different kinds of fruit. We expect the fountain to flow with sweet water at all times, and we expect the fig tree to bear figs and the olive tree to bear olives. Nature reproduces after its own kind.

If the tongue is inconsistent, there is something radically wrong with the heart. I heard about a professing Christian who got angry on the job and let loose with some oaths. Embarrassed, he turned to his partner and said, "I don't know why I said that. It really isn't in me." His partner wisely replied, "It had to be in you or it couldn't have come out of you."

The tongue that blessed the Father, and then turns around and curses men made in God's image, is in desperate need of spiritual medicine! How easy it is to sing the hymns during the worship service, then after the service, get into the family car and argue and fight all the way home! "My brothers, this should not be."

Applying God's Truth:

1. Can you think of anyone whose "inconsistent" tongue significantly damages his or her personal ministry?

2. Think of your comments to others so far today. What percentage of them were "fresh water"? What percentage were "salty" (or bitter)?

3. Can you think of any recent comment for which you need to go back to the person and apologize or otherwise make restitution?

Scripture: Read James 3:13-17

"The wisdom that comes from heaven is first of all pure; then peace loving, consider-ate, submissive, full of mercy and good fruit, impartial and sincere" (James 3:17).

KNOWLEDGE VERSUS WISDOM

Certainly, there is a great deal of knowledge in this world, and we all benefit from it; but there is not much wisdom. Man unlocks the secrets of the universe, but he does not know what to do with them. Almost every-thing he discovers or devises turns against him. Over a century ago, Henry David Thoreau warned that we had "improved means to unimproved ends."

Whenever I ride a bus or elevated train in the city, I often think of the man in Boston who was entertaining a famous Chinese scholar. He met his Oriental friends at the train station and rushed him to the subway. As they ran through the subway station, the host panted to his guest, "If we run and catch this next train, we will save three minutes!" To which the patient Chinese philosopher replied, "And what significant thing shall we do with the three minutes we are saving?"

Man's wisdom is foolishness to God (1 Cor. 1:20), and God's wisdom is foolishness to man (2:14). Man's wisdom comes from reason, while God's wisdom comes from revelation. Man's worldly wisdom will come to nothing (1:19), while God's wisdom will endure forever.

Applying God's Truth:

1. What is some "wisdom of the world" you've heard or read lately that con-flicts with God's wisdom?

2. What do you think are the primary sources of worldly wisdom?

3. On a scale of 1 (least) to 10 (most), rate your levels of wisdom according to each of the following standards: Purity, Peace-producing, Consideration of Others, Submission, Mercy, Impartiality, and Sincerity.

Scripture: Read James 3:18

"Peacemakers who sow peace raise a harvest of righteousness" (James 3:18).

SOWING AND REAPING

The Christian life is a life of sowing and reaping. For that matter, *every* life is a life of sowing and reaping, and we reap just what we sow. The Christian who obeys God's wisdom sows righteousness, not sin; and peace, not war. The life we live enables the Lord to bring righteousness and peace into the lives of others.

What we *are* is what we live, and what we live is what we sow. What we sow determines what we reap. If we live in God's wisdom, we sow righteousness and peace, and we reap God's blessing. If we live in man's worldly wisdom, we sow sin and war, and we reap "disorder and every evil practice" (v. 16).

It is a serious thing to be a troublemaker in God's family. One of the sins that God hates is that of sowing "dissension among brothers" (read Prov. 6:16-19). Lot followed the world's wisdom and brought trouble to the camp of Abraham, but Abraham followed God's wisdom and brought peace. Abraham's decision, in the wisdom of God, led to blessings for his own household and ultimately for the whole world. (Read Gen. 13.)

"Blessed is the man who finds wisdom, the man who gains understanding" (Prov. 3:13).

Applying God's Truth:

1. In what ways have you attempted to "sow in peace" lately?

2. What do you think is the connection between sowing in *peace* and harvesting *righteousness*?

3. Who is the best peacemaker you know? What can you learn from that person to become a better peacemaker yourself?

Scripture: Read James 4:1-6

"You do not have, because you do not ask God. When you ask, you do not receive, because you ask with wrong motives, that you may spend what you get on your pleasures" (James 4:2-3).

AT WAR WITH OURSELVES

The war in the heart is helping to cause the wars in the church! (v. 1) The essence of sin is selfishness. Selfish desires are dangerous things. They lead to *wrong actions* and they even lead to *wrong praying*. When our praying is wrong, our whole Christian life is wrong. It has well been said that the purpose of prayer is not to get man's will done in heaven, but to get God's will done on earth.

Sometimes we use prayer as a cloak to hide our true desires. "But I prayed about it!" can be one of the biggest excuses a Christian can use. Instead of seeking God's will, we tell God what He is supposed to do; and we get angry at Him if He does not obey. This anger at God eventually spills over and we get angry at God's people. More than one church split has been caused by saints who take out their frustrations with God on the members of the church. Many a church or family problem would be solved if people would only look into their own hearts and see the battle raging there.

Applying God's Truth:

1. Can you recall a time when selfish desires led to wrong actions? What did you learn from the experience?

2. Can you think of any times when you may have prayed with improper motives? What led you to eventually discover your selfish motives?

3. What are some things you don't have that you need to ask God for? How can you keep your motives pure as you ask God to provide for your needs?

Scripture: Read James 4:7-12

"Submit yourselves . . . to God. Resist the devil, and he will flee from you. Come near to God and he will come near to you" (James 4:7-8).

CLOSING THE DISTANCE

D r. A.W. Tozer has a profound essay in one of his books, entitled, "Nearness Is Likeness." The more we are like God, the nearer we are to God. I may be sitting in my living room with my Siamese cat on my lap, and my wife may be twenty feet away in the kitchen; yet I am nearer to my wife than to the cat because the cat is unlike me. We have very little in common.

God graciously draws near to us when we deal with the sin in our lives that keeps Him at a distance. He will not share us with anyone else; He must have complete control. The double-minded Christian can never be close to God.

It is possible to submit outwardly and yet not be humbled inwardly. God hates the sin of pride, and he will chasten the proud believer until he is humbled. We have a tendency to treat sin too lightly, even to laugh about it. But sin is serious, and one mark of true humility is facing the seriousness of sin and dealing with our disobedience.

Sometimes we hear a believer pray, "O Lord, humble me!" That is a dangerous thing to pray. Far better that we humble ourselves before God, confess our sins, weep over them, and turn from them.

Applying God's Truth:

1. What are some ways that you try to "draw near to God"? Which ones seem to work best for you?

2. How difficult do you find it to "resist the devil"? What methods do you use?

3. Do you try hard to humble yourself and get as close to God as possible, or do you feel safer or more comfortable when God seems to be at a distance?

Scripture: Read James 4:13-14

"You do not even know what will happen tomorrow. What is you life? You are a mist that appears for a little while and then vanishes" (James 4:14).

COUNTDOWN

We count our *years* at each birthday, but God tells us to number our *days* (Ps. 90:12). After all, we live a day at a time, and those days rush by quickly the older we grow.

Since life is so brief, we cannot afford merely to "spend our lives"; and we certainly do not want to "waste our lives." We must invest our lives in those things that are eternal.

God reveals His will and His Word, and yet most people ignore the Bible. In the Bible, God gives precepts, principles, and promises that can guide us in every area of life. Knowing and obeying the Word of God is the surest way to success.

Man cannot control future events. He has neither the wisdom to *see* the future nor the power to *control* the future. For him to boast is sin; it is making himself God. How foolish it is for people to ignore the will of God. It is like going through the dark jungles without a map, or over the stormy seas without a compass.

When we visited Mammoth Cave in Kentucky, I was impressed with the maze of tunnels and the dense darkness when the lights were turned off. When we got to the "Pulpit Rock," the man in charge of the tour gave a five-word sermon from it: "Stay close to your guide." Good counsel indeed!

Applying God's Truth:

1. If you knew you had only one week to live, list all the things you would want to do during that week.

2. What do you think is the difference between *spending* your life doing something and *investing* it in something?

3. Do you have a way of regularly evaluating how productive you are being for God? If not, what can you do to start such an evaluation?

Scripture: Read James 4:15-17

"You ought to say, 'If it is the Lord's will, we will live and do this or that'" *(James 4:15).*

OBEYING GOD'S WILL

It is important that we have the right attitude toward the will of God. Some people think God's will is a cold, impersonal machine. God starts it going and it is up to us to keep it functioning smoothly. If we disobey Him in some way, the machine grinds to a halt, and we are out of God's will for the rest of our lives.

God's will is not a cold, impersonal machine. You do not determine God's will in some mechanical way, like getting a soft drink out of a pop machine. *The will of God is a living relationship between God and the believer.*

I prefer to see the will of God as a warm, growing, living body. If something goes wrong with my body, I don't die: the other parts of the body compensate for it until I get that organ working properly again. There is pain; there is also weakness; but there is not necessarily death.

When you and I get out of God's will, it is not the end of everything. We suffer, to be sure; but when God cannot rule, He overrules. Just as the body compensates for the malfunctioning of one part, so God adjusts things to bring us back into His will.

Applying God's Truth:

1. On a scale of 1 to 10 where 1 is "Do your own thing" and 10 is "Follow God's will exclusively," where would you say you usually are?

2. What are some ways in which you try to determine God's will for your life?

3. What is one decision you're getting ready to make right now for which you first need to seek God's will?

351

Scripture: Read James 5:1-2

"Now listen, you rich people, weep and wail because of the misery that is coming upon you" *(James 5:1)*.

WANTS AND NEEDS

A magazine advertisement told of the shopping spree of an oil-rich Sultan. He purchased nineteen Cadillacs, one for each of his nineteen wives, and paid extra to have the cars lengthened. He also bought two Porsches, six Mercedes, a $40,000 speedboat, and a truck for hauling it. Add to the list sixteen refrigerators, $47,000 worth of women's luggage, two Florida grapefruit trees, two reclining chairs, and one slot machine. His total bill was $1,500,000, and he had to pay another $194,500 to have everything delivered. Talk about living in luxury!

All of us are grateful for the good things of life, and we would certainly not want to return to primitive conditions. But we recognize the fact that there is a point of diminishing returns. "Tell me what thou dost need," said the Quaker to his neighbor, " and I will tell thee how to get along without it." The rich men James addressed were feeding themselves on their riches and starving to death. The Greek word pictures cattle being fattened for the slaughter.

Luxury has a way of ruining character. It is a form of self-indulgence. If you match character with wealth, you can produce much good, but if you match self-indulgence with wealth, the result is sin.

Applying God's Truth:

1. Do you have any dreams or fantasies of luxury? If so, what do you sometimes dream about?

2. Do you own anything that you feel you absolutely, positively couldn't live without? If so, explain why.

3. Do you think you could be extremely wealthy without being selfish or self-indulgent? Why?

Scripture: Read James 5:3-6

"Your gold and silver are corroded. Their corrosion will testify against you and eat your flesh like fire. You have hoarded wealth in the last days" (James 5:3).

WHAT MONEY CAN'T BUY

It is good to have the things that money can buy, provided you also have the things that money cannot buy. What good is a $500,000 house if there is no home? Or a million-dollar diamond ring if there is no love? James did not condemn riches or rich people; he condemned the wrong use of riches, and rich people who use their wealth as a weapon and not as a tool with which to build.

It is possible to be poor in this world and yet rich in the next world. It is also possible to be rich in this world and poor in the next world. The return of Jesus Christ will make some people poor and others rich, depending on the spiritual condition of their hearts.

A famous preacher, known for his long sermons, was asked to give the annual "charity sermon" for the poor. It was suggested that if he preached too long, the congregation might not give as much as they should.

Yes, money talks. What will it say to you at the last judgment?

Applying God's Truth:

1. What are some things you have that money can't buy? Do you ever wish you could trade any of those things for cold, hard cash?

2. Would you say you are rich or poor in this world? Will you be rich or poor in the next world?

3. How important would you say money is to you? Why?

Scripture: Read James 5:7-9

"See how the farmer waits for the land to yield its valuable crop and how patient he is for the autumn and spring rains. You too, be patient and stand firm, because the Lord's coming is near" *(James 5:7-8).*

A COMING HARVEST

I f a man is impatient, then he had better not become a farmer. No crop appears overnight, and no farmer has control over the weather. He must also have patience with the seed and the crop, for it takes time for plants to grow. Jewish farmers would plow and sow in what to us are the autumn months. The "autumn rain" would soften the soil. The "spring rain" would come in February or March and help to mature the harvest. The farmer had to wait many weeks for his seed to produce fruit.

Why did he willingly wait so long? Because the fruit is "valuable." The harvest is worth waiting for. James pictured the Christian as a "spiritual farmer" looking for a spiritual harvest. There are seasons to the spiritual life just as there are seasons to the soil. Sometimes, our hearts become cold and "wintry," and the Lord has to "plow them up" before He can plant the seed. He sends the sunshine and the rains of His goodness to water and nurture the seeds planted, but we must be patient to wait for the harvest.

Here, then, is a secret of endurance when the going is tough: *God is producing a harvest in our lives.*

Applying God's Truth:

1 What are the situations in which you are usually most impatient? Why?

2. How can a "watchful farmer" mentality help you be more patient during times when your patience tends to wear thin?

3. Why do you think patience is so important as an element of spiritual maturity?

Scripture: Read James 5:10-11

"Brothers, as an example of patience in the face of suffering, take the prophets who spoke in the name of the Lord" (James 5:10).

PROPHET SHARING

The prophets encourage us by reminding us that God cares for us when we go through sufferings for His sake. Elijah announced to wicked King Ahab that there would be a drought in the land for three and one-half years, and Elijah himself had to suffer in that drought. But God cared for him, and God gave him victory over the evil priests of Baal. It has been said, "The will of God will never lead you where the grace of God cannot keep you."

Many of the prophets had to endure great trials and sufferings, not only at the hands of unbelievers, but at the hands of professed believers. Jeremiah was arrested as a traitor and even thrown into an abandoned well to die. God fed Jeremiah and protected him throughout that terrible siege of Jerusalem, even though at times it looked as though the prophet was going to be killed. Both Ezekiel and Daniel had their share of hardships, but the Lord delivered them. And even those who were not delivered, who died for the faith, received that special reward for those who are true to Him.

The impact of a faithful, godly life carries much power. We need to remind ourselves that our patience in times of suffering is a testimony to others around us.

Applying God's Truth:

1. How many instances from the Old Testament can you think of where a prophet modeled patience? (If you can't think of several, you might want to do some research.)

2. Have you ever been in the position of a prophet—taking a public and unpopular stand on an issue at the risk of your reputation (or worse)? What happened?

3. When you are in the minority, but know you are right, how do you keep from caving in to popular opinion?

Scripture: Read James 5:13-18

"Is any one of you in trouble? He should pray. Is anyone happy? Let him sing songs of praise" (James 5:13).

SONGS AND PRAYERS

Prayer can remove affliction, if that is God's will. But prayer can also give us the grace we need to endure troubles and use them to accomplish God's perfect will. *God can transform troubles into triumphs.* Paul prayed that God might change his circumstances, but instead, God gave Paul the grace he needed to turn his weakness into strength (2 Cor. 12:7-10). Our Lord prayed in Gethsemane that the cup might be removed, and it was not; yet the Father gave Him the strength He needed to go to the cross and die for our sins.

James indicated that everybody does not go through troubles at the same time. God balances our lives and gives us hours of suffering and days of singing. The mature Christian knows how to sing *while he is suffering.* (Anybody can sing after the trouble has passed.)

Praying and singing were important elements in worship in the early church, and they should be important to us. Our singing ought to be an expression of our inner spiritual life.

Applying God's Truth:

1. On a scale of 1 (least) to 10 (most), how would you rate yourself at going to God in prayer during times of trouble? How would you rate yourself at singing His praises when things are going well?

2. Do you have a song or songs that seem(s) to bring you closer to God? If not, try to choose one today that you can recall during your next stressful situation.

3. In what ways has God recently transformed some of your troubles into triumphs?

Scripture: Read James 5:19-20

"Remember this: Whoever turns a sinner from the error of his way will save him from death and cover over a multitude of sins" (James 5:20).

WINNING THE SAVED

What are we to do when we see a fellow believer wandering from the truth? We should pray for him, to be sure, but we must also seek to help him. He needs to be "converted"—turned back onto the right path again.

It is important that we seek to win the lost, but it is also important to win the saved. If a brother has sinned against us, we should talk to him privately and seek to settle the matter. If he listens, then we have "won our brother over" (Matt. 18:15).

If we are going to help an erring brother, we must have an attitude of love, for "love covers over a multitude of sins" (1 Peter 4:8). This does not mean that love "sweeps the dirt under the carpet." Where there is love, there must also be truth; and where there is truth, there is honest confession of sin and cleansing from God.

Love not only helps the offender to face his sins and deal with them, but love also assures the offender that those sins, once forgiven, are remembered no more.

Applying God's Truth:

1. On a scale of 1 (least) to 10 (most), how readily do you tend to confront someone you know who is caught up in some kind of sinful behavior? Why?

2. If you were involved in something sinful and harmful, would you want a friend to lovingly help you get rid of the problem and find your way back to a good standing with God? Why?

3. Do you think it's possible to confront someone about a sin without being judgmental or condescending? How?

HOPE

30 Daily Readings from the Book of 1 Peter

THE EMINENT PSYCHIATRIST DR. KARL MENNINGER CALLED HOPE "THE major weapon against the suicide impulse." He said that hope was "an adventure, a going forward—a confident search for a rewarding life" (*The Dictionary of Quotable Definitions*, ed. Eugene E. Brussell, Prentice-Hall).

Those who have trusted Christ as their Savior aren't searching for hope or life because we have both of these priceless possessions in Jesus Christ. Peter called it "a living hope"—a hope that is *alive* and *that gives us life* as we follow the Lord. A living hope makes life worth living.

All of us have days, maybe weeks, when the future looks dim, and we wonder if it's really worth it all to keep going. People, circumstances, health, finances—all of these things and more seem to conspire against us to rob us of our hope. That's when we need the "spiritual prescription" found in the ancient letter we call 1 Peter.

In this letter, the apostle explains what the Christian hope is and how it changes our lives. Peter makes it clear that God's children have no reason to despair no matter how they feel or what they face in life.

So, if you've been trying to manufacture hope in your heart, and the machinery has broken down, a study of 1 Peter is just what you need. The future is always bright when you are possessed by the living hope, trusting the living Word, and guided by the living Christ.

Scripture: Read 1 Peter 5:12

"I have written to you briefly, encouraging you and testifying that this is the true grace of God. Stand fast in it" (1 Peter 5:12).

HOPE: IT'S ALIVE

W hile there's life, there's hope!" That ancient Roman saying is still quoted today and, like most adages, it has an element of truth but no guarantee of certainty. It is not the fact of life that determines hope, but the faith of life. A Christian believer has a "living hope" (1:3) because his faith and hope are in God (v. 21). This "living hope" is the major theme of Peter's first letter. He is saying to all believers, "Be hopeful!"

The writer's given name was Simon, but Jesus changed it to Peter, which means "a stone" (John 1:35-42). The Aramaic equivalent of "Peter" is "Cephas," so Peter was a man with three names. Nearly fifty times in the New Testament, he is called "Simon", and often he is called "Simon Peter." Perhaps the two names suggest a Christian's two natures: an old nature (Simon) that is prone to fail, and a new nature (Peter) that can give victory. As Simon, he was only another human piece of clay, but Jesus Christ made a rock out of him!

Applying God's Truth:

1. If Jesus changed your name (or gave you a nickname), what do you think it would be? Why?

2. Would you say that hope in your life is *living*? To what extent? (Thriving? A little weak? *Barely* alive? etc.)

3. What situation in your life would you say is most in need of new levels of hope?

Scripture: Read 1 Peter 1:1-2

"Peter, an apostle of Jesus Christ, to God's elect, strangers in the world . . . Grace and peace be yours in abundance" (1 Peter 1:1-2).

THREE UNITED THEMES

As we study 1 Peter, we will see how the three themes of suffering, grace, and glory unite to form an encouraging message for believers experiencing times of trial and persecution. These themes are summarized in 5:10, a verse we would do well to memorize.

The cynical editor and writer H.L. Mencken once defined hope as "a pathological belief in the occurrence of the impossible." But that definition does not agree with the New Testament meaning of the word. True Christian hope is more than "hope so." It is confident assurance of future glory and blessing.

This confident hope gives us the encouragement and enablement we need for daily living. It does not put us in a rocking chair where we complacently await the return of Jesus Christ. Instead, it puts us in the marketplace, on the battlefield, where we keep on going when the burdens are heavy and the battles are hard. Hope is not a sedative; it is a shot of adrenaline, a blood transfusion. Like an anchor, our hope in Christ stabilizes us in the storms of life (Heb. 6:18-19), but unlike an anchor, our hope moves us forward, it does not hold us back.

Applying God's Truth:

1. On a scale of 1 (least) to 10 (most), to what level do you currently feel you are experiencing suffering? God's grace? God's glory?

2. How would you explain Christian "hope" to a stranger who asked?

3. Can you think of a time in the recent past when your hope was like "a shot of adrenaline"? What were the circumstances?

Scripture: Read 1 Peter 1:3-5

"In his great mercy he has given us new birth into a living hope through the resurrection of Jesus Christ from the dead, and into an inheritance that can never perish, spoil or fade" (1 Peter 1:3-4).

GLORY BE

On a balmy summer day, my wife and I visited one of the world's most famous cemeteries located at Stoke Poges, a little village not far from Windsor Castle in England. On this site Thomas Gray penned his famous "Elegy Written in a Country Churchyard," a poem most of us had to read at one time or another in school.

As we stood quietly in the midst of ancient graves, one stanza of that poem came to mind:

> The boast of heraldry, the pomp of power
> And all that beauty, all that wealth e're gave,
> Awaits alike the inevitable hour,
> The paths of glory lead but to the grave.

Man's glory simply does not last, but God's glory is eternal; and He has deigned to share that glory with us!

What do we mean by "the glory of God"? The glory of God means the sum total of all that God is and does. "Glory" is not a separate attribute or characteristic of God, such as His holiness, wisdom, or mercy. Everything that God is and does is characterized by glory. He is glorious in wisdom and power, so that everything He thinks and does is marked by glory. He reveals His glory in creation (Ps. 19), in His dealings with the people of Israel, and especially in His plan of salvation for lost sinners.

Applying God's Truth:

1. Prior to this reading, what would have been your definition of God's "glory"?

2. How have you recently witnessed God's glory expressed in creation?

3. How have you recently witnessed God's glory in other ways in your life?

Scripture: Read 1 Peter 1:6-7

"In this you greatly rejoice, though now for a little while you may have had to suffer grief in all kinds of trials" (1 Peter 1:6).

WHY TRIALS?

All God plans and performs here is preparation for what He has in store for us in heaven. He is preparing us for the life and service yet to come. Nobody yet knows all that is in store for us in heaven, but this we do know: life today is a school in which God trains us for our future ministry in eternity. This explains the presence of trials in our lives: they are some of God's tools and textbooks in the school of Christian experience.

Peter illustrated this truth by referring to the goldsmith. No goldsmith would deliberately waste the precious ore. He would put it into the smelting furnace long enough to remove the cheap impurities; then he would pour it out and make from it a beautiful article of value. It has been said that the eastern goldsmith kept the metal in the furnace until he could see his face reflected in it. So our Lord keeps us in the furnace of suffering until we reflect the glory and beauty of Jesus Christ.

Applying God's Truth:

1. What have some of your previous trials taught you about God that you might not have known otherwise?

2. What have your previous trials taught you about *yourself*?

3. As you dwell on many of the trials that you've overcome with God's grace, what are some things you can be sure of as you face *present* trials?

Scripture: Read 1 Peter 1:8-12

"Even though you do not see him now, you believe in him and are filled with an inexpressible and glorious joy, for you are receiving the goal of your faith, the salvation of your souls" (1 Peter 1:8-9).

IF YOU COULD SEE IT, IT WOULDN'T BE FAITH

We must live by faith and not by sight. An elderly lady fell and broke her leg while attending a summer Bible conference. She said to the pastor who visited her, "I know the Lord led me to the conference. But I don't see why this had to happen! And I don't see any good coming from it." Wisely, the pastor replied, "Romans 8:28 doesn't say we *see* all things working together for good. It says that we *know* it."

Faith means surrendering all to God and obeying His Word in spite of circumstances and consequences. Love and faith go together: when you love someone, you trust him. And faith and love together help to strengthen hope; for where you find faith and love, you will find confidence for the future.

How can we grow in faith during times of testing and suffering? The same way we grow in faith when things seem to be going well: by feeding on the Word of God (Rom. 10:17). Our fellowship with Christ through His Word not only strengthens our faith, but it also deepens our love. It is a basic principle of Christian living that we spend much time in the Word when God is testing us and Satan is tempting us.

Applying God's Truth:

1. Even though you can't see God, would you say your faith is "blind"? Explain.

2. What is an issue of faith you are really struggling with at this time because you can't "see" an answer? As you struggle, what is your goal?

3. When you are facing difficult times, do you have favorite passages of Scripture you go to? (Ask this question to three other people this week and "trade" favorite verses to expand your collection.)

Scripture: Read 1 Peter 1:13-16

"Prepare your minds for action; be self-controlled; set your hope fully on the grace to be given you when Jesus Christ is revealed" (1 Peter 1:13).

MIND CONTROL

Prepare your minds for action" (or, "Gird up the loins of your mind" [KJV]) simply means, "Pull your thoughts together! Have a disciplined mind!" The image is that of a robed man, tucking his skirts under the belt, so he can be free to run. When you center your thoughts on the return of Christ, and live accordingly, you escape the many worldly things that would encumber your mind and hinder your spiritual progress.

Outlook determines outcome; attitude determines action. A Christian who is looking for the glory of God has a greater motivation for present obedience than a Christian who ignores the Lord's return.

Not only should we have a disciplined mind, but we should have a sober and optimistic mind as well. The result of this spiritual mind-set is that a believer experiences the grace of God in his life. To be sure, we will experience grace when we see Jesus Christ, but we can also experience grace *today* as we look for Him to return. We have been saved by grace and we depend moment by moment on God's grace. Looking for Christ to return strengthens our faith and hope in difficult days, and this imparts to us more of the grace of God

Applying God's Truth:

1. In what ways do you "prepare your mind for action" in a spiritual sense?

2. Do you feel that you are "self-controlled" when it comes to your thoughts and attitudes? In what areas do you need improvement?

3. To what extent do you feel that you "experience the grace of God in your life"? What might you do to increase your awareness of His grace?

Scripture: Read 1 Peter 1:17

"Since you call on a Father who judges each man's work impartially, live your lives as strangers here in reverent fear" (1 Peter 1:17).

THE PRIVILEGE NOT GRANTED

God will give us many gifts and privileges as we grow in the Christian life, but He will never give us the privilege to disobey and sin. He never pampers His children or indulges them. He is not a respecter of persons. He "shows no partiality and accepts no bribes" (Deut. 10:17). "For God does not show favoritism" (Rom. 2:11). Years of obedience cannot purchase an hour of disobedience. If one of His children disobeys, God must chasten (Heb. 12:1-13). But when His child obeys and serves Him in love, He notes that and prepares the proper reward.

Peter reminds his readers that they were only "sojourners" (KJV) on earth. Life was too short to waste in disobedience and sin (see 1 Peter 4:1-6). It was when Lot stopped being a sojourner, and became a resident in Sodom, that he lost his consecration and his testimony. Everything he lived for went up in smoke! Keep reminding yourself that you are a "stranger and pilgrim" in this world.

In view of the fact that the Father lovingly disciplines His children today, and will judge their works in the future, we ought to cultivate an attitude of godly fear. This is not the cringing fear of a slave before a master, but the loving reverence of a child before his father. It is not fear of judgment, but a fear of disappointing Him or sinning against His love. It is "godly fear," a sober reverence for the Father.

Applying God's Truth:

1. Have you given up sins that you occasionally wish you could indulge in again—perhaps just for a few minutes?

2. Do you think it's fair that Christians are expected to obey God's law *all* the time while the rest of the world lives it up as they please? Explain.

3. What would you say is the difference between fear and "godly fear"?

Scripture: Read 1 Peter 1:18-21

"You know that it was not with perishable things such as silver and gold that you were redeemed . . . but with the precious blood of Christ" *(1 Peter 1:18-19).*

LEAVING SLAVERY BEHIND

The love of God is the highest motive for holy living. Peter reminded his readers of their salvation experience, a reminder that all of us regularly need. He reminded them of what they were. They were slaves who needed to be set free.

There were probably 50 million slaves in the Roman Empire! Many slaves became Christians and fellowshipped in the local assemblies. A slave could purchase his own freedom, if he could collect sufficient funds; or his master could sell him to someone who would pay the price and set him free. Redemption was a precious thing in that day.

We must never forget the slavery of sin. Not only did we have a life of slavery, but it was also a life of emptiness. At the time, these people thought their lives were "full" and "happy," when they were really empty and miserable. Unsaved people today are blindly living on substitutes.

While ministering in Canada, I met a woman who told me she had been converted early in life but had drifted into a "society life" that was exciting and satisfied her ego. One day, she was driving to a card party and happened to tune in a Christian radio broadcast. At that very moment, the speaker said, "Some of you women know more about cards than you do your Bible!" Those words arrested her. God spoke to her heart, she went back home, and from that hour her life was dedicated fully to God. She saw the futility and vanity of a life spent out of the will of God.

Applying God's Truth:

1. What types of "slavery" did you experience prior to becoming a Christian?

2. Does "holy living" ever seem like "boring living" to you? If so, how do you generate more excitement about living as God has instructed?

3. What are some "substitutes" that people try (rather than a personal relationship with God) as they seek to fill the emptiness in their lives?

Scripture: Read 1 Peter 1:22–2:3

"Like newborn babies, crave pure spiritual milk, so that by it you may grow up in your salvation, now that you have tasted that the Lord is good" (1 Peter 2:2-3).

MILK: IT DOES A BODY GOOD

God's Word *has* life, *gives* life, and *nourishes* life. We should have appetites for the Word just like hungry newborn babes! We should want the *pure* Word, unadulterated, because this alone can help us grow. When I was a child, I did not like to drink milk (and my father worked for the Borden Dairy!), so my mother used to add various syrups and powders to make my milk tastier. None of them really ever worked. It is sad when Christians have no appetite for God's Word, but must be "fed" religious entertainment instead. As we grow, we discover that the Word is milk for babes, but also strong meat for the mature (Heb. 5:11-14; 1 Cor. 3:1-4). It is also bread (Matt. 4:4) and honey (Ps. 119:103).

Sometimes children have no appetite because they have been eating the wrong things. Peter warned his readers to "lay aside" certain wrong attitudes of heart that would hinder their appetite and spiritual growth. When Christians are growing in the Word, they are peacemakers, not troublemakers, and they promote the unity of the church.

Applying God's Truth:

1. If you received physical nourishment with the same regularity that you receive spiritual nourishment from God's Word, what kind of shape would you be in?

2. In what way(s) does God's Word *give* you life? How does it *nourish* your life?

3. Can you think of anything you've been "nibbling on" lately that might affect your spiritual appetite?

Scripture: Read 1 Peter 2:4-8

"As you come to him, the living Stone—rejected by men but chosen by God and precious to him—you also, like living stones, are being built into a spiritual house" *(1 Peter 2:4-5).*

ALL TOGETHER NOW!

Peter wrote this letter to believers living in five different provinces, yet he said that they all belonged to one "spiritual house." There is a unity of God's people that transcends all local and individual assemblies and fellowships. We belong to each other because we belong to Christ.

A contractor in Michigan was building a house and the construction of the first floor went smoothly. But when they started on the second floor, they had nothing but trouble. None of the materials from the lumber yard would fit properly. Then they discovered the reason: they were working with two different sets of blueprints! Once they got rid of the old set, everything went well and they built a lovely house.

Too often, Christians hinder the building of the church because they are following the wrong plans. When Solomon built his temple, his workmen followed the plans so carefully that everything fit together on the construction site (1 Kings 6:7). If all of us would follow God's blueprints, given in His Word, we would be able to work together without discord and build His church for His glory.

Applying God's Truth:

1. On a scale of 1 (least) to 10 (most), how much unity would you say your immediate family has? Your church? Your workplace?

2. Can you think of a time when you tried to "build" according to your own blueprints rather than God's? What happened?

3. Think of three people you have frequent conflicts with (or whom you try to avoid). What might you do to try to create better unity with each person?

Scripture: Read 1 Peter 2:9-10

"You are a chosen people, a royal priesthood, a holy nation, a people belonging to God, that you may declare the praises of him who called you out of darkness into his wonderful light" (1 Peter 2:9).

FAMILY, STONES, PRIESTS, CITIZENS

We belong to one family of God and share the same divine nature. We are living stones in one building and priests serving in one temple. We are citizens of the same heavenly homeland. It is Jesus Christ who is the source and center of this unity. If we center our attention and affection on Him, we will walk and work together; if we focus on ourselves, we will only cause division.

Unity does not eliminate diversity. Not all children in a family are alike, nor are all the stones in a building identical. In fact, it is diversity that gives beauty and richness to a family or building. The absence of diversity is not *unity*; it is *uniformity*, and uniformity is dull. It is fine when the choir sings in unison, but I prefer that they sing in harmony.

Christians can differ and still get along. All who cherish the "one faith" and who seek to honor the "one Lord" can love each other and walk together (Eph. 4:1-6). God may call us into different ministries, or to use different methods, but we can still love each other and seek to present a united witness to the world.

St. Augustine said it perfectly: "In essentials, unity. In nonessentials, liberty. In all things, charity."

Applying God's Truth:

1. Which of Peter's analogies (family, stones, priests, citizens) do you think best describes God's people? Why?

2. What are some examples where people try to substitute uniformity for unity, and only end up making things worse?

3. Can you think of a personal example where diversity of individuals combined for the unity of a group and resulted in the glory of God?

Scripture: Read 1 Peter 2:11-12

"Live such good lives among the pagans that, though they accuse you of doing wrong, they may see your good deeds and glorify God on the day he visits us" *(1 Peter 2:12).*

PEOPLE ARE WATCHING

In the summer of 1805, a number of Indian chiefs and warriors met in council at Buffalo Creek, New York, to hear a presentation of the Christian message by a Mr. Cram from the Boston Missionary Society. After the sermon, a response was given by Red Jacket, one of the leading chiefs. Among other things, the chief said:

"Brother, you say there is but one way to worship and serve the Great Spirit. If there is but one religion, why do you white people differ so much about it? Why not all agree, as you can all read the Book?

"Brother, we are told that you have been preaching to the white people in this place. These people are our neighbors. We are acquainted with them. We will wait a little while and see what effect your preaching has upon them. If we find it does them good, makes them honest and less disposed to cheat Indians, we will then consider again of what you have said."

Peter encouraged his readers to bear witness to the lost, by word and deed, so that one day God might visit them and save them. When these people do trust Christ, they will glorify God and give thanks because we were faithful to witness to them even when they made life difficult for us.

Applying God's Truth:

1. Can you recall a time when you were trying to follow another person's example, only to be disappointed when he or she let you down in some way? How might you avoid such disappointments in the future?

2. Who are the people who look at you as an example for what a Christian should be?

3. Are you satisfied with the example you set for others? If not, how can you improve it?

Scripture: Read 1 Peter 2:13-25

"Show proper respect to everyone: Love the brotherhood of believers, fear God, honor the king" (1 Peter 2:17).

POLITICALLY CORRECT

A true Christian submits himself to authority because he is first of all submitted to Christ. He uses his freedom as a tool to build with and not as a weapon to fight with. A good example of this attitude is Nehemiah, who willingly gave up his own rights that he might help his people and restore the walls of Jerusalem.

If we are sincerely submitted to authority "for the Lord's sake," then we will show honor to all who deserve it. We may not agree with their politics or their practices, but we must respect their position. (See Rom. 13.) We will also "love the brotherhood," meaning, of course, the people of God in the church. This is a recurring theme in this letter. One way we show love to the brethren is by submitting to the authority of the "powers that be," for we are bound together with one another in our Christian witness.

We honor the king because we do fear the Lord. It is worth noting that the tenses of these verbs indicate that we should *constantly* maintain these attitudes. "Keep loving the brotherhood! Keep fearing God! Keep honoring the king!"

Applying God's Truth:

1. Do you know Christians who frequently criticize national or local politicians? Do *you*? Do you think such criticism has anything to do with submitting to their authority? Explain.

2. When *you* are in a position of authority, what do you do to try to earn the respect of those under your control?

3. On a scale of 1 (least) to 10 (most), where would you stand on loving the brotherhood? Fearing God? Honoring political leaders?

Scripture: Read 1 Peter 3:1-2

"Wives, in the same way be submissive to your husbands so that, if any of them do not believe the word, they may be won over without talk by the behavior of their wives (1 Peter 3:1).

COMMOTION VERSUS COMMITMENT

While standing in the checkout line in a supermarket, I overheard two women discussing the latest Hollywood scandal that was featured on the front page of a newspaper displayed on the counter. As I listened (and I could not *help* but hear them!), I thought: "How foolish to worry about the sinful lives of matinee idols. Why clutter up your mind with such trash? Why not get acquainted with decent people and learn from their lives?"

When Christian couples try to imitate the world and get their standards from Hollywood instead of from heaven, there will be trouble in the home. But if both partners will imitate Jesus Christ in His submission and obedience, and His desire to serve others, then there will be triumph and joy in the home.

A psychiatrist friend of mine states that the best thing a Christian husband can do is pattern himself after Jesus Christ. In Christ we see a beautiful blending of strength and tenderness, and that is what it takes to be a successful husband.

We cannot follow Christ's example unless we first know Him as our Savior, and then submit to Him as our Lord. We must spend time with Him each day, meditating on the Word and praying, and a Christian husband and wife must pray together and seek to encourage each other in the faith.

Applying God's Truth:

1. How many celebrity marriages or break-ups can you recall from the "news" during the past several months? Why do you think so many people find such things newsworthy?

2. What couple do you know who best demonstrates the meaning of real love? What do you think is their "secret"?

3. In order of priority, what are the top ten characteristics you admire (or desire) in your spouse (or potential spouse)?

Scripture: Read 1 Peter 3:3-6

"Your beauty . . . should be that of your inner self, the unfading beauty of a gentle and quiet spirit, which is of great worth in God's sight" (1 Peter 3:3-4).

SUBMISSION AND ATTRACTION

It is the character and conduct of the wife that will win the lost husband—not arguments, but such attitudes as submission, understanding, love, kindness, patience. These qualities are not manufactured; they are the fruit of the Spirit that comes when we are submitted to Christ and to one another.

One of the greatest examples of a godly wife and mother in church history is Monica, the mother of the famous St. Augustine. God used Monica's witness and prayers to win both her son and her husband to Christ, though her husband was not converted until shortly before his death. Augustine wrote in his *Confessions*, "She served him as her lord, and did her diligence to win him unto Thee . . . preaching Thee unto him by her conversation [behavior]; by which Thou ornamentest her, making her reverently amiable unto her husband."

In a Christian home, we must minister to each other. A Christian husband must minister to his wife and help to "beautify her" in the Lord (Eph. 5:25-30). A Christian wife must encourage her husband and help him grow strong in the Lord. If there are unsaved people in the home, they will be won to Christ more by what they see in our lives and relationships than by what they hear in our witness.

Applying God's Truth:

1. What letter grade would you give yourself in each of the following "subjects": Submission? Understanding? Love? Kindness? Patience?

2. Can you think of a specific instance when you chose to be submissive and accomplished much more good than if you had argued your case?

3. If an unsaved person had witnessed your actions this past week, do you think he or she would want to become a Christian? Why?

Scripture: Read 1 Peter 3:7

"Husbands, in the same way be considerate as you live with your wives, and treat them with respect as the weaker partner and as heirs with you of the gracious gift of life, so that nothing will hinder your prayers" (1 Peter 3:7).

IGNORANCE IS AMISS

Somebody asked Mrs. Albert Einstein if she understood Dr. Einstein's theory of relativity, and she replied, "No, but I understand the Doctor." In my premarital counseling as a pastor, I often gave the couple pads of paper and asked them to write down the three things each one thinks the other enjoys doing the most. Usually, the prospective bride made her list immediately; the man would sit and ponder. And usually the girl was right but the man wrong! What a beginning for a marriage!

It is amazing that two married people can live together and not really know each other! Ignorance is dangerous in any area of life, but it is especially dangerous in marriage. A Christian husband needs to know his wife's moods, feelings, needs, fears, and hopes. He needs to "listen with his heart" and share meaningful communication with her. There must be in the home such a protective atmosphere of love and submission that the husband and wife can disagree and still be happy together. When either mate is afraid to be open and honest about a matter, then you are building walls and not bridges.

Applying God's Truth:

1. What are three things you might like to do on your next free night? (If married, see how many of these thing your spouse predicts you will say.)

2. If one spouse isn't very good at "listening with the heart," what are some things the other spouse might try?

3. What are three things you can do to be able to disagree with someone else (especially a spouse) and still be happy together?

Scripture: Read 1 Peter 3:8-12

"Do not repay evil with evil or insult with insult, but with blessing, because to this you were called so that you might inherit a blessing" (1 Peter 3:9).

RESPONSE OPTIONS

As Christians, we can live on one of three levels. We can return evil for good, which is the satanic level. We can return good for good and evil for evil, which is the human level. Or, we can return good for evil, which is the divine level. Jesus is the perfect example of this latter approach (2:21-23). As God's loving children, we must not give "eye for eye, and tooth for tooth" (Matt. 5:38-48), which is the basis for *justice*. We must operate on the basis of *mercy*, for that is the way God deals with us.

We must always be reminded of our *calling* as Christians, for this will help us love our enemies and do them good when they treat us badly. We are called to "inherit a blessing." The persecutions we experience on earth today only add to our blessed inheritance of glory in heaven someday (vv. 10-12). But we also inherit a blessing *today* when we treat our enemies with love and mercy. By sharing a blessing with them, we receive a blessing ourselves! Persecution can be a time of spiritual enrichment for a believer. The saints and martyrs in church history all bear witness to this fact.

Applying God's Truth:

1. Can you think of a relationship you have with someone that continues to be bad because neither of you will make the first move toward reconciliation? What would it take for you to be willing to make the first move this week?

2. When is the last time you returned good for evil? Why do you think this is such an infrequent option for most people?

3. How much of an effort do you make to genuinely love your enemies? What are some new things you might try?

Scripture: Read 1 Peter 3:13-17

"Who is going to harm you if you are eager to do good? But even if you should suffer for what is right, you are blessed" (1 Peter 3:13-14).

FEARLESS (OR, AT LEAST, LESS FEAR)

As Christians, we are faced with crises, and we are tempted to give in to our fears and make the wrong decisions. But if we "set apart Christ as Lord" in our hearts, we need never fear men or circumstances. Our enemies might *hurt* us, but they can never *harm* us. Only we can harm ourselves if we fail to trust God. Generally speaking, people do not oppose us if we do good; but even if they do, it is better to suffer for righteousness' sake than to compromise our testimony.

Instead of experiencing fear as we face the enemy, we can experience blessing, if Jesus Christ is Lord in our hearts. When Jesus Christ is Lord of our lives, each crisis becomes an opportunity for witness. We are "always prepared to give an answer." Every Christian should be able to give a reasoned defense of his hope in Christ, *especially in hopeless situations.* A crisis creates the opportunity for witness when a believer behaves with faith and hope, because the unbelievers will then sit up and take notice.

Applying God's Truth:

1. Do you ever experience elements of fear in any part of your spiritual life?

2. What is the worst you've ever suffered because of your faith?

3. Under what situations are you most tempted to compromise your faith? Or are you consistently firm when dealing with bosses, strangers, skeptics, and such?

Scripture: Read 1 Peter 3:18-20

"[Christ] went and preached to the spirits in prison who disobeyed long ago when God waited patiently in the days of Noah while the ark was being built" (1 Peter 3:19-20).

ACT NOW

Jesus Christ is the only Savior, and the lost world needs to hear His Gospel. Some people try to use this complex passage of Scripture to prove a "second chance for salvation after death." But even if these "spirits" were those of unsaved people, this passage says nothing about their salvation. And why would Jesus offer salvation (if He did) *only to sinners from Noah's day?* And why did Peter use a different verb meaning "proclaim as a herald" instead of the usual word for preaching the Gospel?

Hebrews 9:27 makes it clear that death ends the opportunity for salvation. This is why the church needs to get concerned about evangelism and missions, because people are dying who have never even heard the Good News of salvation, let alone had the opportunity to reject it. It does us no good to quibble about differing interpretations of a difficult passage of Scripture, if what we *do* believe does not motivate us to want to share the Gospel with others.

Peter made it clear that difficult days give us multiplied opportunities for witness.

Are we taking advantage of our opportunities?

Applying God's Truth:

1. How might this difficult passage be used in a discussion of "Is there life after death"?

2. When you consider that "death ends the opportunity for salvation," can you think of anyone whom you want or need to spend more time with in order to share some spiritual truths?

3. Have you set any spiritual goals that you hope to accomplish before your own death?

Scripture: Read 1 Peter 3:20-22

"In it only a few people, eight in all, were saved through water, and this water sym-bolizes baptism that now saves you also" *(1 Peter 3:20-21)*

NOAH WAY

W hat relationship did Peter see between his readers and the ministry of Noah? For one thing, Noah was a "preacher of righteousness" (2 Peter 2:5) during a very difficult time in history. The early Christians knew that Jesus had promised that, before His return, the world would become like the "days of Noah" (Matt. 24:37-39); and they were expecting Him soon (2 Peter 3:1-3). As they saw society decay around them, and persecution begin, they would think of our Lord's words.

Noah was a man of faith who kept doing the will of God even when he seemed to be a failure. This would certainly be an encouragement to Peter's readers. If we measured faithfulness by results, then Noah would get a very low grade. Yet God ranked him very high!

But this is another connection: Peter saw in the Flood a picture (type) of a Christian's experience of baptism. The Flood pictures death, burial, and resurrection. The waters buried the earth in judgment, but they also lifted Noah and his family up to safety. The early church saw in the ark a picture of salvation. Noah and his family were saved by faith because they believed God and entered into the ark of safety. So sinners are saved by faith when they trust Christ and become one with Him.

Applying God's Truth:

1. What sinful things have you witnessed this week that would have made Noah feel right at home?

2. What aspects of being a Christian might seem as absurd to outsiders as Noah's building an ark? How do you handle skepticism others may have toward your faith?

3. If Noah were to offer advice about being a godly example in a sinful world, what do you think he might tell you?

Scripture: Read 1 Peter 4:1-3

"Since Christ suffered in his body, arm yourselves also with the same attitude, because he who has suffered in his body is done with sin" *(1 Peter 4:1).*

USED TO THE DARK?

The picture in verse 1 is that of a soldier who puts on his equipment and arms himself for battle. Our attitudes are weapons, and weak or wrong attitudes will lead us to defeat. Outlook determines outcome, and a believer must have the right attitudes if he is to live a right life.

A friend and I met at a restaurant to have lunch. It was one of those places where the lights are low, and you need a miner's helmet to find your table. We had been seated several minutes before we started looking at the menu, and I remarked that I was amazed how easily I could read it. "Yes," said my friend, "it doesn't take us long to get accustomed to the darkness."

There is a sermon in that sentence: It is easy for Christians to get accustomed to sin. Instead of having a militant attitude that hates and opposes it, we gradually get used to sin, sometimes without even realizing it. The one thing that will destroy "the rest of our earthly life" (v. 2) is sin. A believer living in sin is a terrible weapon in the hands of Satan.

Applying God's Truth:

1. In what ways have your attitudes of the past week been "weapons"?

2. What are some sins that many Christians gradually get used to?

3. Can you identify any "dim" areas in your own life where the light of God's truth needs to shine through more brightly?

Scripture: Read 1 Peter 4:4-6

"[The pagans] think it strange that you do not plunge with them into the same flood of dissipation, and they heap abuse on you" (1 Peter 4:4).

LOST PATIENCE

U nsaved people do not understand the radical change that their friends experience when they trust Christ and become children of God. They do not think it strange when people wreck their bodies, destroy their homes, and ruin their lives by running from one sin to another! But let a drunkard become sober, or an immoral person pure, and the family thinks he has lost his mind!

We must be patient toward the lost, even though we do not agree with their lifestyles or participate in their sins. After all, unsaved people are blind to spiritual truth (2 Cor. 4:3-4) and dead to spiritual enjoyment (Eph. 2:1). In fact, our contact with the lost is important *to them* since we are the bearers of the truth that they need. When unsaved friends attack us, this is our opportunity to witness to them (1 Peter 3:15).

The unsaved may judge us, but one day, God will judge them. Instead of arguing with them, we should pray for them, knowing that the final judgment is with God.

Applying God's Truth:

1. Do you know an unsaved person who is a real annoyance, yet for whom you may be the sole contact with Christianity? What do you do to maintain that relationship?

2. When you are annoyed or antagonized by lost people, what steps can you take to remain patient?

3. You may feel you are making no progress with your unsaved associates, but do you think the situation might change the next time they go through an intense emotional crisis? In what ways?

Scripture: Read 1 Peter 4:7-11

"The end of all things is near. Therefore be clear minded and self-controlled so that you can pray" (1 Peter 4:7).

TIME MATTERS

My wife and I were in Nairobi where I would be ministering to several hundred national pastors at an Africa Inland Mission conference. We were very excited about the conference even though we were a bit weary from the long air journey. We could hardly wait to get started, and the leader of the conference detected our impatience.

"You are in Africa now," he said to me in a fatherly fashion, "and the first thing you want to do is put away your watch."

In the days that followed, as we ministered in Kenya and Zaire, we learned the wisdom of his words. Unfortunately, when we returned to the States, we found ourselves caught up again in the clockwork prison of deadlines and schedules.

Peter had a great deal to say about *time*. Certainly the awareness of his own impending martyrdom had something to do with this emphasis (John 21:15-19; 2 Peter 1:12ff). If a person really believes in eternity, then he will make the best use of time. If we are convinced that Jesus is coming, then we will want to live prepared lives. Whether Jesus comes first, or death comes first, we want to make "the rest of the time" count for eternity. And we can!

Applying God's Truth:

1. In what ways do you tend to get too caught up "in the clockwork prison of deadlines and schedules"?

2. In what ways do you tend to squander time, and not get around to what you feel is important?

3. What do you need to do to achieve the right balance—to do what you want to do without becoming a slave to the clock?

Scripture: Read 1 Peter 4:12-16

"Rejoice that you participate in the sufferings of Christ, so that you may be over-joyed when his glory is revealed" (1 Peter 4:13).

THE PRIVILEGE OF SUFFERING

I t is an honor and a privilege to suffer with Christ and be treated by the world the way it treated Him. "The fellowship of His sufferings" is a gift from God (Phil. 1:29; 3:10). Not every believer grows to the point where God can trust him with this kind of experience, so we ought to rejoice when the privilege comes to us (Acts 5:41).

Christ is with us in the furnace of persecution. When the three Hebrew children were cast into the fiery furnace, they discovered they were not alone (Dan. 3:23-25). The Lord was with Paul in all of his trials, and He promises to be with us "to the very end of the age" (Matt. 28:20). In fact, when sinners persecute us, they are really persecuting Jesus Christ (Acts 9:4).

"Suffering" and "glory" are twin truths that are woven into the fabric of Peter's letter. The world believes that the *absence* of suffering means glory, but a Christian's outlook is different. The trial of our faith today is the assurance of glory when Jesus returns (1 Peter 1:7-8). This was the experience of our Lord (5:1), and it shall also be our experience.

Applying God's Truth:

1. Does suffering ever *feel* like a privilege to you? If not, how can you try to keep a positive mind-set as you suffer?

2. How do you think suffering is connected with glory?

3. Do you think you can ever suffer anything that Jesus doesn't completely understand? Explain.

Scripture: Read 1 Peter 4:17-19

"Those who suffer according to God's will should commit themselves to their faithful Creator and continue to do good" (1 Peter 4:19).

ACTS OF FAITH

I f we really have hope, and believe that Jesus is coming again, then we will obey His Word and start laying up treasures and glory in heaven. Unsaved people have a present that is controlled by their past, but Christians have a present that is controlled by the future (Phil. 3:12-21). In our very serving, we are committing ourselves to God and making investments for the future.

There is a striking illustration of this truth in Jeremiah 32. The Prophet Jeremiah had been telling the people that one day their situation would change and they would be restored to their land. But at that time, the Babylonian army occupied the land and was about to take Jerusalem. Jeremiah's cousin, Hanamel, gave Jeremiah an option to purchase the family land *which was now occupied by enemy soldiers.* The prophet had to "put his money where his mouth is." And he did it! As an act of faith, he purchased the land and became, no doubt, the laughingstock of the people of Jerusalem. But God honored his faith because Jeremiah lived according to the Word that he preached.

Applying God's Truth:

1. In what ways is your present controlled by your past? How is it controlled by your future?

2. Can you think of an act of faith you've performed along the lines of Jeremiah's buying a field—something that made absolutely no sense to the rest of the world, yet that showed your complete trust in God?

3. Rather than focusing on obstacles, what things can you list that should tend to help you "commit yourself to your faithful Creator and continue to do good"?

Scripture: Read 1 Peter 5:1-3

"Be shepherds of God's flock that is under your care, serving as overseers—not because you must, but because you are willing, as God wants you to be" (1 Peter 5:2).

FORWARD HO!

The pastor of the local assembly must be a man who walks with God and who is growing in his spiritual life. Paul admonished young Timothy: "Be diligent in these matters; give yourself wholly to them, so that everyone may see your progress" (1 Tim. 4:15). The word "progress" in the original means "pioneer advance." The elders must constantly be moving into new territories of study, achievement, and ministry. If the leaders of the church are not moving forward, the church will not move forward.

"We love our pastor," a fine church member said to me during a conference, "but we get tired of the same thing all the time. He repeats himself and doesn't seem to know that there are other books in the Bible besides Psalms and Revelation." That man needed to become a "spiritual pioneer" and move into new territory, so that he might lead his people into new blessings and challenges.

Sometimes God permits trials to come to a church so that the people will be forced to grow and discover new truths and new opportunities. Certainly Peter grew in his spiritual experience as he suffered for Christ in the city of Jerusalem. He was not perfect by any means, but Peter was yielded to Christ and willing to learn all that God had for him.

Applying God's Truth:

1. On a scale of 1 (least) to 10 (most), how would you rate your pastor in terms of being a "spiritual pioneer"? How would you evaluate your own recent "advances"?

2. What have you done lately to encourage your pastor and/or church officers?

3. Can you think of an example of how trials have helped your church grow spiritually? What can you learn from those past trials?

Scripture: Read 1 Peter 5:4

"When the Chief Shepherd appears, you will receive the crown of glory that will never fade away" (1 Peter 5:4).

REWARD OFFERED

A Christian worker may labor for many different kinds of rewards. Some work hard to build personal empires; others strive for the applause of men; still others seek promotion in their denomination. All of these things will fade one day. The only reward we ought to strive for is the "Well done!" of the Savior and the unfading crown of glory that goes with it. What a joy it will be to place the crown at His feet (Rev. 4:10) and acknowledge that all we did was because of His grace and power (1 Cor. 15:10; 1 Peter 4:11). We will have no desire for personal glory when we see Jesus Christ face to face.

Everything in the local church rises or falls with leadership. No matter how large or small a fellowship might be, the leaders must be Christians, each with a vital personal relationship with Christ, a loving concern for the people, and a real desire to please Jesus Christ.

We lead by serving, and we serve by suffering. This is the way Jesus did it, and this is the only way that truly glorifies Him.

Applying God's Truth:

1. Be honest. What kinds of reward do you hope to receive *now* for your Christian service? What *eventual* rewards do you desire?

2. In what ways do you lead by serving? How do you serve by suffering?

3. What would you tell someone complaining that it's unfair to have a life of suffering *now* in order to receive rewards *later*?

Scripture: Read 1 Peter 5:5-7

"Clothe yourselves with humility toward one another, because, 'God opposes the proud but gives grace to the humble' " (1 Peter 5:5).

A FASHION STATEMENT

Younger believers should submit to the older believers, not only out of respect for their age, but also out of respect for their spiritual maturity. Not every "senior saint" is a mature Christian, of course, because quantity of years is no guarantee of quality of experience. This is not to suggest that the older church members "run the church" and never listen to the younger members! Too often there is a generation war in the church, with the older people resisting change, and the younger people resisting the older people!

The solution is twofold: (1) all believers, young and old, should submit to each other; and (2) all should submit to God. "Clothe yourselves with humility" is the answer to the problem. Just as Jesus laid aside His outer garments and put on a towel to become a servant, so each of us should have a servant's attitude and minister to each other. True humility is described in Philippians 2:1-11. Humility is not demeaning ourselves and thinking poorly of ourselves. It is simply not thinking of ourselves at all!

Applying God's Truth:

1. Would you say you're usually submissive to older Christians? Are there exceptions? Explain.

2. How would potential problems with submitting to other people be avoided if everyone regularly submitted to God?

3. Would you say you "clothe yourself with humility"? In what ways? How might you improve in this area?

Scripture: Read 1 Peter 5:8-11

"Be self-controlled and alert. Your enemy the devil prowls around like a roaring lion looking for someone to devour" (*1 Peter 5:8*).

TAKE IT FROM PETER

Never discuss things with Satan or his associates. Eve made this mistake, and we all know the sad consequences. Also, never try to fight Satan in your own way. Resist him the way Jesus did, with the Word of God (Matt. 4:1-11). Never get the idea that you are the only one going through these battles, because "your brothers throughout the world" are facing the same trials. We must pray for one another and encourage each other in the Lord. And we must remember that our personal victories will help others, just as their victories will help us.

Had Peter obeyed these instructions the night Jesus was arrested, he would not have gone to sleep in the Garden of Gethsemane, attacked Malchus, or denied the Lord. He did not take the Lord's warning seriously; in fact, he argued with Him! Nor did he recognize Satan when the adversary inflated his ego with pride, told him he did not have to "watch and pray," and then incited him to use his sword. Had Peter listened to the Lord and resisted the enemy, he would have escaped all those failures.

Before we can stand before Satan, we must bow before God. Peter resisted the Lord and ended up submitting to Satan!

Applying God's Truth:

1. What do you suppose was Peter's biggest regret from his life?

2. When Christians feel they are alone in their spiritual struggles, how is Satan's influence more effective? How can this problem be alleviated?

3. It's easy to see how Peter could have avoided some of his failures, but can you look back on your own life and see what *you* could have done differently to avoid some major failures?

Scripture: Read 1 Peter 5:12-14

"Greet one another with a kiss of love. Peace to all of you who are in Christ" (*1 Peter 5:14*).

A PEACE AT A TIME

Paul always ended his letters with a benediction of grace (2 Thes. 3:17-18). Peter closed this epistle with a benediction of peace. He opened the letter with a greeting of peace (1 Peter 1:2), so the entire epistle points to God's peace from beginning to end. What a wonderful way to end a letter that announced the coming of a fiery trial!

Four times in the New Testament we will find the admonition about "a holy kiss" (Rom. 16:16; 1 Cor. 16:20; 2 Cor. 13:12; and 1 Thes. 5:26). Peter called it "a kiss of love." Keep in mind that the men kissed the men and the women kissed the women. It was a standard form of greeting or farewell in that part of the world at that time, just as it is in many Latin countries today. How wonderful that Christian slaves and masters would so greet each other "in Jesus Christ"!

Peter has given to us a precious letter that encourages us to hope in the Lord no matter how trying the times may be. Down through the centuries, the church has experienced various fiery trials, and yet Satan has not been able to destroy it. The church today is facing a fiery trial, and we must be prepared.

But, whatever may come, Peter is still saying to each of us—be hopeful! The glory is soon to come!

Applying God's Truth:

1. Do you think it's unusual that a message about "fiery trials" would have such an emphasis on peace? Explain.

2. Do you have a greeting that's equivalent to "a kiss of love"? If not, can you think of one you might want to initiate?

3. Are you any more hopeful now than when you started reading 1 Peter? If so, in what ways?